The End of
BUSINESS
AS USUAL

The End of BUSINESS AS USUAL

Rewire the Way You Work to Succeed
in the Consumer Revolution

BRIAN SOLIS

WILEY

John Wiley & Sons, Inc.

Published by John Wiley & Sons, Inc., Hoboken, New Jersey.
Published simultaneously in Canada.

For general information on our other products and services or for technical support, please contact our Customer Care Department within the United States at (800) 762-2974, outside the United States at (317) 572-3993 or fax (317) 572-4002.

Wiley publishes in a variety of print and electronic formats and by print-on-demand. Some material included with standard print versions of this book may not be included in e-books or in print-on-demand. If this book refers to media such as a CD or DVD that is not included in the version you purchased, you may download this material at http://booksupport.wiley.com. For more information about Wiley products, visit www.wiley.com.

Library of Congress Cataloging-in-Publication Data:

Solis, Brian.
   The end of business as usual : rewire the way you work to succeed in the consumer revolution / Brian Solis. — 1st ed.
       p.   cm.
   Includes index.
   ISBN 978-1-118-07755-9 (acid-free paper); ISBN 978-1-118-17158-5 (ebk); ISBN 978-1-118-17157-8 (ebk); ISBN 978-1-118-17156-1 (ebk)
      1. Consumer behavior.   2. Customer relations.   3. Social media.
   4. Internet marketing—Social aspects.   5. Management—Social aspects.
   6. Information technology—Management.   I. Title.
      HF5415.32.S599 2011
      658.8'72—dc23   2011029304

Printed in the United States of America

10 9 8 7 6 5 4 3 2 1

Contents

Foreword

Over the summer I invited a few friends and colleagues to my house for lunch. When they arrived, hugs and greetings were exchanged and my guests headed for the dining room while I finished up in the kitchen, mixing the homemade potato salad, and, well, let's say "supervising" the grilling out on the patio.

While I put the finishing touches on the plates I noticed something strange about the chatter coming from the other room ... there *was* none. They had either all been so bored they dozed off or they had quietly left and stuck me with way too much salmon and salad.

But, in fact, they were still there, seated at the table, one reading an iPad, two texting on iPhones, and one clicking away fervently on a BlackBerry.

I insisted that lunch would have to be a device-free meal.

You notice it at restaurants, at ball games, even at movies and plays. People can't seem to stop letting their fingers do the walking, as the Yellow Pages commercial goes.

Today the digital world pervades every aspect of our lives. I used to wonder what people did before call waiting. Now, phones are tiny laptops, and while you once had to be on a computer to engage online, you can now do it from anywhere, no wires required.

The world has changed at such warp speed in the past decade it's as if Henry Ford, the Wright Brothers, and Thomas Edison had gathered at some cosmic convention and unleashed all of their innovations the very next day.

When I was asked to record a video for YouTube's fifth anniversary, I have to admit my first thought was, "Wow, it's only been five years." After all, it wasn't that long ago that Bryant Gumbel and I had trouble explaining what the "Internet" was to *Today* show viewers. (And yes, I now know what the "@" symbol means!)

The advent of social media has also rapidly changed the way we do business, particularly in my field. Viewers and consumers of news now interact with information in a much more dynamic way. They aren't just watching a broadcast passively. They tweet about it, post and discuss stories on Facebook, and, yes, send their comments instantly.

I met Brian Solis last year when he interviewed me for his webshow. I have to admit I was a bit intimidated because I consider myself a tech novice, an information hunter trying to find her way through the World Wide Woods that the Web can be. I had begun to engage in social media just two years earlier. First a YouTube channel, then Facebook, Twitter, and webshows of my own. But I certainly didn't, and still don't, consider myself an expert.

When I relayed that thought to Brian, he told me that he sometimes feels that way, too. That this change is happening so fast it is impossible to be an expert. We're all just students, literally learning something new every day.

That instantly put me at ease. Some tech experts can be smug know-it-alls, as if only they have the keys to the digital castle. But Brian, in a world of aggregators and content providers, is a navigator, a sort of digital Sherpa who understands we all must climb at our own pace . . . but we do need to climb.

While I am fully engaged in the digital world, I do see pros and cons to our connectivity. As I have said before, the good thing about social media is it gives everyone a voice. The bad thing is . . . it gives everyone a voice.

Other books have been written about negativity, anonymity, and brutal bombs of bad information that can spread like wildfire online.

But I have also seen the very positive impact our global connectedness has brought to journalism and to information sharing in general.

As a news anchor I could tell my audience about unrest in Iran surrounding the 2009 elections there, but nothing could bring home the struggle in the streets like a cell phone video of Neda Agha-Soltan. This beautiful and brave young Iranian woman was killed at a protest and a citizen journalist captured the horrific images and was able to share them with the world. The anonymous cell phone video went on to win the prestigious George Polk Award.

After the fall of Hosni Mubarak's regime in Egypt I interviewed Wael Ghonim, the patriot and revolutionary whose Facebook page began a youth movement against oppression in his nation. He told me that Facebook didn't make people brave, it just helped that bravery spread and grow. But it was technology that spread the word and gave voices to millions of disenfranchised Egyptians demanding change.

These are dramatic and powerful examples, but there are many others, perhaps more mundane, that highlight the power of information campaigns in the digital world.

We each need to find the way to most effectively and productively utilize social media and digital technology in our professional and personal lives. It can be daunting. But Brian is the ultimate technological tour guide, and thanks to his patience, knowledge and understanding, you too can climb to the digital mountaintop and enjoy the view of this brave new world.

KATIE COURIC

Introduction

(R)evolution: How Internet Culture Has Created a New Era of Social Consumerism

This is a book about the new era of business, consumerism, and your role in defining the future of everything....

Let me start by saying thank you for picking up this book. If you read only these few lines, realize that you are part of a consumer revolution that is changing the future of business, media, and culture. You did not intentionally enlist in this movement, but you are indeed part of it.

Consumers are connecting with one another, creating a vast and efficient information network that shapes and steers experiences and markets. Whether you're a business professional or a consumer, you are part of this new era of connected or social consumerism and individually and collectively, the effects of your actions and words are nothing short of extraordinary when concentrated. Together, you ... me ... we have the power to change things around us. Every day, we're learning and practicing how to make sense of these emerging privileges. Businesses and consumers have the power to change the course of the economy and it's nothing short of disruptive.

People are now investors in and beneficiaries of a new genre of collective intelligence that informs and guides people in real time. Information, whether we contribute or learn, is now a wonderful commodity that's on demand. Needless to say, people are informing and are informed.

In just a few short years, we witnessed how people-powered Wikipedia displaced industry giant Britannica as the world's encyclopedia. The so-called wisdom of the crowds is now forming a *power* of the crowds, creating a new form of group buying to unlock amazing deals online and in the real world. Groupon, LivingSocial, Facebook Deals, and the countless others that are emerging empower groups of people to buy and save together, and in turn, share these opportunities with those to whom they're connected online and offline.

Simply by discussing the experiences we've had with brands and businesses on review sites, in blogs, and in online communities, we've created a new world of consumer influence. People make decisions based on the shared experiences of others. And that influence is sweeping, as consumers are increasingly connecting to one another.

Remember the Yellow Pages? Websites such as Yelp, Craigslist, Angie's List, and even Foursquare collectively displaced what was once the community staple for local businesses and service providers by moving information and experiences to online communities and social networks.

Once "too big to fail" businesses such as Borders, Tower Records, Wherehouse, Circuit City, and Blockbuster are now gone. Each business is a victim of Digital Darwinism, the evolution of consumer behavior when society and technology evolve faster than the ability to exploit it. Digital Darwinism does not discriminate. Every business is threatened.

This is just a little taste of how consumer behavior has changed the landscape for buying and selling—and this transformation is just getting started. It's nothing new. What *is* different, though, is that change forces just that: change. Those businesses that recognize disruption and develop a culture and process for innovation now and over time will survive the perpetual threat of Digital Darwinism.

The consumer revolution is already underway. The question is: How do you better understand the role you play in this production as a connected or social consumer as well as a business professional? As a stakeholder, it's now your obligation to study how, when, where, and why consumers are connecting and how they're making and influencing decisions. Doing so brings clarity to your work to create and steer consumer experiences to your advantage.

This book reveals how digital culture is changing the landscape of business, consumerism, and the workplace, and what you should do about it.

■ THIS IS NONE OF YOUR BUSINESS, SO MAKE IT YOUR BUSINESS

This book was written to groom a new generation of leaders, people who want to lead and are looking for the answers and inspiration necessary to guide others into uncharted territory. It's an exploration of culture, society, and how to unravel trends and hype to find the meaning in all of this. It's how we'll grow personally and professionally. For many of us, applying these insights at work will also teach us how to embrace new media in our personal lives.

What are the pillars of a successful business? Competitive prices? Great service? Widespread distribution? Better products? Maybe. But experience has taught us that ambition, practicality, and achievements are the traits of successful leaders. As a result, we sometimes compromise consumer experiences for numbers...business goals, minimized expenses, and increases in efficiencies, forecasts, and sales. Find any business owner or executive and they'll tell you that's just good business. But is that enough to survive Digital Darwinism? If marketing and PR departments serve as the voices of companies, how are we to really know?

It's the difference between being market-driven and marketing-driven. The true voice and personality of a company is rarely heard unless a customer calls in to the service department or visits the business in person to demand personalized attention and resolution. Suddenly marking is no longer "the voice." The front-line service representative is in charge of defining the consumer experience and the next steps a consumer may take, including sharing that experience with others. But how are representatives instructed to steer experiences today? How are they rewarded for cultivating memorable and satisfying engagements to encourage the sharing of positive experiences? Representatives are instead often motivated with incentives for increasing sales or churning through customer calls and emails faster than their peers, measured by time to resolution and transactional satisfaction.

Following these interactions, customers would walk away percolating with emotion. Whether positive, negative, or ambivalent, it's human nature to share these experiences with peers and quite honestly, anyone who'll listen. Again, none of this is new. It's human nature. Businesses have long known that a happy customer tells a few people, but an unhappy customer tells many, many more.

But everything was business as usual, until it wasn't. And, that's where this story begins.

Of course, no matter the business, the only factor as significant as customer acquisition is customer retention. But it's exponentially more expensive to acquire new customers than it is to retain them. Some businesses embrace this reality and hold it sacred. Others see the allure of saving money at the expense of positive experiences to placate customers rather than continually earn their affinity and loyalty.

The true character of any business is revealed in the collective experiences of its customers. It's about what people say when you're not around. With the rise of social media, people are connecting with one another to create vast networks rich with interaction. The social graphs that people create as a result are increasingly becoming interconnected, creating an audience that, too, boasts an audience with audiences. And guess who's in control of the information that circulates within each network? It's not the brand or its clever messaging, attractive promotions, or creative gimmicks. People are in control. The choices they make and the experiences they share through their words, relationships, and actions, influence those around them.

This book will introduce you to the connected consumer and how they search for, discover, and share information, and ultimately, make decisions. In many significant ways, they're not at all the customer you think you know.

Some of us are becoming the very consumers we're trying to reach and as a result, we are changing everything. By placing ourselves in the spotlight, we gain a more personal view of the change unfolding before us, without the obstruction of our business blinders we unknowingly wear in our professional lives. It's this perspective that's usually missing from today's business approach and prevailing philosophy.

Understanding this new connected consumer will help us gain two critical business traits long absent from the hallmark of typical business culture, the ability to feel and show empathy and the ability to change. To best earn residence in the minds and hearts of customers, we must invest in shaping exceptional experiences worth sharing.

Understanding this new consumer and what moves them will help businesses compete for tomorrow, today. It's the acceptance of this perspective that will allow us to uncover and affect the decisions that orbit and define the brands we represent.

The businesses that aspire to a higher purpose will outperform businesses that focus on the bottom line.

People aspire to be part of something bigger than themselves. Give them something to align with to create a sense of belonging. Give them something to talk about. Give them a reason to share experiences. After all, you are part of the new digital culture that is defining the future of all of this. Change is upon us. Change is because of us.

It is not the strongest of the species that survives, nor the most intelligent that survives. It is the one that is most adaptable to change.

—*Charles Darwin*

A Quiet Riot: The Information Divide and the Cultural Revolution

I woke up one morning only to find that the whole world changed around me. . . .

For 20 years, I collected fountain pens. The beauty and shape of the pen, the fine detail of the nib, and the careful balance of the design introduced a sense of importance to every stroke and every word I wrote. Writing to me is an art, but the reality is that I just don't practice my handwriting as I did in the past. The last addition to my collection was just over seven years ago. Not only is my penmanship deteriorating, the pen feels foreign in my grasp. I'm realizing that with every day that passes, I lose simple muscle memory that took most of childhood and young adulthood to train. Now, my thumbs are far more dexterous on a mobile phone than my index finger adjoined to my thumb on the best of my fountain pens.

The reality is that almost everything I write these days is composed on either a PC, mobile phone, tablet, microphone/webcam, or anything with a keyboard. One day soon, I'm sure I will only have to think what I want to say and it will appear before me on screen.

This is just the beginning of how communication is changing. A simple pinch of the thumb and index finger is now more agile and capable, thanks to Mr. Steve Jobs and the iOS team at Apple. The pinch is becoming the standard for interacting with devices and content. While it's something most of us have adapted to, younger generations view this motion as second nature. They don't think twice to pinch a screen to enlarge the text. Nor do they have to think about how to scroll through pages of content. Because the technology is so accessible, it is one of the first methods they learn.

Displacing landlines is one thing. The cell phone's impact on behavior is something different altogether. For years, we frowned on bringing anything to the dinner table that might detract from the interactions that meals foster. But then cell phones quietly took over our attention one by one, until the table was surrounded by people with their heads focused downward and their thumbs texting away. To an outsider, this conduct would appear nothing less than rude. In her book, *Table Manners for Kids,* published in 2009, Emily Post says bluntly, "Do *not* use your cell phone or any other electronic devices at the table."[1]

Unraveling the reasons behind why this behavior has become acceptable will help us bridge the digital and cultural divide. While some people use their gadgets to escape conversation, there are usually other factors at work. In some cases, it's a symptom of introversion or shyness. In other cases, it's simply how certain people cope with a pervasive feeling of missing out. The world moves much faster with every generation, and rapid-fire text messaging and social networks allow people to stay connected. This statement seems contradictory in nature. However, people are balancing virtual and real-world relationships in the moment. Perhaps they need a constant sense of belonging and outside reinforcement to reinvigorate the here and now.

With that said, it is the responsibility of the host to realize the changing nature of human interaction to not discourage outside interaction, but to steer the experience to include everyone in one's own way. Are you encouraging distraction? Are you enabling distraction? You betcha. Controlling the moment is so last decade. It's now up to the host, or in the world of business, the brand, leader, or champion, to create moments that are nothing short of engaging. Yes, that's right. Attention is distracted and there's very little that you can do to reverse the evolution of the human psyche. Instead, you can steer experiences to your benefit by becoming the focal point or creating one.

In these cases, a smartphone can enhance conversations rather than inhibit them. In a piece that ran in the *New York Times* in December 2010, Bruce Feiler explored the advantages of using Google during meals to foster engaging dialogue:

> *If you could invite any five people from history to dinner, who would it be? That game seems to have lost popularity of late, and I'm beginning to think I know why. These days, everybody I know invites the same guest to dinner. Who's this ubiquitous invitee? The answer is sitting in your pocket. Google. . . . What if a few clicks of the smartphone can answer a question, solve a dispute, or elucidate that thoughtful point you were making? What if that PDA is not being used to escape a conversation but to enhance it?*[2]

Banning the phone from the table is easier than it sounds. The need for constant connectedness is reshaping what we consider acceptable behavior. The constant desire for interaction comes down to shared experiences and staying connected.

The truth is that we're always on.

There I was, in Lisbon having dinner with 20 of Portugal's leading digerati. I had no choice but to leave my phone in my bag as the international data functions were down at that time and the establishment did not offer Wi-Fi (but they did serve great food!). Without the ability to check emails, text, or update social networks, I channeled all of my attention on the people at the table. To my surprise, I found a table surrounded by new friends with their heads pointed down toward their laps. Some were live tweeting the event. Others were texting with friends. A few were checking email. Others were checking Facebook updates and searching for real-time mentions of their name online.

Without a phone, I took it upon myself to unite the table around good old-fashioned conversation, but not just with those in the room, those to whom they're also connected online. I asked guests to ask their online friends questions to see how we can channel a discussion with greater reach and input. I also played the role of sociologist and asked questions that explored the reasons why each immediately took to their iPhones and BlackBerrys before placing their napkins on their laps. I learned something interesting. To engage an entire table and prevent them from mobile temptation is impossible. It was the beginning of a realization for me that would affect my work. If I could steer experiences, I could connect with people at the table as well as those they're engaging with on the other side of the device.

Had my phone worked, I probably would have joined them. The fact that we're becoming an always-on society combined with the responsibility of hosting very public online presences (Facebook, Google Plus, Twitter, LinkedIn), we are now all full-time brand managers—even if that brand is just our individual online presence. Now we're paying attention to what others are saying about us.

People will always talk about you, so give them something to talk about.

But this conversation is not just about whether you choose to stay connected through meals. The access to people and information, whenever, wherever is powerful and addictive. Students are focusing more on their smartphones than the lessons they are being taught in the classroom. Drivers are paying less attention to the roads and instead, are interacting with friends and associates at the risk of crashing into those nearby.

Texting was an early culprit. Then the world was diagnosed with BlackBerry thumbs. And now Twitter, Facebook, and other social networks constantly vie for our attention as well. Bringing electronics to the table, the classroom, or our cars is a symptom of our always-on society. We indeed bring our connections with us everywhere we go. The experiences and sentiment we share are just a different, but no less meaningful, way we invest in our relationships. It's how we maintain relevance within our social network, which is our society. The question is, where's the balance? Or, better asked, how can this be used more productively? How can we keep people engaged and encourage the sharing of meaningful and beneficial experiences? How can outside interaction strengthen real world interaction?

Again, this behavior is already beyond the attention Rubicon. As heads of households, educators, friends, and peers, it's our responsibility to find opportunities to stay engaged in person, and when necessary, digitally. But there is an informational and digital divide that still exists within greater society and it extends across generations and demographics. Whether consumers are online or offline, technology is evolving faster than the majority of businesses or consumers can adapt or assimilate.

■ THE HUMAN GENOME MEETS DIGITAL DNA

There's an expression that's often used to explain why we perform the simplest, uncommonsensical, or most mundane of tasks, over and over: it's because "we're just wired that way."

As difficult as it can be to accept, things around us are constantly changing, causing society, life, and humanity to change along with them. We initially question or resist the events unfolding before us until they either recede or prevail. We then adapt, constantly changing our routines, even if in the slightest of traces. Every so often though, the events that emerge and play out before us are so transformative that evolution is disrupted, giving way to a revolution. The effects affect social development, human behavior, and ultimately, the course of history.

How we were wired is quickly becoming outdated. The new models of us are wired for the modern lifestyle. How we interact, learn, and mature is different. Everyone else is left feeling antiquated, out of touch, or simply unaware of the differences. But for those who get it ... like you ... you're constantly looking for ways to get rewired to keep up. The simple truth is that things, and people, are changing right before us. We live in interesting times and the change we're experiencing now is nothing less than historic.

The more I study technology and its impact on behavior, the more I find myself revisiting a widely accepted notion: technology changes, people don't. But nowadays, I'm not so sure. Technology is indeed changing, but it is also changing us along with it. Whether it's through social networks or digital lifestyle products such as iPhones, iPads, and Kindles, we are adapting and evolving as a result. Technology has become a form of self-expression. What we use and how we use it says everything about us . . . and we want it to. We no longer live in an era in which we make decisions based solely on form or function; we're moving toward a genre of picking the electronics and online services that define our persona. Are you an iPhone or Android person? Either way, they're extensions of our identity, who we are today and who we want to be tomorrow.

With the pervasiveness of iPods, iPads, and other digital devices, everyday people now march to their own soundtracks, moving throughout their lives quite literally to the beat of their own drummer. In curious ways, we're creating an introverted nation of *earbudsmen*, small armies of people with white earbuds absorbed in what they're listening to, the people they're texting, and the videos they're watching, all while moving.

It's not just about the iGeneration of earbudsmen either. With the universality of social networks such as Facebook and Twitter and the rise of geolocation networks such as Foursquare, we are learning to live our lives online, revealing a bit more about ourselves with every status update, check-in, tweet, and social object we publish.

■ DON'T BLAME IT ON THE YOUTH

With the rise of the Golden Triangle of technology (mobile, social, and real-time), technology is not just for the geeks; it's now part of our lifestyle. How we use this technology says everything about us, and we're starting earlier and earlier.

A study by security company AVG and Research Now surveyed 2,200 mothers in North America (the United States and Canada), the EU 5 (the United Kingdom, France, Germany, Italy, and Spain), Australia/New Zealand, and Japan, and found that 81 percent of children under the age of two currently have some kind of digital profile or footprint, with images of them posted online.[3] Ninety-two percent of U.S. children have an online presence created for them by the time they are two years old. In many cases, a digital presence is born before the child, with sonograms (23 percent) actively published and shared on social networks and blogs. A digital presence is now just a way of life. For these children, managing their online persona and relationships is all they know.

■ CH-CH-CHANGES

The rapid evolution in technology is completely transforming society and human behavior. Technology is changing us, and as it does, it can improve how we learn, share, and communicate.

The result ultimately affects and alters our personal and professional worlds. Human relationships, interaction, consumerism, education, media, government, and business are all forever changed.

To reach this always-on consumer, we can no longer continue operating under a banner of business as usual. Instead we must appreciate that we don't understand all that is changing, but we must learn to understand and eventually become part of the (r)evolution.

As change is omnipresent and sweeping, time is of the essence. The only way to understand new culture and behavior is to go native. Going native refers to the process of observing, learning, and deepening the involvement of an anthropologist with their hosts and their hosts' cultures through long-term fieldwork and participation.[4] In the process, we become digital natives, uncovering the facts we need to improve our communication, customer relationships, and overall business opportunity.

One way to go native is through immersion.

To best understand the effects of human behavior on business, it is best to be immersed in new consumerism directly. Through immersion, we'll gain perspective and develop the empathy needed to later make meaningful connections and shape productive experiences worth sharing.

Understanding the connected consumer requires sincerity. By identifying their challenges, we actually go beyond observing their behavior to become part of their society. Though this is the end of business as usual, this is the beginning of a new genre of business, one that presents an opportunity to earn customers by becoming relevant to their needs and aspirations.

Centers of Attention

➤ We need to explore avenues to shape and steer experiences rather than discount how technology is changing behavior.

➤ Mobile is becoming increasingly important in how people, regardless of generation, find and share information.

➤ We are becoming brand managers and are responsible for managing our online reputations.

➤ How people are connecting is setting the foundation for a powerful distribution network that rivals the greatest of news and broadcast networks.

➤ To succeed in the business of the future, we have to become the very people we're trying to reach.

Chapter 2

Youthquake: Millennials Shake Up the Digital Lifestyle

The Millennial generation, or as they are often called, Generation Me, represent one-quarter of the American population.[1] Seventy-seven million Americans were born between the mid-1970s and the late 1990s.

In 2011, the youngest of the Millennial generation hit their mid-teens. The oldest Millennials recently entered their thirties. And in between there's an entire segment of maturing adults who are now settling into their twenties. But this generation will also change the world before taking ownership of it.

In February 2011, Edelman Digital published its annual 8095 report—a survey of 3,100 Millennials across eight countries. The report brings to life the greater theme of this book, "Why Millennials matter to every brand."[2] As described in the introduction to the study, "While many still view Millennials as punky kids playing on their tablets between high school classes, the reality is that two-thirds of Millennials are now over the age of 21, and many have established careers, families and an incredible amount of influence."

According to the report, within the past 30 days, Millennials had recommended online that a friend or family member purchase a specific product in the following categories:

Food—54 percent

Electronics—39 percent

Personal care—37 percent

Clothing—35 percent

Beauty—35 percent

Cleaning—24 percent

Cooking—19 percent

Pet—19 percent

Other—13 percent

The most interesting part of the report is of the level of brand loyalty shared among the Millennials. Worldwide, 70 percent feel that once they find a company or product they like, they keep coming back. Fifty-eight percent are willing to share more personal information with trusted brands. And as a brand fits into their lifestyle, it becomes an extension of their persona, creating a personal bond between brand and customer. On average globally, 86 percent will share their brand preference online, creating a new and powerful form of self-expression using digital presences for discovery, articulation, and definition.

While the value of relevant and expert information is hardly limited to Millennials, the Edelman study found that younger consumers seek more product information for purchase consideration—an average of 7.4 times per month. Millennial moms seek additional information 9.2 times per month. When considering a purchase, Millennials will seek input from the following:

Family—77 percent

Friends—64 percent

Search engine—21 percent

Expert website—21 percent

Co-worker—20 percent

Social networks—13 percent

Solo—8 percent

The percentage of people looking to social networks for information on products or services is not indicative of how consumers are seeking information when shopping. Instead, those interactions are often included in the percentage attributed to friends and family. Why? Because friends and family are connected within social networks and also through technology. These networks are merely hubs for insights, both gleaning and sharing it.

It's not just friends and family that Millennials are connecting with, however; they're also forming alliances with brands. Nearly 20 percent of Millennials attended a brand-sponsored event in the past 30 days. Of those who attended, 65 percent purchased the featured product. But that's not all. Twenty-five percent worldwide have joined seven or more brand-sponsored communities online!

This influential generation is moving beyond the role of traditional consumer and assuming the role of self-ordained experts. Forty-seven percent will write about their positive experiences with companies and products online. On the flipside, 39 percent will share negative encounters. Also, 70 percent of U.S. Millennial consumers will try a new product from a trusted brand and most will post a review online to promote the experience. That same number of younger consumers also relies on friends to learn about new trends. A whopping 36 percent said that they purchased a product that was introduced to them by a friend within the preceding week.

When it comes to customer service, Millennials do not see call centers as centers for customer service. Less than 1 percent of Millennials will actually let companies know they have a problem through a traditional call center or email. For them, the first line of resolution is through...

The company website—50 percent

Search—48 percent

Store location—45 percent

Friends—30 percent

Family—22 percent

Social networks—20 percent

It's easy to disregard the Millennials as different, but they're the next generation. They were born this way and technology is just part of their DNA. After all, 65 percent are disconnected as little as just one hour per day or less while they're awake because any longer creates an unnerving sense of disconnectedness. Their social network, even while sleeping, is within arm's length.

■ BOOM

When an aircraft hits supersonic speeds it creates a sonic boom. As it travels, that boom becomes known as the boom carpet. Here, it's a play on words, as Millennials *and* boomers are causing shockwaves in consumer markets, creating an economic sonic boom. But they are not alone in the important roles each generation plays in socioeconomics. Generation X is sandwiched between boomers and Millennials and they're connecting with one another online too.

Millennials come after the similarly tech-savvy Generation X, a generation that helped put a smartphone user into the United States White House. This generation, my generation, born between 1965

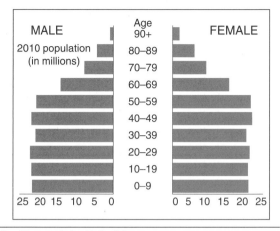

Figure 2.1   The Shape of the United States
Source: U.S. Census Bureau.

and 1980, also gets tech: We were among the earliest adopters of new technology and media. With the advent of social media, we were its earliest inhabitants.

The Millennials are juxtaposed against the Boomers, balancing a society divided today by technology savvy and well-established behavior. (See Figure 2.1.) After World War II, the Baby Boom generation numbered more than one-third of the U.S. population in 1965, when the boom had just ended. While Gen Y is similar in size to the Boomers, they represent less than a quarter of the population. Families back then simply had more children. Now lifestyle choices are changing the demographic makeup of the population, transforming the age breakdown from a pyramid to a rectangle.

In the United States, the median age is 36.8, falling squarely in the zone of Generation X. It is this age that divides a population into two numerically equal groups, half of whom are younger (Millennials) and half of whom are older (Boomers) than this age.[3] Around the world, that number fluctuates from a low of about 15 in Uganda and the Gaza Strip to 40 or more in many European countries and Japan. The average age of the world population is 28 and by 2015, it will hover around 25.[4]

In 2010, The Pew Internet and American Life Project, which studies how technology is affecting American culture, revealed that Internet users aged 65 and older flocked to social media, growing by 100 percent over the previous year. One in four people (26 percent) in that age group are now logging in to Facebook or Twitter, among others, to stay connected. Boomers aged between 50 and 64 grew by

88 percent. Americans over 55 who were online grew from 1 million in early 2009 to 10 million in early 2010. This trajectory shows no sign of leveling off. They're learning to connect and communicate as part of a new digitally literate society. And, they're becoming connected customers in the process. As I said in an interview with CBS on the trend:[5]

> *The ability to reconnect with family and old friendships is the primary driver that (causes) Boomers to start to experiment with Facebook. One of the things they learn almost immediately is that when their profile is public they (receive a lot of) inbound connection requests of other friends and family and it takes on a new life for them. It's a baptism-by-friend-request, learning the value of social networking. Social consumerism in general is shifting to social media. Consumers can connect with brands directly. Social media provides access to exclusive content and information, as well as discounts, promotions, and special offers.*

Children, relatives, and friends are flocking to social networks and spending less time sending pictures or calling with updates. As such, moms, dads, grandparents, aunts, and uncles have no choice but to follow their loved ones to these new services. When digital chasms divide you and your loved ones, you find a way to build bridges because you have to, because you want to.

■ DIGITAL DARWINISM: CONTROLLING YOUR WAY TO OBSOLESCENCE

While the Youthquake rocks the foundation of consumerism, Generation X and Boomers serve as the seismic retrofitting that keeps everything together.

This is a global movement that is creating a global culture bound through a series of networks. Buying behavior is indeed changing and the role the customer plays in the greater scheme of business is gaining in prominence. There is a great shift occurring and power is moving away from businesses and toward people, kept in balance through dynamic stabilization. Collaboration, engagement, empowerment, and investment each contribute to the balance in equal parts.

Consumer experiences shared in networking and in review sites create a living *Consumer Reports* study whereby collective intelligence is the new consumer influence. Businesses are no longer the sole creator of a brand; it is co-created by consumers through shared experiences and defined by the results of online searches and conversations.

In the Edelman Digital 8095 report, Michael Penman, senior director of global marketing, Levis Strauss recognized this new genre of customer influence:

We have to let go a lot. As a brand, I think we were a company, among others, who felt that tight control of the brand and saying what our voice is was crucial up until probably a couple of years ago. We're essentially a brand now that is based on co-creation, self-expression, and originality.

The effect of connected consumers reverberates across markets and societies, online and offline, and it's both good and bad for brands. When asked to share the reasons as to why they recommend products, one 8095 Millennial respondent spoke on behalf of that generation, "Quality of the product and reputation of the company. Not the kind of reputation where they are hip and they're cool and so I must purchase their products, but companies that have a long history for caring for their customers."

Namely, caring for them, not simply servicing them, becomes paramount.

Wait, what's that you say? You want a company to pay attention to you, demonstrate that you're a valued customer, help you make the right decisions, deliver exceptional or useful experiences, and respond when you need help? Nonsense! Businesses are in business to do business. This is about boosting sales, reducing costs, increasing margins, operationalizing around efficiencies, all at the expense of the customer experience, all while still increasing our Net Promoter Score!

This type of thinking is a tell-tale sign of the coming obsolescence that ultimately succumbs to digital Darwinism if not met with an intervention of reality.

Connected customers will feel a celebrated sense of schadenfreude at the demise of the businesses that refuse to adapt. As I said in the original *Social Media Manifesto*[6] for business in 2007, "Engage or Die!" Now it's clear that businesses must also "Adapt or Die!"

It is in fact this organizing demand for customer centricity that is at the heart of the future of what I call the adaptive business. It's easy to pin change on the emergence of a new generation that is gaining prominence in the market. Blame it on the youth, right? No. Digital consumers are becoming connected.

The pivot of any business is not whether it can reach consumers, it's the reality of whether consumers, especially connected customers, wish to connect with them now and over time. The definition of creating a desirable brand now takes on an entirely new meaning. To earn the attention and business of the connected consumer, the brand, product, or service must connect with its consumer personally—emotionally and intellectually. This creates a new caliber of relationship, one that is balanced in stature between consumer and brand, between referral or censure.

Regardless of age or demographic, a brand is a reflection of the customer's own personal brand and lifestyle. Consumers are taking action on their own terms and sharing every step of the experience through their networks.

The democratization of information is connecting everyone, not just Millennials, distributing influence and making the role of the consumer and its impact on business more important than ever before. And it is through this unfiltered access to information that empowerment defines the future of business, where brands and their respective markets are not created, but co-created. This is about finding a role within the lives of connected customers, recognizing them as partners and not just as consumers. Welcome to a new era of marketing and service in which your brand is defined by those who experience it.

Centers of Attention

➤ The millennial age spans from 17 to 32 as of 2012.

➤ Millennials are active influencers and consumers and they are ready to engage with those brands that demonstrate empathy and a substantial value proposition that extends who they are.

➤ Millennials are loyal; can your company say the same thing?

➤ This group represents almost a quarter of the total market.

➤ They don't want to call your customer service department when they have a problem, and that will change the structure of your company ... and they're not the only generation sharing the distaste for the customer service grind.

➤ While digital connectedness is in their DNA, older generations are undergoing technology transfusions to stay connected.

➤ Boomers were the fastest growing demographic in social networks in 2010; no generation can be discounted.

➤ In the United States, the median age is 36.8.

➤ The era of command and control is over.

➤ Customer care will first serve as a valuable differentiator, but great service will become a necessary ingredient in any successful business.

Chapter

3

The Medium Is No Longer the Message

I never intended to start a revolution, I was simply trying to tell the world that I had something to say . . . and learn.

When you go online, where do you go? What do you do? If you were similar to the people studied by Nielsen in 2010, you would spend a majority of your time on social networks. In a study that illustrates the ever-changing landscape of U.S. Internet time,[1] 22.7 percent of people use social networks such as Twitter and Facebook. This number is up by 43 percent over the previous year and represents a new reality. Online games followed with 10.2 percent, which in turn, was trailed by email with 8.3 percent. While email was once a critical point of inbound and outbound interaction, it is becoming less important.

People are spending more time on social networks because there's more reason for them to be there. Friends, family, and peers all connect through shared experiences. The social graph represents those relationships we maintain online. To many, it represents much more than the nodes that define their social network, the act of social networking offers a sense of belonging. And as such, it pulls people online over and over. These networks become a home away from home as social technology brings people together. But ultimately, it is the value of each relationship and the merit of corresponding interactions that magnetize time and attention.

The media channels that compete for our attention are transforming our behaviors, empowering users to take control of the information that reaches them. The era of mass broadcasting and consumption is winding down only to be reborn through context and the relevant experiences of people and organizations we value. The relationships that people form online and the nature of their connections define the paths for information and content to travel beyond their intended medium.

> ➤ Television programs are now live-tweeted.
> ➤ News no longer breaks, it tweets.
> ➤ Online video networks are destinations for engaged entertainment, no longer just temporary distractions.
> ➤ Local businesses are gaining greater visibility based on the reviews and social check-ins of patrons over traditional advertising or the Yellow Pages.
> ➤ The cycle of decision making is becoming a public practice. While people may start their search in Google, the results are qualified in social networks.
> ➤ Mobile is the new point of purchase and consumers are scanning products, searching other consumer experiences, seeking deals, and asking questions online before finalizing the transaction.

In 2010, Experian Hitwise, a part of Experian Marketing Services, analyzed the top 1,000 search terms in 2010. For the second straight year, Facebook was the number-one term people searched.[2] But more importantly, Hitwise documented an important shift in online behavior. For the first time, Facebook was ranked the top-visited website, accounting for 8.93 percent of all U.S. visits between January and November 2010. Facebook surpassed Google, signaling a shift in attention from search to social. Google is quite aware that individuals are increasingly relying on their social networks for just about everything. Over the years, the company has introduced a series of socialized products such as Social Search, GoogleWave, and GoogleBuzz only to learn that developing products with an engineering focus was no match for a social network that placed people and their relationships front and center. Don't count Google out, though. In 2011, it introduced Google Plus (or Google+) and became the fastest social network to reach 10 million users. In just 16 days it accomplished what took Facebook 852 days and Twitter 780 days. Innovation is constant, however, and regardless of the network de jour, people are learning that online connections are just a way of life.

As a result, budgets and resources for reaching customers should be focused on intercepting consumer attention. While we are seeing businesses shift greater budgets to new media, most decision makers lack the insights necessary to bring meaning and value to these numbers. But that's why you're reading this book. It's not just about moving businesses toward Facebook, Google+ or Twitter; it's about identifying the various groups of customers within the network, extracting intelligence, and reverse-engineering programs to activate desired responses and outcomes. Basically, start with the end in mind and work backward from there.

■ SOCIAL NETWORKS AS YOUR PERSONAL OPERATING SYSTEM (OS)

The medium is no longer just the message. Now, the medium is the platform and people now represent both the medium and the message. Their digital relationships define the nature of information discovery and its course through the social graph.

For example, Facebook started out as a social network, but it is growing into a personal operating system of sorts, where friends and experiences are interconnected and apps and brand pages connect people through interests. Every month, the Facebook population invests over 700 billion minutes interacting with their social graphs and creating and sharing content and experiences. Facebook is a hub for people and information. And at this moment, at the center of everything, is you and every customer or client you interact with. Facebook is a platform within which relationships create the construct for what I call the 3Cs of information commerce: content creation, curation, and consumption. We review this in greater detail later in the book.

The acts of sharing and consuming content in social media represent the social dealings between people and set the stage for interaction and education, but it is a platform for development and a solid foundation for social architecture. It is the websites that feature Facebook interconnects that weave the fabrics of relationships and the ties that bind us.

➤ People on Facebook install 20 million applications every day in the popular network.

➤ 250 million people engage with Facebook on external websites every month.

➤ More than 2.5 million websites have integrated with Facebook, including 80 of comScore's U.S. top 100 websites and over half of comScore's global top 100 websites.[3]

Indeed, according to comScore, Facebook traffic soared by 55.2 percent, hitting 151.1 million in October 2010, up from 97.4 million visitors at the same time last year.[4] It's also important to note that Facebook was home to 300 million active denizens in 2010 and it now has a population of more than 750 million.

➤ 50 percent of active users log on to Facebook in any given day.
➤ The average user has 130 friends.

Facebook is becoming an epicenter for all online activity. It's where individuals pool all that they are and all that interests them into an organized, presentable, and searchable framework. We can learn a lot about someone based on what they share as well as what they don't share.

The more we interact on Facebook through Likes, Shares, and Comments, the more we feed what's referred to as the social effect, the ability for information to travel quickly from person to person around the world, building new relationships in the process. The next Web is predicated on this very premise. Facebook knows what you like, and as a result, your actions inside Facebook and any site running Facebook technology can transform the surrounding content on the page to better match your preferences.

Aside from our favorite bands, movies, TV shows, and destinations, we reveal more than we realize. Democracy UK, a UK-focused political campaigning initiative run by Facebook,[5] released some very telling facts and figures in its snapshot report of Facebook in 2010.[6] Let's take a look at relationships in one year:

➤ 43,869,800 changed their status to single.
➤ 3,025,791 changed their status to "It's complicated."
➤ 28,460,516 changed their status to in a relationship.
➤ 5,974,574 changed their status to engaged.
➤ 36,774,801 changed their status to married.

We now know that more than 700 billion minutes are clocked every month on Facebook. But, what does 20 minutes look like? In the same report by Democracy UK, we are able to look at the events that unfold every 20 minutes.

➤ Every 20 minutes, more than one million links are shared.
➤ 1.3 million photos are tagged.
➤ 1.5 million invites are sent.
➤ 1.6 million Wall posts are published.

➤ 1.9 million status updates are published.

➤ 2 million friend requests are accepted.

➤ 2.7 million photos are uploaded, making Facebook the largest photo network online.

➤ 10.2 million comments are shared.

➤ 4.6 million messages are sent.

The extent of interaction that takes place in 20 minutes reveals a glimpse of the sheer size of Facebook. On a monthly basis, this translates to:

➤ The average user creates 90 pieces of content each month.

➤ More than 30 billion pieces of content (web links, news stories, blog posts, notes, photo albums, and so on) are shared each month.

■ DON'T GOOGLE ME, FACEBOOK ME

Connected customers no longer take to search engines' insight first; they now take to their social streams.

What lies ahead is a cold war between Google and Facebook, where your social graph is at stake. Facebook is taking large steps to move you away from Google and Google is fighting back with Google+. Facebook is vying to become your home page. The company believes that your social graph should be the starting point to your online experience each and every time you fire up your browser. While Google+ hit 10 million users in 16 days, it took only an additional week to double its size to 20 million. Google+ isn't the last social network to hope to compete for the attention of the connected consumer, either. Regardless of network, connected consumers are increasingly leaning on their friends for empowerment, entertainment, and enlightenment. Social networks are now personal hubs that bring information, people, and businesses together.

■ TWITTER ME THIS . . . THE FACEBOOK GENERATION

And what of Twitter? The year 2010 will be forever commemorated as the year Twitter matured from a cool but undecided teenager into a more confident and assertive young adult. While there's still much room to mature and develop, Twitter's new direction is crystallizing.

With a new look, Dick Costolo as the new CEO, and an oversold new advertising platform, Twitter is growing into something not yet fully identifiable, but formidable nonetheless. In fact, in 2010, Twitter attracted more than 100 million users, its largest growth rate in the history of the company. In just one year, 44 percent of its total population moved into the micro-utopia in the hopes of finding and sharing something that has been missing elsewhere online and in real life (IRL).

At a minimum, Twitter is an extension of each one of us. It feeds our senses and amplifies our voice. We're connecting to one another through shared experiences, creating a hybrid social network and information exchange tied by emotion and interest. While Twitter provides the technology foundation, it is we who make Twitter so unique and consequential by simply being human and sharing what we see, feel, and think—in Twitter time. It's both a gift and a harbinger of enlightenment. As new media philosopher and good friend, Stowe Boyd, once said, "It's our dancing that makes the house rock, not the planks and pipes. It is us that make Twitter alive, not the code."

Twitter is like a moon that orbits a networked planet. It turns the tides. It defines its rotation. Twitter is your window to relevance, but Facebook is your home page for the Social Web.

We are witnessing the dawn of a more social consumer. In the United States, we have a few top traditional TV networks that compete for our attention: CBS, ABC, and NBC. In social networking, we now have three networks to compete for the online attention of not only Americans, but also the world—Facebook, Twitter, and Google+. Each in their own way serves as the foundation for our social operating system and in turn, we continue to change how information and experiences travel. With every post, comment, and photo we share, we trigger a reaction. With our relationships serving as the construct for any social network, we are realizing that the social effect is ours to define.

Centers of Attention

➤ Social networking is about connecting, but also staying connected... maintaining a sense of belonging and relevance.

➤ People are creating distribution networks within and across social networks. They are the gatekeepers for the new channels tied to your work.

➤ Facebook and Google+ are no longer just social networks, they are burgeoning online societies that rival some of the largest countries in the world. It's where you maintain an identity, invest in relationships, and share the things that are important to you.

➤ Twitter is also important, but different. Facebook is your home in the Social Web and Twitter is your window to engagement and real-time belonging.

➤ Invest in F-Commerce.

Chapter 4

The Attention Deficit Crises and Information Scarcity

Saturday Night Live's spoof about moms on Facebook[1] represented just how deeply social networking has permeated popular culture. The mock commercial playfully offered young adults a solution for masking updates from curious moms. The "Damn it, my mom is on Facebook filter" used in the skit is as humorous as it is telling of the challenges we all face in social networking. In one example, a stereotypical mother comments on a picture of her son holding a beer next to a female partygoer who's visibly intoxicated. The comment, "Who's your new friend? She looks ill," gives us a taste of how we're willfully living our lives in public, open to interpretation from family, friends, schools, employers, basically . . . everyone, 24 hours a day, seven days a week.

While the commentator in the mock commercial is joking when he says, "Now you have to watch everything you say," the reality is, you really do.

Interaction is all very public and it's all very addictive. What we share is seen by various groups of people and as a result, each update requires thoughtful consideration. In the near future, deliberate curation in how we weave our networks will improve our experiences. People are realizing that the democratization of information is a giant buffet of which, at some point, becomes too much to digest. Noise is a byproduct of networking, but deliberate curation offers a cure for information overload to help people get out of these experiences what it is they value.

In six short years and through a series of waves, Facebook recruited college kids, Silicon Valley geeks, and everyday people to join the network. Since then, checking Facebook has become an indispensible ritual for the social and connected. Facebook aside, social networking as technology and as a way of life is competing for your attention and, in many ways, thinning it to the point of distress. Text messaging, tweets, email, and other forms of connecting also thrive off of your participation. This is at the root of our always-on society and the thinning of attention, making it increasingly difficult for information, especially marketing messages, to reach desired audiences. But it is when you're not participating in online networks that a curious form of missing out builds. It's this sense of belonging and an insatiable appetite for information that keeps us addicted and connected. Relevance, as we learn, is earned through constant participation and self-expression and for businesses, relevance is difficult to earn.

■ REMORSE AND SOCIAL NETWORK FATIGUE

Social networks unite us and challenge us at the same time. Many of us have learned behavioral traits from our parents, role models, or peers. In our professions as well as in everyday situations, we were taught how to navigate obstacles and opportunities in preparation for what lay ahead. But, we were not, and in many ways are still not, conditioned for social networking. Lessons in how to engage are missing from curricula. We learn the hard way. However, in social networking, we learn in public and we're gaining digital street smarts through positive and negative experiences. The tough lessons for many of us are rife with overfriending and oversharing.

This overabundance of access will continue to change how we interact in the real world as well. As Denise Hayes, president of the Association for University and College Counseling Center Directors, told *The Chronicle of Higher Education,* "If you develop that sense of intimacy over the Internet, it can create a void in one-on-one interaction."[2]

In October 2010, the Associated Press and mtvU released the results of a survey revealing a correlation between social networking and stress for college students.[3] More than 2,200 students were surveyed across 40 colleges. It was discovered that the majority of participants used Facebook, with more than 40 percent amassing more than 500 friends. Managing these large networks proved to be an added stressor to the already stressful college experience.

But relief is but a power button away. While most students felt pressure to answer texts or voice mails immediately and also reported feeling anxiety if their messages did not receive an immediate reply, 25 percent of students said that they would experience a sense of relief upon shutting off their cells phones and PCs. A staggering 57 percent said that they would feel stressed without access to social media. This data adds credence to the omnipresent need to network online as a means of maintaining relevance and social stature. When we fuse technology with social media, we build a series of interconnects between people that forms a new type of lifeline. When we pull the plug, we disconnect people.

Eighty-five percent say social networking helps individuals feel more connected to people, not less. Fifty-four percent believe that an increased use of technology also makes it easier to feel close to people. On the other hand, 28 percent state that digital interaction actually impedes closeness.[4] As society finds its footing in networking, what's already obvious is that some find that virtual connectedness improves relationships while others do not. Either way, online experimentation continues, and as a result, how information is exchanged and how people connect only continues to evolve.

The point at which attention is in short supply and information no longer reaches us in an effective way, or, the Attention Rubicon, as I call it, may be closer than we realize. But that didn't stop Harrisburg University of Science and Technology from experimenting in connectivity abstinence. In September 2010, the university imposed a blackout in the use of Facebook, Twitter, instant messaging, and other social media to see how the technology affects the lives of students and faculty.[5]

Indeed. Many of the college professors and teachers that I've worked with during the rise of new media expressed a great deal of frustration over the inability to maintain the attention of students in the classroom. All devices have their vices and social networking is not alone. Eric Darr, the college provost, noted the experience of one student that heightened the need for the ban, "One student felt compelled to check Facebook 21 hours a day and blocked posts between 2 and 5 in the morning to get some sleep."

What's clear is that no matter how difficult it is to find the balance, people are not abandoning social networks in favor of traditional channels. To reach people now takes an incredible amount of intelligence, relevance, and value.

■ POSTER'S REMORSE

You've heard it before. If you don't have anything interesting or productive to say, then don't say it...no, really, don't say it. The truth is that at one time or another, we've all said or shared something that we regret. When sense finally catches up with our actions, we delete the questionable content or update. But, most times it's too late. Like the way a light illuminates the room upon flicking a switch, our update was viewed and shared before we realized the momentary lapse of reason. But, we learn.

Retrevo studied the relationship between oversharing and remorse in a study published in May 2010, "Preserve Your Facebook Privacy, Post Cautiously."[6] Among the 1,000 people interviewed, more than one-third expressed poster's remorse over inappropriate comments made on Facebook, Twitter, and other social networks. As social networking moves toward mobile, the numbers are more profound. Fifty-four percent of smartphone users and 59 percent who own iPhones felt poster's remorse.

When inner monologue and reflection meet a trigger update finger, our filters become clouded. According to the study, 54 percent of people under 25 and 27 percent over 25 wished they hadn't posted certain thoughts or moments online. It's just far too easy to click before we think.

Over time, we'll mature. We'll find our voice, and once we do, our collective intelligence will be far more influential than it is today.

For organizations hoping to connect with connected customers, the same philosophy holds true. If you don't have anything interesting to say or any value to contribute, consumers will either learn to not pay attention or disconnect altogether. Poster's remorse in this case carries tremendous economic risks. It's not as much as engagement as it is about being engaging.

■ **DOES ATTENTION BANKRUPTCY LOOM BEHIND THE THIN VEIL OF POPULARITY?**

The average person on Facebook maintains a social graph of 130 people, but we also see more active users building networks with far greater connections. In the AP-mtvU study, the average student friended 500 people. Facebook and Google+ impose a 5,000-friend limit, claiming that it's impossible for anyone to have that many friends. If we introduced social physics to this equation, social networking causes a measurable increase in the velocity of information and interaction, in both directions, resulting in a change in the position of any object—namely us. Simply said, the more connections we weave, the more interaction we invite. It's just human nature to feel compelled to respond, until we can no longer keep pace with the social graphs we've fabricated.

Aside from stress and remorse, productivity may also be dwindling. Students reported falling behind in their schoolwork as a result of plugging in. The *New York Times* shared the story of Vishal Singh, a

17-year-old student in Redwood City, California, who was assigned to read Kurt Vonnegut's *Cat's Cradle* as part of his summer reading.[7] In two months, he read all of 43 pages. Rather than learning the story of Dr. Felix Hoenikker and the development of the atomic bomb through traditional reading, Singh chose instead to watch the video summary on YouTube. He shared his reason with the *New York Times,* telling them, "[On YouTube] you can get a whole story in six minutes. A book takes so long. I prefer the immediate gratification."

Explained in three words, we're *wired for distraction.* Attention is elastic, and certain aspects, such as reading comprehension, must snap back. Other nuances, such as multitasking and appreciation for short forms of content, will evolve as well.

Researchers believe that the lure of social networks and the gadgets that link us to one another are rewiring our brains to constantly switch tasks. In the process, we lose our ability to preserve attention and focus. This is particularly powerful for young people.

Fourteen-year-old Allison Miller was profiled in the *New York Times* piece. Miller sends and receives 27,000 texts per month, carrying on as many as seven conversations simultaneously. Aside from learning the importance of paying for unlimited text and data plans for our children, we're witnessing the effects of technology and digital interaction on our persona and responsibilities. She blames her lower grades on these social responsibilities.

Michael Rich, an associate professor at Harvard Medical School and executive director of the Center on Media and Child Health in Boston, believes that young adults are potentially subjected to lingering effects, "Their brains are rewarded not for staying on task but for jumping to the next thing. The worry is we're raising a generation of kids in front of screens whose brains are going to be wired differently."

But, they're not alone. Adults are also struggling with information overload. Social network fatigue or attention bankruptcy is very real. And it's contributing to a form of attention deficit disorder in the greater realm of society.

Up to this point, we've examined the inherent growing pains of embracing new media. The question is, if plugging in causes such grief, then why use it? We connect and share to earn desirable reactions and connections. It helps us mature and stay relevant.

I live in social media. It's where I work, reinvigorate my productivity, and stay connected with friends, family, and peers. It's where I learn. It's where I seek entertainment. It's how I stay in sync with the rest of my world. But just writing this book is sometimes a daunting mission. The lure of distractions is considerable. I face the same challenges as other social or connected consumers.

Should I check my tweets? Maybe I need to update my status? What new posts were published that I need to read? What is everyone talking about? What is everybody sharing in my social graph? What's trending?

Momentum and depth of due diligence are often in jeopardy. My stream of consciousness is always open to derailment. What should take a few hours creeps along like an Olympic sprinter running neck deep in a pool of water. But like the connected consumer, I'm struggling and adapting at the same time.

And here we are, still Facebooking, Googling, tweeting, and checking in. Debates are never-ending as to the value and the future of social networking. But you and I, we're not here to argue or speculate. We're here to learn. And while the theorists wax philosophical (of which I'm guilty as well), we have work to do. Back to social physics for a moment...for every action, there is always an equal and opposite reaction. Social networking appears to also offer positive effects. And when harnessed, it will only continue to change the course of human and technological evolution. As a result, people will balance their relationships so that they reduce stress and increase productivity. This isn't a one-time affair; the process of auditing relationships is constant. Your customers are connected. This will only become more pervasive. Where are you?

■ IF YOU CAN'T TWEET 'EM, JOIN THEM

As social networking migrates from the edge of outliers to the center of humanity, one by one we will find balance. We gain confidence in a new frontier that transforms our avatars into dynamic representations of who we are and who we want to be.

Employers are not so sure, however, that social networking positively affects the bottom line, and many are blocking access to Facebook, Twitter, and the like in the workplace.

In 2009, Robert Half Technology found that 54 percent of U.S. companies block social networks completely and another 19 percent permit it only for business purposes. Of that, 10 percent of companies surveyed permit social networking for personal use and 16 percent allow limited personal use.[8] Subsequent studies strengthen this side of the discussion.

Nucleus Research found that nearly half of office employees access Facebook during work, resulting in an average decrease of 1.5 percent in total office productivity.[9]

In 2010, *Wired* magazine published a story[10] that referenced a study by Morse PLC, currently named 2e2. The research estimated on-the-job social networking cost British companies $2.2 billion a year. But is social networking really detracting from work performance?

Brendan Koerner, author of the aforementioned *Wired* story, concluded his article with some very compelling thoughts on why introducing opportunities for intentional distraction can actually increase productivity.

Studies that accuse social networks of reducing productivity assume that time spent microblogging is time strictly wasted. But that betrays an ignorance of the creative process. Humans weren't designed to maintain a constant focus on assigned tasks. We need periodic breaks to relieve our conscious minds of the pressure to perform—pressure that can lock us into a single mode of thinking. Musing about something else for a while can clear away the mental detritus, letting us see an issue through fresh eyes, a process that creativity researchers call incubation.

Everything in moderation, of course.

In the book *Creativity and the Mind*,[11] authors Thomas B. Ward, Ronald A. Finke, and Steven M. Smith blend leading scientific research with experiences to help readers unlock their creative potential. The authors believe that encouraging or distracting employees to temporarily step away from a problem enhance problem-solving skills significantly. These acts force workers to explore memories in search of relevant clues.

Toward the end of 2010, the University of Melbourne released research declaring that social networks, including Facebook, Twitter, and YouTube, are the most productive ways employees can relax at work.[12] According to Dr. Brent Coker, a lecturer in the University of Melbourne's Department of Management and Marketing, the team discovered that accessing social networks refreshes deskbound employees.

The study was an extension of the University of Melbourne's earlier study that also found that "people who surf the Internet for fun—for less than 20 percent of their work time—were 9 percent more productive than those who don't."[13]

Dr. Coker explained the results to *The Age*, "The enjoyable stuff is better for people than the mundane stuff . . . the more escapist, relaxing type of feeling [the better] . . . reading what your friends are saying on Facebook, playing a little Mafia Wars or whatever . . . so when you go back to work your mind is refreshed and you can really hammer it." He continued, "A fresh mind can do a lot more in a short period of time than somebody's who's tired. It'll take them five times longer to do the same task."[14]

Indeed, with training, either officially or through self-education, we are conditioning ourselves to process new tasks even while distracted. With intentional, timed distractions, we are potentially much more productive than succumbing to social networks without governance.

■ THE PROGRESS OF PROGRESS

Over time, human nature will force discipline into how we find information and grant access to our social graph. We will focus our activities and attention to preserve happiness and ultimately gain from each interaction. We can clearly see that generations are struggling with the delicate art of maintaining balance while also unearthing new benefits for social immersion. Our path of learning and progress is righted through self-analysis and self-correction.

Sometimes we need not look further than our children for evidence of behavioral development. Some teens realize the importance of compartmentalizing their social experiences and protecting their digital identity. Teens and young adults are already experimenting with the creation of multiple accounts in social networks, one as an almost strategic façade for family and peers and the other to interact with friends online just as they do in every other facet of their life. Rarely do they cross the streams.

Living in an always-on society, we take measures for self-preservation when we feel threatened. In some cases, it's to preserve productivity, in others our sanity. For many teens, innovation in social networking is driven by the protection of their digital persona.

danah boyd (yes, it's lowercase) is a researcher at Microsoft Research New England and a Fellow at Harvard University's Berkman Center for Internet and Society, and one of the world's leading digital anthropologists studying new media today. Referred to as Risk Reduction Strategies on Facebook,[15] she shows how teens are taking control over who posts what and when to their Facebook page. Younger users have figured out that Facebook has an on/off switch as well as a handy eraser.

boyd shares the story of Mikalah, a young Facebook user who deactivates her account each time she logs out. This practice is called *super-logoff* because it doesn't completely delete the account. When Mikalah logs back in and activates the account, her connections and published content are immediately restored. So why would anyone use this super-logoff technique? Mikalah and others like her realized that by deactivating their account, they protect their Facebook wall, eliminate unwanted browsing, as well as shut off her Facebook messaging channel to control the flow of inbound information. Brilliant!

Through boyd's work, we're also introduced to Shamika. Unlike Mikalah, Shamika doesn't switch her profile on and off. Instead, she deletes every wall message, status update, and Like shortly after it's posted. The act of engagement is visible long enough to reach and resonate with the affected parties. But, once done, she sweeps away her digital footprints. This exercise is referred to as *whitewashing* or *whitewalling*. Shamika explained to boyd that she does this to avoid "too much drama." She believes that people are nosy and that it's too easy to get into trouble for the things you write and share long after they're forgotten by the poster. The window for context usually closes at some point. For her and other maturing social consumers, it's easy to maintain a clean slate that is always ready and relevant in the moment.

This isn't a scientific fact, nor am I referring to the traditional definition of the intelligence quotient (IQ), but in my experience studying and practicing new media, connected consumers boast higher social IQs. Their understanding and mastery of social media is becoming second nature. Necessity is the mother of reinvention. Shamika and Mikalah represent the evolution of the connected consumer. Their needs cause adaptation, and in the process, they become more discerning in how they consume and share information.

Attention is a precious commodity. I don't believe in attention bankruptcy, however. I don't believe that our attention spans will stretch to the point of snapping. While the attention span may be thinning, it is also adapting. The efficacy of attention is rooted in how it's shaped and focused. Our culture is undergoing yet another series of transformations, which is nothing new. We just need to learn how to change so that we can lead.

At this point, you should feel the pain of those online consumers who are at an inflection point in how they change their digital diets. We should also feel the sensation of hope. Shamika and Mikalah are representatives of the emerging class of social, or connected, consumers. Of course, there are also traditional consumers still struggling with adaptation, but our goal here is gaining a better understanding of the role of the social consumer.

As individuals, and also as brands, we are perpetually competing for the moment, and earning it requires personalization, understanding, and individual engagement.

Social media amplifies the noise. But as it is freely available to anyone to embrace, the question is how you will amplify the signal. And, how will you extract insights from the deafening volume of conversations? Doing so is how we begin to earn relevance with connected, but distracted, consumers. It's how we add to the signal.

To best engage the connected consumer, you have to feel a day in the life. Distraction is a reality and our job is predicated on capturing attention and driving action and outcomes. Social media is a privilege, and with it comes great responsibility.

Centers of Attention

➤ Each update requires thoughtfulness based on our desired audiences.

➤ In the near future, deliberate curation in how we weave our networks will improve our experiences.

➤ Developing a sense of intimacy over the Internet can create a void in one-on-one interaction.

➤ Social graphs are an extension of media networks.

➤ We are creating syndication networks around us, bringing degrees of separation to life, not just by who we know, but who we're connected to.

➤ People feel that if they shut off their attention to social networks, they become disconnected from their life.

➤ We were not, and in many ways are still not, conditioned for social networking—we are all learning together.

➤ Social Physics: Social networking causes a measurable increase in the velocity of information and interaction, in both directions, resulting in a change in the position of any object.

➤ According to research, we are becoming wired for distraction.

➤ With intentional, timed distractions, we are potentially much more productive than succumbing to social networks without governance.

➤ Social media amplifies the noise, but it's your job to amplify the signal.

➤ At the moment, there are three classes of consumers: traditional, online, and social/connected.

➤ Competing for attention and relevance is the foundation for success in engagement.

The Evolution of the Network Economy and the Human Network

The fourth edition (1867) of Walt Whitman's historic *Leaves of Grass* contains a profound statement about humankind: *I sing the body electric.* Historians and pundits alike have long debated the meaning of this important line. Of the various analyses, I find inspiration in the idea that Whitman celebrated the body as not just a thing of beauty, but the very essence of who we are. After all, it is our experiences and emotions that define who we are as well as our place in the world.

At this moment, we now sing the *digital* body electric. As in, the body we create online. There's a beauty in the idea of a digital persona. What we say, do, share, and create online defines our presence and our individuality. In many ways, it's different from who we are offline ... but that's changing. And while self-expression is central to shaping our identity, the fabric of our social graph is equally representative. For the genre of tomorrow's connected consumer, the networks that form and the roles people play in the distribution and consumption of information and experiences become the infrastructure for the *next* network economy.

More than 5 billion people are wirelessly connected through cell phones. Two billion individuals are wired to the Internet globally.[1] Add to the mix an escalating array of tablets and ultraportable PCs bridging the divide between access and information, and we start to realize something quite profound. We have become *the* information network.

The degree of connectivity between us is as staggering as it is powerful. How information travels is evolving. Through our online interactions, the devices we use, the networks we join, and the people we befriend we are becoming the architects of tomorrow's information highway. The ties that bind us are symbolized through online relationships and it is through these relationships that our experiences are shaped and shared. But today, our network is still in its infancy. We're making mistakes, overconnecting and oversharing, and hopefully learning as we go. How this network evolves will affect the way information travels and the people at the epicenter of the new (r)evolution—a simultaneous revolution and evolution in media, culture, and communications. We live in an era in which content and connections are in abundance but relevance and context are scarce. To improve the network, order must eclipse chaos. The future of information and connectivity reside in the hands of the connected consumer... you and me.

■ CONTENT WAS KING

As social networks are attracting users by the hundreds of millions, connected consumers, the savvier of the bunch, are busy figuring out how to use their social networks to gain personal and professional rewards. What started as a gold mine for consumers quickly materialized into a different kind of content commodity. People are connecting with people because they can. Information overload, as we've seen in earlier examples, was inevitable by design. Facebook, Twitter, Google, YouTube, and other social networks have captivated our attention over the years. We've been excited to connect to loved ones, rekindle forgotten friendships, and interact with scores of newfound friends. But these networks do not ship with instructions. To excel, we've been left to our own devices.

In the Web 1.0 era, during the 1990s and early 2000s, the online experience was defined by content. In fact, content long reigned as king. For almost 20 years, online sites relied upon visitors to consume the content they published and hosted. Still today, online business is predicated on the methodology of traffic and conversion. Content and marketing around content is at the center of how visitors are lured. In the era of Web 2.0, which emerged in the mid-2000s, the Web revolved around personal connections. Content suddenly became a commodity. The reality is that there was and is too much content, but not all of it matters to the people engaging within one another.

Social Media gave rise to the greatest disruption to the already disrupted business of content creation, distribution, and consumption. Social and mobile networks are now the destinations of online consumers and each individual curates his social graph differently from the next. You are the center of your egosystem. Your connections and networks build a framework for how, when, and where information finds you. Without realization, you are building an elaborate and increasingly efficient network for information ebb and flow. Our networks, whether intentional in design or not, overturn the era of content as a destination and instead demand that information comes to us.

➤ News now finds you. Special offers or deals are sent directly to you and others like you to unlock and activate.

➤ Brands come to you with invitations to join their community or to reward you for your stature within online communities.

➤ Politicians seek your endorsement by reaching out to you directly in your social stream.

➤ Local businesses are extending their services to you in geolocation networks through tips and specials.

In addition to expecting information to come to us, we are also demanding personalization. The content that is of greater interest entices us to click through. Each time a story appears in the social stream of any given network, individuals are presented with a gateway to leave their social network for a moment to help them learn more about what was shared. What's most fascinating about all of this, however, is that information needs to appear multiple times within the social stream before someone actually sees and responds to it.

In the social stream, information is curated and qualified by the people in one's network. Therefore, most of the content that flies through attention dashboards are worthy of a click. This is why many businesses and media properties are realizing that sending people aimlessly to a traditional dotcom is no longer effective for increasing traffic or conversions. Many progressive companies are experimenting with augmentation by packaging information differently for important segments and then hosting content within Facebook, YouTube, and other social networks. Also, companies are moving the clickpath to these networks where clicks-to-action begin and end in the social network or a customized landing page designed exclusively for the connected consumer. For example, the Mayo Clinic monitors what individuals are asking and sharing in social networks and connecting relevant content directly to each instance. From there, a distinct clickpath is in place to guide individuals in beneficial directions to learn more, respond, share with others, or get in contact with a representative.

This is only the beginning, however. To best capture the attention of the connected consumer, content must now also be market and/or customer-driven to speak directly to individuals as if it was designed specifically for them.

■ CONTEXT IS KING: DEFINING OUR EXPERIENCES

As we learned during the rise of social and mobile networking, users over-friended. It was all so new that we welcomed the never-ending lines of friends and the content they shared. We subjected ourselves to information overload even when it deflated the fun and diluted the enlightenment of our social experience. The connected consumer, however, is now far more self-regulating, placing greater emphasis on the quality of their social graph rather than quantity. With the increasing demands for inbound information and increased personalization and relevance, the era of content as king is officially over. Context becomes paramount in the business of engagement and the connected consumer is now in control of how relevant content moves in their direction and influences their next steps.

If the attention of this emerging class of connected consumers is fleeting, it is also focusing on what captures it.

Any medium in which information revolves around us begets elements of existentialism. *I tweet, therefore I am . . .*

In many ways, we are each responsible for the development of connected experiences through shared emotions, actions, responsibilities, and thoughts. The *me* in social media is, after all, at the core of the egosystem and why individuals willingly jump on to social networks. If we are to justify the existence of not just social networks, but our place within them, we must invest in the caliber of relationships, as well as the caliber of the content we consume, create, and share.

The answer to what customers value lies in context. How we find the right information depends on the people and organizations to whom we connect. Here misguided online consumers are learning the hard way. They are connecting to as many people as they can to help them boost their numbers because they believe it's important. On the other hand, connected consumers understand that through the concentration of connections, their social experiences, digital literacy, and the value of content that populates their streams are intensified.

Context in social and mobile networks is king and the result is amplification in signal and a decrease in overall noise. Context represents the catalyst for the overdue shift from a top-down information architecture to one that employs the laws of attraction to pull relevant content toward the center of the egosystem. In the realm of context, connected consumers are already segmenting their social networks into a series of nicheworks. Each represents something far more methodical than undeveloped social graphs. We are now weaving interest graphs, distinctive connections around the various satellites of all that interests us in the orbit of our egosystem.

Our networks will expand and contract until we find a comfortable cadence and caliber of relationships and information that falls between overload and scarcity. This balance is the essence of the next network economy. Technology isn't going to save us from information overload. We are in control of to whom we connect and why. Our social streams will improve through the quality of our connections, not the quantity. The net result of honing our relationships will be a dramatic renovation and upgrade in the relevance and value of information and people who come to us.

The pressure to connect is not insignificant. If you decide not to follow or friend someone back, don't take it personally when guilt or disappointment is tweeted your way. With everything consumers share, they are investing in an alternative form of currency and capital. Meaningful connections are not driven by reciprocity; they're fortified in mutual value. The ability to publish is a right that marks a rite of passage. And in the end, connected consumers define their persona through their actions and words and earn the relationships they deserve.

Businesses and media networks looking to attract connected consumers must earn every click by providing contextually relevant information and deliberate value. This changes the game for content production and engagement strategies. No one said this would be easy, but that's what separates the enlightened from the unenlightened.

Context and relevance aren't only prevalent in social streams. Destination brands are realizing power in contextualizing social graphs. For example, visitors to CNN.com or the Huffington Post are presented with the stories that their Facebook friends have "Liked." If we employ the cognizant act of curating nicheworks around the interests of connected consumers, the information they see becomes immensely pertinent.

Context predicates relevant content, and at the center of every experience are the individuals interacting in the network. Consequently, the future of all business is defined through shared experiences and the connections that build an efficient, people-driven information network.

■ THE SHIFT IN NETWORKING: NICHEWORKS BRIDGE SOCIAL AND INTEREST GRAPHS

As noted earlier, the genesis of a human network is being created through relationships, and forged through context. The evolution of these relationships is composed of interest groups in which each consists of strong, weak, and temporary ties. How you network on-line and network in the real world may be different, but they're both redefining how you live in the moment—offline or online. We are at the cusp of creating and *using* networks within networks (*nicheworks*, if you will) to effectively channel information inbound and outbound.

Let's take a look at why this is important to connected consumers and how the management of their networks affects how information finds them, and in turn, is shared.

As a connected consumer, the infrastructure of your egosystem places your updates and the activities of others in your social stream and the content that flows through it in a way that is unique to you. When you share, your social graph as it exists today is essentially your broadcast network. What you say once is sent to many. It is not unlike how news media publishes information today. The future of network-ing is a convergence of one-to-many publishing (social graphs) and also a more focused one-to-one-to-many approach (interest graphs). For example, you have many interests and you most likely maintain different sets of relationships around each. You may have some rela-tionships that span all or some interests, but in many cases, interest groups are distinct. Even though you have many contacts in your life (the social graph), they are grouped on the basis of common threads, thus creating a series of interest graphs.

As such, a new formula for relationships and how information travels starts to take shape: one plus one = many.

While social networks may offer elementary controls to select who sees what, the majority of status updates are published for everyone—*one to many*. But that's simply not at all how human inter-action works in the real world.

Social networks are designed to facilitate the creation and cultiva-tion of discrete social graphs, or nicheworks, which set the foundation for interest graphs—*one to one to many*. The people who populate each and also what we say and do are different across each group.

Paul Adams once worked on the UX (user experience) team at Google before jumping ship to Facebook. In 2010, he gave a presen-tation that discussed the idea of contextual networking and the need for nicheworking.[2] His research and observations demonstrated how context, relevance, and interest are at the core of the future of media and connections. His work would later lead to what would become Google Circles, a feature in Google+ that allows people to group their friends by interest and the nature of their relationship.

Mr. Adams's presentation is the result of years of research in how people network online and offline. His conclusions demonstrate the need for us to intentionally channel our activity in its most favor-able directions. Also, his research demonstrates the nature of how

individuals will group businesses over time, based on how they perceive the nature or the value of the relationship.

The example Paul shared could be any one of us. By the time we
reach the end of Adams's example, we will see an inflection point
from a social consumer to an informed, connected consumer.

Adams introduced us to Debbie. And to help us get a better sense
of her world, I borrowed some of his slides to share with you here. (See
Figures 5.1 through 5.7.)

Debbie moved to San Diego, but is still connected to a group of
friends she made when she lived in Los Angeles. She now also maintains a network of new friends in San Diego. Of course, she is still
in contact with her family as well. These three groups of friends and
family currently reside in the same social graph, Debbie's egosystem.

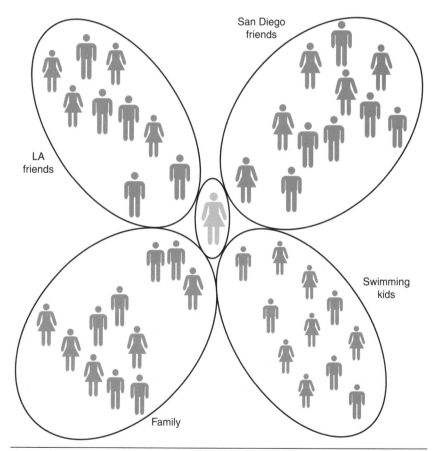

Figure 5.1   Debbie's Egosystem

Source: Paul Adams, "The Real Life Social Network," June 2010.

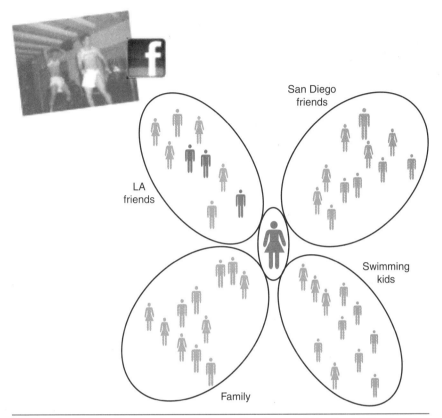

Figure 5.2   Debbie Comments on Photos in One Group of Her Social Graph

Source: Paul Adams, "The Real Life Social Network," June 2010.

Debbie is also an active swimmer and trains 10-year-old kids in competitive swimming. She has also befriended other trainers and some of the kids in her class.

Back in Los Angeles, some of Debbie's friends work in a gay bar. They share photos on Facebook of wild and memorable nights in the bar.

Debbie loves the pictures and often comments on them.

By the nature of social graph design, the 10-year-old kids that have friended Debbie can see her activity as well as the pictures she's commented on.

Debbie realized, for the first time, that the kids could see this activity and she was upset at herself for not realizing this earlier. She blamed the system for letting it happen. Experiences on social networks are not compartmentalized today. They are shared blindly and as a result, the human network as designed is asymmetrical, skewed to noise rather than signal.

This is true for every one of us. We share in a one-to-many approach without realizing that we're mass broadcasting to an audience much like traditional media today.

As Adams observed, the problem isn't Facebook. The problem is that one social network does not represent how we network in real life and exposes discrete groups to one another intentionally or unintentionally. We contribute to information overload by not segmenting our content or channeling our experiences to corresponding nicheworks.

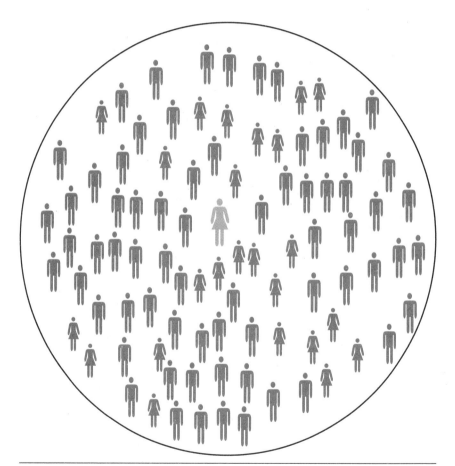

Figure 5.3   The Online Experience: One Large Social Network Does Not Represent How We Network in Real Life

Source: Paul Adams, "The Real Life Social Network," June 2010.

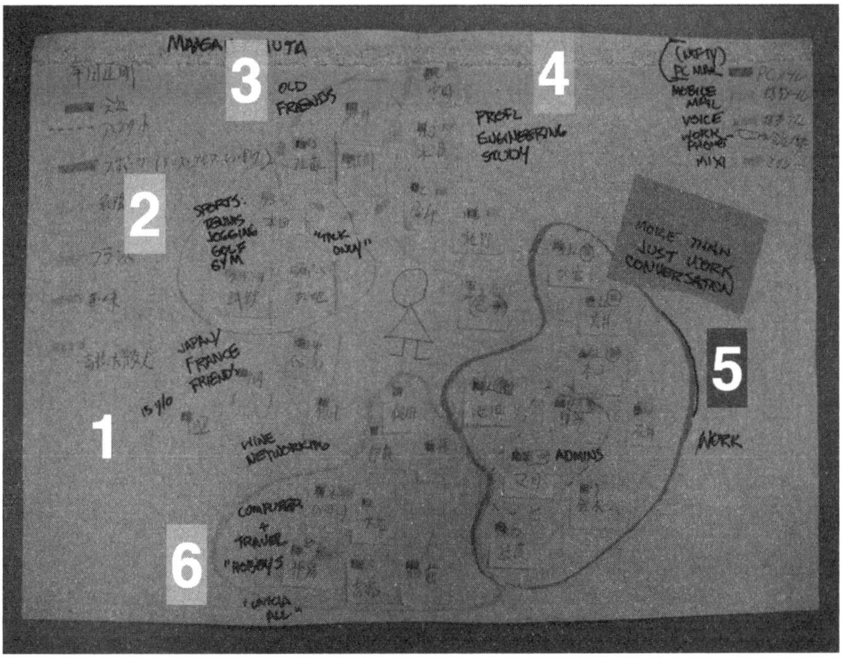

Figure 5.4   A Look at Real-World Social Networks Offline

Source: Paul Adams, "The Real Life Social Network," June 2010.

In reality, we do not have just one group of friends. Nor should we have only one social graph. We maintain networks of friends, peers, associates, and family. And each is governed by varying levels of interest, themes, intimacy, and expectations.

According to Adams's work at Google, people tend to have between four and six real-life groups. For some, it's school, church, family, sports, hobbies, and so on. And each of those groups tends to have between 2 and 10 people.

In social networking, the patterns appear to be very similar. While social networks such as Facebook and Twitter make it easier to connect, we still maintain relationships (strong ties) and also relations (weak ties). What's changing is the abundance of weak ties, driven by context and interest. This is also a reflection of the intermingling of our personal and professional contacts.

According to Adams, a study of 3,000 randomly selected Americans showed that we maintained just four strong ties. Many held between two to six.

A separate study of 1,178 adults found that on average, people maintained regular contact with 10 friends on a weekly basis.

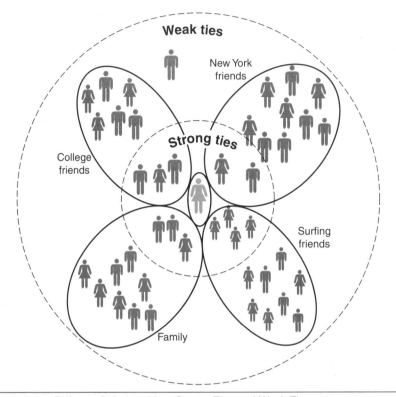

Figure 5.5   Different Relationships: Strong Ties and Weak Ties

Source: Paul Adams, "The Real Life Social Network," June 2010.

On Facebook, the average size of the social graph is 130. However, studies show that the vast majority of Facebook users interact regularly with just four to six people.

As the size of social graphs increases and as we start to include new connections based on various interests, we're introduced to the idea of temporary ties. These fleeting relationships emerge through projects, current decisions, events, or other circumstances in which the need for information and communication results, but usually dissipates over time. For example, Debbie is considering a trip to Paris. As she begins her preparation, she'll most likely start with research on Google and also within social networks. She'll ask questions of her social graph and as a result, she'll meet new people, join new groups, follow lists or other experts related to the Paris experience, and she'll interact with people and their respective social graphs all over the world. She may in fact, meet some of these new friends during her travel. After her trip to Paris, most of these ties will dissolve

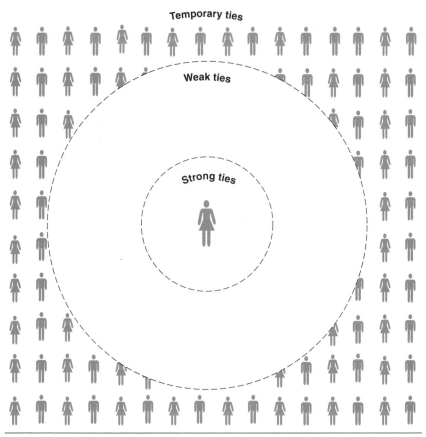

Figure 5.6   New Category for Online Relationships: Temporary Ties
Source: Paul Adams, "The Real Life Social Network," June 2010.

because they were created only as a temporary means to insight and information. For social graphs and interest graphs to mature into networks of relevance, however, Debbie would then need to unfollow, unfriend, and unsubscribe to the temporary groups that are no longer of value to her.

■ **RECOGNIZING THE VALUE OF NICHEWORKS**

In 2010, Facebook reinvented its Groups product, giving us the ability to create nicheworks within our social network for the different audiences with which we'd like to communicate. Before doing so, Groups were elementary in their design and did not facilitate the type of interaction necessary to help leaders engage members or help members communicate and collaborate effectively. Now, Facebook Groups represents something much more meaningful than a collection of people for idle chatter. This work served as the foundation for Google Circle. People can now build social networks based on interests. Like Google Circles, Facebook Groups are platforms for improving focus, increasing collaboration, and fostering dedicated relationships around interest and purpose. They're designed to help interest groups flourish.

As such, privacy is now a process of boundary management. Through settings within the devices and networks we use—to whom we decide to connect—and what we decide to share—privacy is by all means in our control to define how much other people know about us, what they see, and the impressions they form. At the same time, the onus is on businesses to navigate these nicheworks in ways that offer value for the community. At a minimum, studying the nature and dynamics of nicheworks is enlightening. The intelligence contained within nicheworks on Facebook, Google, Twitter, and so on reveal short- and long-term opportunities.

Nicheworks and interest graphs represent the future of social networking and business relevance. Recognizing the value of microengagement delivers value at a macro level. Businesses are now presented with a unique view into how connected customers communicate, collaborate, and co-create to market with purpose.

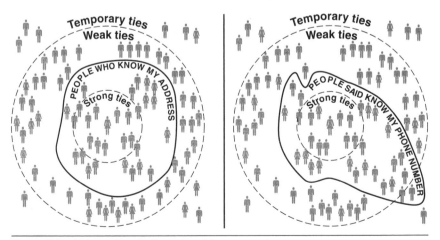

Figure 5.7   Privacy Equals Boundary Management

Source: Paul Adams, "The Real Life Social Network," June 2010.

■ INTEREST GRAPHS ARE THE CONSTRUCTS OF MATURING INFORMATION NETWORKS

From content to context and from networks to nicheworks, the connected consumer is fabricating a much more efficient network for the exchange of information and the expansion and contraction of long-term relationships and short-term relations. The velocity of information is tied to the architecture of social networks. Efficiency is created through improvements in how we connect and interact with one another. As such, the future of business will be defined by relevance.

The path of relevant information advances as shared interests shape interest graphs. The interest graph expedites and sharpens how the right information finds the connected consumer and how the content and experiences they share also reach interested parties. Through the ongoing investment of shared experiences related to interest, these focused networks are strengthened and enhance the experience of everyone connected.

While we're left to our own devices to improve our network and ultimately the network effect, we do get a little help from our friends and our network hosts. Facebook, Twitter, Google, LinkedIn, and others, recommend like-minded people to us for connection. The algorithm originally served up the avatars of those who were connected to people we know. As technology and social networking has evolved, the algorithm uncovered people who share similar interests based on the information and experiences they already share and consume. Businesses can benefit as well.

The livelihood of social and mobile networks relies on us to cultivate and define our connections. By investing in meaningful and beneficial relationships, we become vested in the community. By investing in the caliber of connections and their nature, we improve not only how information flows between us, but also how social networks sell and serve us paid content. Interest graphs are incredibly monetizable, and may in fact represent the future of marketing, service, media, and advertising. More on this later. . . .

As a result of our vested relationships, we place greater value and emphasis on our attention streams. As we progress, we are subsidizing a powerful exchange for information commerce. We also advance the foundation of literacy by improving how people learn, discover, share, and communicate.

As we examine our online relationships, how we view the nature of relationships and what defines them changes, and as a result, this affects how we connect with one another and businesses alike. What started as the social graph, the network of people we knew and connected to in social networks is now spawning new branches that resemble how we interact in real life. The difference is that attention becomes an even more precious commodity and businesses must adapt in order to capture it.

We're now looking beyond the social graph as we move into focused networks that share more than just a relationship. This is the era of the interest graph—the expansion and contraction of social nicheworks around common interests and events.

I personally maintain a series of interest graphs within my social graph. I follow and communicate with individuals who share interests in new media, digital anthropology, technology, marketing, business, and wine. When I communicate publicly, I realize that at any one moment, I'm addressing only a subset of the group, not the entire group. When I consume, I focus on specific lists or groups to satisfy my craving for relevant content for each contextual moment. Doing so prevents digital schizophrenia and enriches my experience.

Interest graphs represent a potential gold mine for brands, media, and any other person or organization needing your attention and action. But before we jump into the commercial aspects of interest graphs and connected consumers, we'll close this chapter with one last thought. The potential of social networking is far from realized. We are building the pipes for information commerce through every connection we make. It almost sounds like a science fiction movie, but the machines are not building a matrix. We, instead, are the architects of our online experiences.

Centers of Attention

➤ People are forming the foundation of a sophisticated information network.

➤ Content is important, but it is no longer king.

➤ Context is king and is the key to earning relevance.

➤ People are at the center of their own experiences, creating personal egosystems.

➤ Connected consumers no longer start their online experiences by visiting destinations; they visit their streams.

➤ Information must now find people directly; otherwise, it goes unseen.

➤ Attention must be captured where and when it's focused.

➤ Businesses, media companies, and brands are moving experiences from their websites to social networks.

➤ Social networks are spawning nicheworks for focused interaction.

➤ Technology isn't going to save us from information overload; connected consumers are innovating solutions on their own.

➤ Relationships are not about quantity, but instead quality to improve signal-to-noise ratios.

➤ Social networking today doesn't mimic how we network in real life, but that's changing.

➤ Social graphs are evolving into interest graphs.

➤ Interest graphs introduce a new formula to the information equation, from one-to-many to one-to-one-to-many.

➤ Networks are maturing and represent the future for media and how information reaches people.

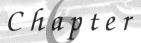

Chapter 6

The Nextwork: Defining Tomorrow's Information Network

We are who we are because of who we know and who we admire . . . this is the nexus of self-actualization and information commerce.

In 2010, the Audit Bureau of Circulations documented that newspaper subscriptions in the United States decreased by almost 9 percent.[1] Subscription trends aside, the *Wall Street Journal, USA Today,* and the *New York Times* collectively possess a circulation of less than 5 million.

Television viewership is on the decline as well. In January 2011, the Nielsen Company released its primetime ratings revealing the top programs and viewers. CBS, NBC, Fox, and ABC combined reached an estimated 35 million people.[2]

However, the erosion of viewers or subscribers isn't the story here. This is about the shrinking role of traditional information networks and the rise of what I call the *nextwork,* the interconnected relationships that traverse across multiple social networks. The reach of these networks is practically limitless. With Facebook housing more than 750 million residents and Twitter sheltering over 200 million digital natives among other emerging and established networks, over 1 billion nodes propel information around the world every second of every day.

Denying or ignoring the reality of a new information landscape doesn't change the actual flow of information. Audiences, individuals, are progressively tuning in to their social networks for information and, in turn, they may already be tuning you out.

Several leading pioneers who carried the banner for traditional media are already realizing the need to extend beyond traditional circulation and web visitors to increase reach and relevance. These brands are taking to social networks to connect with the connected, to offset losses, and gain traction with a different genre of information consumers. At the time this book was printed...

➤ CNN amassed an audience of 4 million followers on Twitter and 500,000 fans on Facebook.

➤ The *New York Times* scored 3 million followers and 1.1 million Likes.

➤ The *Wall Street Journal* possessed 600,000 Twitter followers and 200,000 followers on Facebook.

➤ The *Guardian* (UK) accumulated 125,000 Twitter followers and 62,000 fans on Facebook.

➤ Satirical news outlet *The Onion* earned 2.5 million followers and 1.5 million Likes.

➤ *People* actively advertised its Facebook page to collect 1 million Likes and also attracted 2.3 million Twitter followers.

But this is just the beginning. Brands are realizing the importance of becoming visible when and where the attention of their consumers is focused. Many early adopters are betting on the importance of the connected consumer, investing in the cultivation of communities in areas where they don't necessarily control, but as participants earn the privilege to steer experiences and interaction. With investment, we learn that there is indeed reward. Several of the top brands on Facebook and Twitter have already eclipsed the very media that traditional and online consumers look to for information.

➤ Coca Cola was Liked more than 30 million times on Facebook.

➤ Starbucks earned 25 million Likes on Facebook and 1.3 million Twitter followers.

➤ Skittles invested in Facebook and was Liked by 20 million people.

➤ Converse All Star followed Skittles' footsteps and accumulated 20 million fans on Facebook.

➤ Victoria's Secret also invested in Facebook, accumulating 15 millions Likes on Facebook and 50,000 fans on Twitter.

An interesting observation is that for some brands, Facebook is an essential home base within which individuals can interact with not only representatives, but also interact around content for a more engaging experience. Media properties, however, witnessed greater adoption among connected consumers on Twitter. The human networks are conductors in the spark of information dissemination. Of the top accounts on Twitter for example,

➤ E! Online boasted 3 million followers.
➤ *Time* connected with 2.3 million.
➤ BBC Click garnered 1.8 million.

However, when we look at Facebook, the same media properties didn't connect with consumers in the same numbers as seen on Twitter:

➤ E! Online: 93,000 fans
➤ *Time:* 230,000
➤ BBC Click: 2,247

The community is only as strong as our investment in earning the attention of connected consumers and nurturing a community that engages and provokes the sharing of information.

The distance between a brand and its customers is measured by shared experiences.

■ DO I KNOW YOU? OH YES, YOU'RE FRIENDS WITH THEIR FRIENDS WHO ARE FRIENDS WITH THOSE WHO ARE FRIENDS OF MINE

In 2012, the human population is estimated at 7 billion.[3] With every new medium, how we connect and relate to one another changes. As the world of information and connections experiences dramatic tectonic shifts, people are moving closer together. The result is an increasingly connected society in which the flow of information discovery and sharing accelerates exponentially.

In 1929, Hungarian author Frigyes Karinthy published a series of short stories titled "Everything Is Different" (Minden masképpen van).[4] This work inspired generations of study by mathematicians and social scientists around Karinthy's postulation that the world was shrinking, not literally, but figuratively. His hypothesis was based on ever-increasing connectedness. As human networks evolved, geographic distances between people diminished as relationships grew in density. In one of the short stories, titled "Chains" or "Chain Links," Karinthy introduced us to a game we've heard of, but never quite knew its origin.[5] He believed that any two individuals anywhere in the world could trace the connections between them within five steps:

> *A fascinating game grew out of this discussion. One of us suggested performing the following experiment to prove that the population of the Earth is closer together now than they have ever been before. We should select any person from the 1.5 billion inhabitants of the Earth—anyone, anywhere at all. He bet us that, using no more than five individuals, one of whom is a personal acquaintance, he could contact the selected individual using nothing except the network of personal acquaintances.*

Karinthy's work served as the foundation for the renowned and still contested idea of Six Degrees of Separation and it inspired the work of many studying social networks in the real world and eventually online.

Years later, scientists conducted a series of studies known as the small world experiments. In 1961, Michael Gurevich published a landmark study on the structure of social networks in his Massachusetts Institute of Technology PhD dissertation under Ithiel de Sola Pool.[6] Austrian mathematician Manfred Kochen sampled Gurevich's empirical results in a mathematical manuscript, *Contacts and Influence*, deducing that in a U.S.-sized population without social structure, "It is practically certain that any two individuals can contact one another by means of at least two intermediaries."[7]

Several years later, Stanley Milgram continued Gurevich's experiments at Harvard University where he reported the Small World Problem.[8] Milgram's approach focused on recruiting random people in diverse cities across the Midwest to pass a letter through their social network to reach one of two Massachusetts residents.[9] The number of relays in each successful case averaged 5.5.

As technology evolved, the study was revisited in 2001. Instead of using letters as the social object, this time Duncan Watts, a professor at Columbia University, recreated Milgram's experiment using the Internet and email. This time, an email message was the package requiring delivery. With 48,000 senders, 19 targets, and 157 countries, Watts's results were strikingly similar to those of Milgram, averaging six steps.[10]

■ IT'S A SMALLER WORLD, AFTER ALL

Through social and mobile networks, human relationships are forming new, extensive channels for information to travel. As in the real world, we are connected to one another through varying degrees of separation online. Through networks such as Facebook and Twitter, the connected consumer is redrawing the lines between them, showing us that online social networking is indeed a smaller and more connected world after all.

Fifty-seven percent of Americans feel more connected to people now than they did previously and 56 percent keep in touch with more friends now than in the past.[11] This information was shared in late 2010 as part of the Harris Poll conducted by Harris Interactive, a leading custom market research firm. Interestingly, 58 percent of online adults feel more connected even though they are not directly interacting with one another. And 54 percent are actually seeing people less often, yet still feeling a greater sense of connectedness.

Harris Interactive found that almost 9 in 10 online Americans use social media. Of those social media users, 44 percent prefer to interact with acquaintances using social media rather than face to face.

While this isn't representative of the overall global population, it is a sign that the connected consumer is unique and therefore requires a unique approach for engagement, marketing, and ultimately product customization.

Starting in 2009 and published in early 2010, the Department of Computer Science at the Korea Advanced Institute of Science and Technology performed a multipart analysis of Twitter with an emphasis on interconnectivity and the ability for the network to filter quality information.[12] The study showed the efficiency of how information travels within the egosystem. Within a few rapid hops through retweets, a significant percentage of the Twitter population is exposed to news and events as they happen. Much like Milgram's letters and Watts's emails, this experiment used retweets as the conduit. The report documented an average person-to-person travel path length on Twitter of 4.12 and shrinking.

The findings in these studies are paramount in the distinction between traditional and connected consumers. Connected consumers are the architects of a future information system that is already significant as it stands today and is only growing in prominence. Whereas brands and media outlets existed on proprietary networks and distribution channels to control the flow of information, the egosystem is a far more efficient system. The future of commerce is linked to the human network or what I call the "nextwork." While it doesn't eliminate the need to build and cultivate proprietary networks, the social and interest graphs woven by connected consumers serve as vital arteries in the circulation of the lifeblood of any business.

■ INFORMATION AT THE SPEED OF TWEETS

When 2011 arrived in Japan, Twitterers wished their friends and followers a fond "Akemashite omedetou gozaimasu" ("Happy New Year!"). On Oshogatsu, we not only welcomed a new year, but also a new record for the number of tweets per second (TPS) reaching 6,939.[13] This shattered the previous record of 3,283 TPS, which was set when Japan defeated Denmark in the World Cup in the summer of 2010. Four short months later, the number of tweets per second soared when news of the death of Osama Bin Laden hit Twitter. While it didn't break the record set during the 2011 New Year, tweets about Bin Laden flew at a blistering rate of 5,106 TPS, which also shattered the record once set during the 2010 World Cup.

The *nextwork* sends and receives information at blinding speeds, creating an efficient human switchboard and network that in theory and in practice, outperforms telephone, terrestrial, cell, emergency, and web networks for the speed and precision at which relevant experiences are shared and re-shared. I call this the new information divide, the delta between an event and the time it's officially reported (Figure 6.1). It is in this space where today's human network comes alive. Filling the gap is also representative of opportunities for innovation and engagement. By plugging into the information ecosystem and participating through the creation and curation of information, organizations can augment existing information channels.

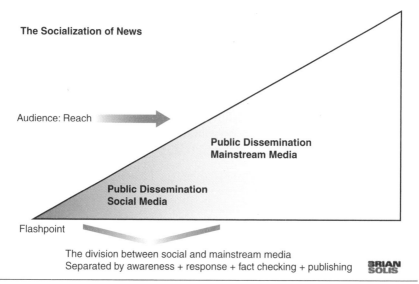

The Socialization of News

Audience: Reach

Public Dissemination
Mainstream Media

Public Dissemination
Social Media

Flashpoint

The division between social and mainstream media
Separated by awareness + response + fact checking + publishing

BRIAN SOLIS

Figure 6.1   The Information Divide

Indeed social media is changing, documenting, and also making history, and revolutionizing once invincible industries that are now paralyzed by confusion, fear, and ignorance. Although they're reacting now, it will take more than the iPad, Kindle, Nook, and other digital readers to revitalize the business of media.

Information moves with or without destination media. . . .

News no longer breaks, it tweets—demonstrating the efficiency, momentum, and influence of the human network. With every new iterative update, social graphs transform into a highly organized information distribution system that resembles an Amber Alert network for the social Web—with far greater speed, reach, impact, and resonance. The future of all media is rooted in engagement and its worth is measured by contribution, collaboration, and the extent of consequential relationships within any and all online networks of relevance.

Human networks can be used as a seismograph of sorts that channels important events and relevant information online and offline. As a result, active connections serve as the pulse of society.

If information's reach, velocity, and impact are measured by this human seismograph, organizations must now employ social seismologists to measure and source the information that will enable them to effectively compete for the future as well as mindshare, right now. Participating in the information egosystem is how we identify information gatekeepers and the corresponding nodes for information dissemination. It is also how any individual or organization can identify how to bridge the information divide with insight, direction, and valuable information as needed. It is context, though, that stitches together the fabric of the human network. As such, the quality of connections designates velocity and distance. We can no longer ignore the importance of this powerful information architecture in which people are at the center of dissemination. Our ability to embrace it and earn a role among the connected will catapult us beyond the reach of even the most sophisticated traditional networks of today.

Centers of Attention

➤ Traditional and online consumers' support for traditional media is dwindling.

➤ Media companies are finding new touchpoints in human networks.

➤ Brands are following suit and building networks that already outperform media networks in these new networks.

➤ Connected consumers are making the online world a much smaller place, shrinking the degrees of relationships from six down to four on Twitter.

➤ Egosystems require attention and nurturing in each respective network to gain traction and build communities.

➤ Information travels faster through the egosystem than any other network; it takes only a few key shares to reach the masses.

➤ Any individual or organization can identify the networks, gatekeepers, and channels important to their business to participate in and steer the flow of information.

➤ Savvy consumers are forming the foundation for nextworks, creating more efficient information networks.

Chapter 7

Your Audience Is Now an Audience of Audiences with Audiences

When I joined the global speaking circuit many years ago, I marveled at the composition and behavior of the audience and how it changed each and every time I presented. Yes, I was there to engage my audience, but unbeknownst to them, I, too, was their audience, observing how their attention slowly shifted its focus from me to me plus their social graph. Slowly, but inevitably, laptops, tablets, and mobile phones originally intended for note taking were being used as a portal for shared experiences among the connected. The number of faces I could see slowly dipped and the battle for eye contact was lost until the only objects that remained fixed on me were the logos or the lenses of the devices in the room.

The reactions of other speakers were as interesting as they were telling. In the speaker rooms for events, each speaker expressed varying levels of concern for the obvious lack of attention in their sessions. Many believed it was rude or disrespectful. Some were deeply concerned that it would lead to revolt or be used as a way to bash the presenters. Others worried about whether or not their message got through to attendees. But personally, I was indifferent. I was fascinated by the idea that attention was only partially focused on me, yet the events I was speaking at were significant enough to warrant in-person presence. I decided not to challenge or complain about what was clearly becoming a widespread reality; I embraced the inevitable and committed to better understanding the phenomenon.

Make no mistake. The audience of today is not the audience we think we know. We are now contending with something new, different, and honestly, better for presenters and brands alike. If they recognize this distinction, they can amplify their message.

I completely redesigned the format of my presentation to trigger the sharing of experiences. I realized that if I could encourage attendees to share my words, I could at once get my message across to those in the room as well as to their online friends and followers. My slides, to this day, are rich with visuals and statements made with fewer than 140 characters—usually 120 to leave room for potential retweets.

See, at the center of the transformation of the audience is the ability for individuals to capture a moment through text, video, audio, or still images and share them in real time to the hundreds or thousands of individuals in their social and interest graphs. To me, it was the manifestation of the nextwork to take a one-to-many distribution channel and reshape it into a one-to-one-to-many-more syndication network that invited others outside the realm of the event to participate and ultimately connect with me.

This observation is not unlike what businesses must contend with now as they attempt to engage connected consumers. This is the dawn of an audience with an audience with audiences.

The update box in any social network is the hub of the connected consumer, and the experiences shared there are the ties that bind. Each update we share quite literally becomes a social object, a form of media that invites interaction whereby reach resonates and extends like concentric circles with every instance. Social objects represent the asphalt that paves the roads between us.

For anyone with a story to tell, from speakers to brands to politicians to causes and everything in between, connecting with the connected consumer is how we stay relevant and spark reactions that are mutually beneficial. The trick is capturing attention right now and competing not just for the future, but also for the moment.

■ SHORT ATTENTION SPAN THEATER

Let's go back some years to talk a bit about how we got here so that I can connect the dots to the notion of the audience with audiences and what comes next.

During the Web 2.0 Expo in San Francisco in April 2008, social business analyst Jeremiah Owyang (my colleague at Altimeter Group), startup entrepreneur and technology developer Gregory Narain, social business architect Stowe Boyd, and I were asked to present on the emergence of microblogging and micromedia. At the time, Twitter was leading the foray of connected micromessaging networks along with early Twitter competitors FriendFeed, Jaiku, and Pownce. In our planning discussions, we focused the outline on the impact of these tools on business, but we also realized the importance of demonstrating how micromedia would eventually affect human behavior. At the time, Twitter search was extremely young, as was Twitter itself. Hashtags were just hitting the scene.[1] Organizing conversations and channeling them into a real-time stream didn't really exist at that time. But even then, we realized that the people in the room would indeed share their experiences from that event with their online connections.

To shake things up, we explored the possibility of developing a dedicated application that would channel every live tweet published about our session and feature it on two large screens on either side of the stage. To our knowledge, this was the first time the audience became part of the session using Twitter. The application development led by Narain was packaged as "Front Channel, bringing conversations from the back channel into the spotlight." As you can imagine, it was a bit controversial. Remember, Twitter was young and its users weren't quite sure what to share and why. When the audience was presented with an opportunity to share their thoughts with the rest of the room, they indeed said what was on their mind. Here are some examples of tweets shared from that session:

➤ "The guy next to me smells."
➤ "I'm humping your pixels."
➤ "I don't get Twitter."

The audience giggled each time something funny was posted, incentivizing others to follow suit. We realized quickly that by democratizing the conversation, the conversation could spin out of control; we therefore channeled their questions and observations through a moderator to be addressed between our commentaries. Once harnessed, the conversation focused and was suddenly very productive. Narain, who was the event's moderator, also noticed how quickly the discussion spread across Twitter. There were 500 people in the room and thousands of individuals connected to them, each tweeting their views and reactions to our discussion. At one point, more than 700 tweets were published about that session in a span of only 45 minutes (Figure 7.1).

As you can see, the conversation reached well beyond those in the room and sparked a global conversation that would continue to reverberate for weeks.

It was later dubbed as the panel "heard 'round the world." As social media blogger and strategist Lee Odden noted in his summary of the session, "The effect of the session was felt 'round the world and in real time. That's powerful."[2]

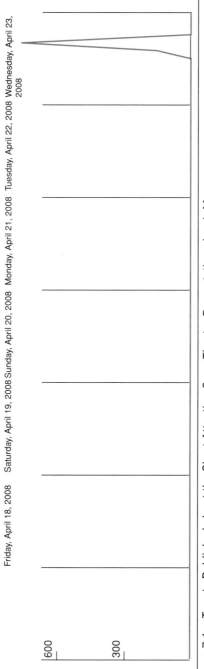

Figure 7.1   Tweets Published about the Short Attention Span Theater Presentation: Jacob Morgan

Source: www.jmorganmarketing.com/web-20-expo-microblogging-micromedia/.

This experiment led to the eventual inclusion of live tweets in conferences everywhere, each experimenting with rules and directions to keep the conversations focused and productive. The ability to share real-time experiences became part of the conference ecosystem. While powerful, it struck fear into the hearts of presenters. The thought of rallying negative commentary into a highly visible medium in which interaction only spurred attention, would force many to rethink adoption.

The back channel originally lent to the perception of real-time chatter as immature, negative, or unproductive. However, individuals and their understanding of this personal real-time medium would, in fact, mature. For example, the tweets shared from live conferences would serve as their notes for future reference. The key for a presenter to unlock a channeled experience was relevance and the establishment of a personal connection. The same is true for anyone seeking to reach their audience. Brands can now dramatically amplify their story, value proposition or message by connecting with an audience in a way that triggers sharing. This changes everything, as it's no longer simply about broadcasting, but rather engaging with consumers. Remember, one plus one equals many.

This coming of age, so to speak, is consequential to the engagement and adaption of any organization. The connected consumer literally shapes experiences and perceptions based on their interaction with content or information. Ignoring these new networks is not an option, as ignorance is bliss until it's not. Our silence says everything and nothing at the same time.

■ AN AUDIENCE WITH AN AUDIENCE OF AUDIENCES

Several years ago, Mollie Sterling shared a picture of a classroom at her alma mater, the Missouri School of Journalism. The picture eventually went viral and in 2008, Apple used it in a press conference announcing a next-generation Macbook event.[3]

In her post titled "How Do You Like Them Apples?," Sterling featured the now-famous picture (Figure 7.2) with a statement that documented the rapid evolution in human computing and networking, "It does my heart good to see these photos from my alma mater, the Missouri School of Journalism. Back in the fall of 2001 when I was a freshman, it was me and two other kids in the back row with our glowing Apples. Now I feel almost sad for that poor kid with the Windows machine in the front row:)."[4]

To say it's a captivating photo is an understatement. It's the kind of picture that evokes exercises in existentialism and introspection.

Figure 7.2   A Visualization of the Connected Consumer and an Audience with an Audience of Audiences

At the very least, it makes us question the future of handwriting. As an aside, there is only one person in the audience taking notes manually.

Sterling's picture is more than an advertisement for Apple. It serves as both a time capsule immortalizing this important transition and evidence of the emergence of new information nextworks, a series of audiences with extended audiences. Every single one of these students is a representation of the connected customer. They are each connected to others in the room and around the world, figuratively and literally. They are nodes in the human network, playing an instrumental role in the dissemination of information and also the experiences that unite us online and in real life (IRL). Your job is now to influence what they share.

■ THE PEOPLE FORMERLY KNOWN AS THE AUDIENCE

We live in interesting times and the dose of reality contained within that photo is intoxicating and frightening at the same time. The classroom, however, is merely one setting in which we can expect to see the impact of the connected individual and the networked audiences they weave.

The audience with audiences populates conferences, webinars, and meetings. The audience with audiences redefines the living room. It is the new consumer landscape.

Each update we share quite literally becomes a social object, a form of media that invites interaction in which reach resonates and extends like concentric circles with every instance. Social objects represent the asphalt that paves the roads between us.

Good friend and NYU journalism professor Jay Rosen famously wrote in 2006, "We are the people formerly known as the audience."[5] His work served as the stimulus for humanizing the audience, challenging content producers to consider the very people they were attempting to reach so as to earn personal connections and galvanize meaningful interaction.

And now the audience has ripened to earn an audience of its own. To connect with this audience requires awareness and appreciation. It requires an understanding that they are impervious to anything that doesn't clearly offer value in exchange for ongoing attention and connection.

■ THE PSYCHOLOGY OF THE AUDIENCES WITH AUDIENCES

Remember, at the heart of the egosystem is you. And it is the events you attend, the news that grabs you, the sounds you hear, the activity you see, and the things that move you that make their way from your world to mine. This is the information network erected to facilitate the distribution of information and the interaction that transpires where and when they appear in our social streams.

The audience with audiences is bound by sharing under a mantra, "I'm living this right now and I want to share this moment with you so that we can experience it together."

But it's more than just sharing. There's a real psychological need to do so. So you or your management can rest assured that social and mobile networks are not going away. At a minimum, sharing is representative of the growing responsibility and increasingly pulling people's feelings as their audiences grow. As individuals cultivate their networks, the care and feeding of it naturally develops. It comes back to the idea that individuals feel disconnected from their friends when they are not interacting with them through their preferred networks. In between interaction, shared experiences fill the void and keep us connected. This keeps us relevant or gives us a semblance of relevance.

It's no longer surprising to attend a social event and see one or more parties checking into locations, tweeting their activity, texting other contacts, updating their Facebook status, checking emails—all while interacting in the real world. It's a delicate balance to jostle online and offline engagement in real time, but the digerati can manage quite well. Because they're always on, they are perpetually living in the moment. They share and seek reactions, and it is these reactions that satisfy and reward the activity. As a result, our attention is constantly lured from the physical to the virtual realm to manage our networks and the experiences we're compelled to share.

Is this behavior a reflection of introverted socializing or is it a sign of something more remarkable? It's both. Online interaction instills a sense of confidence with every action, reaction, Like, follow, request, and share we earn. In a sense, we move one step away from online introvert and one step closer toward becoming digital extroverts. With each update we publish, we're validated and motivated.

Experiences are steerable through relevance and thoughtfulness, but their design must be intentional.

Nowadays, when I present at conferences, I ask, "How many of you are live tweeting this event right now?" Glancing once again at the powerful imagery conveyed through the snapshot of the Missouri School of Journalism class, it's not unrealistic to expect that almost every hand will rise.

As I tell audiences and brands alike, my job now is to speak to you and through you at the same time. The goal, of course, is to share our words and ideas across social graphs and interest graphs connecting to those in the room and the people to whom they're connected around the world.

This is the beginning of the understanding necessary to activate new information networks to reach intended audiences and qualified audiences with audiences to attract attention and drive actions.

■ ZUCKERBERG'S LAW

During Facebook's inaugural F8 Developers Conference in 2008, Facebook founder Mark Zuckerberg introduced us to a formula for online sharing that would later become known as Zuckerberg's Law.[6]

His point was that social networking was just about connecting with people whom we knew. The network would evolve to facilitate sharing and collaboration and accordingly our behavior would evolve along with it. Zuckerberg defined the future of sharing this way, "I would expect that next year, people will share twice as much information as they share this year, and next year, they will be sharing twice as much as they did the year before. That means that people are using Facebook, and the applications and the ecosystem, more and more."

Whether or not the law still holds true is immaterial. People are in fact sharing and consuming more information online than ever before. Nielsen reported that Americans spend nearly a quarter of their time online (906 hours) each month in social networks.[7] And that number is going only up. Between 2009 and 2010, Americans spent more time in social networks while using the Internet than any other service and that activity is up 43 percent between 2009 and 2010 alone. Social networking commanded 22 percent of our attention, followed by online games at 10.2 percent and email at 8.3 percent. Facebook reports that people spend over 700 billion minutes per month Facebooking.[8]

If we examine the principle behind Zuckerberg's Law, we can get an idea of just how powerful this human-powered information network is becoming. According to Facebook statistics, more than 30 billion pieces of content (web links, news stories, blog posts, notes, photo albums, and so on) are shared each and every month. If Zuckerberg's Law holds true, that number will double every year.

It's not so much about how much content we share, it's more about what happens after we click publish, share, or Like. There's an inherent social effect built into social networking and it is the essence of a new, more efficient information delivery system powered by a much more vigorous form of word of mouth. Upload a picture to Facebook and depending on the time, day, and nature of the image, you will see varying levels of responses, from Likes to comments to tags.

The information and experiences people share are inherently tied to a one-to-many network. As people comment, Like, and share, the resulting network effect multiplies each action by a number likely lower than 130, but far greater than one. If we apply Zuckerberg's Law, the number of experiences and objects shared will double every year. This does two things: It increases the number of social objects introduced into the social stream, creates a more connected consumer landscape, and it causes connected consumers to become more discerning in what they share, when, and how. As a result, the focus of the connectivity mindset will change from quantity to quality, targeting relevance over abundance. This behavior was illustrated earlier in the form of interest graphs. I refer to this phenomenon of exploratory intelligent networking as social graph theory.

■ INTEREST GRAPH THEORY

Social graph theory states that online ties—including strong, weak, and temporary connections—will expand and contract, as individuals wrestle with the balance between the semblances of popularity versus gainful experiences. Like Zuckerberg's Law, I once thought that the size of the individual social graph would double every year. Certainly networks benefit from large social networks allowing a greater reach for in-network advertising. After all, there's a reason why social networks present like-minded individuals once you're logged in. They want you to follow and connect with more people just like you. Ideally, you expand your social graph based on shared interests, giving advertisers and marketers a greater pool of consumers. But the risk of course is that even with context at the center of connections, the social and interest graphs are diluted to the point at which you no longer have a grip on the tiered hierarchy of your relationships, regardless of frames of reference.

Interest graph theory (Figure 7.3) explores the idea that our online networks change size and shape based on interests increasing and decreasing to the associated signal and noise. Depending on our mood, focus, work, and state of interests, our time and attention will fluctuate across each network until we find our comfort zones.

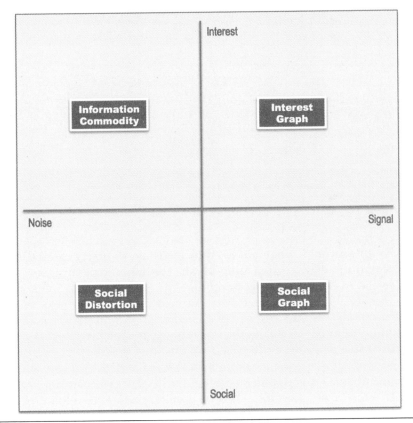

Figure 7.3   Interest Graph Theory

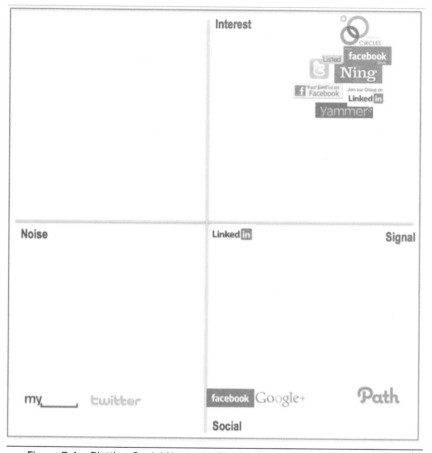

Figure 7.4   Plotting Social Networks Based on Social and Interest Graphs

As an example, when we need to focus on interests or qualified conversations with trusted individuals, the tools we may choose to use reside in the upper right-hand quadrant of Figure 7.4. Tools such as Facebook Groups, Google Circles, LinkedIn Groups, Yammer, Ning, and Facebook Brand Pages are designed to channel relevant activity and thus improve experiences in both signal and interest. On the opposite side of interest and signal, we find Twitter lists. While curated from points of interest, the streams are diluted with the natural flow of average updates that populate the stream in between relevant tweets.

In most cases, services such as LinkedIn and Namesake straddle shared interests with social networking, facilitating more professional connections and interactions, but not necessarily those tied to just one focus. To the bottom left of the quadrant, networks such as Twitter and MySpace facilitate any and all conversations within the social graph. The caliber of friends and followers within these networks are unfocused, whereas Facebook is uniting people that may indeed know one another, thus improving the signal. Facebook employs relationship caps to prevent the news feed of individuals from completely diluting. In the bottom right-hand corner, we find Path, a new service that focuses on increasing the signal within the social graph.

Interest graph theory isn't conjecture in how the social will shift to a more online collection of antisocials. It speculates instead on how individually connected information networks improve experiences and paths over time. Interest graph theory illustrates the need for and eventual shift to the creation of channeled conversations and information streams in which the size of the graph can grow while it systemizes around who we reach and who potentially reaches us. But we choose the information that ultimately compels us to click, which also places us in control of what's shared, specifically to whom and to what extent.

We will eventually think before we update, to answer the following questions:

➤ What do I share with everyone?

➤ How do I interact with a smaller group of more intimate friends and peers?

➤ How do I see only the content that's shared by a more relevant subset of qualified connections?

➤ How do I accomplish tasks or collaborate with others on specific projects?

➤ How do I share and learn within a specific context of interests?

Likewise, businesses must also be cognizant of interest graph theory to prevent the brand from becoming antisocial. To do so, answer the following questions:

1. Why would a connected consumer Like us on Facebook, follow us on Twitter, or connect with us on Google+ or any other network?

2. Why would they value the experience or how could we deliver value?

3. What is the experience they will take away and what is it we want them to share?

4. Why would they want to stay connected over time?

5. Why would they choose to engage our updates in their social stream over those of their real friends?

6. What incentive do they have to tell everyone they know to follow us?

7. Why would they share our content with their audience of peers?

8. Why would they invest their time and express loyalty in their networks?

9. Why should they come back?

■ ON-DEMAND NETWORKING: INVESTING IN NARROW *AND* WIDE EXPERIENCES

Our desire for context and relevance will inspire us to shape social networks to improve our experiences. Doing so mimics how we interact in the real world. Let's take a look at one example as many more similar solutions will emerge inside and outside the world's biggest networks.

In 2010, former Facebook executive Dave Morin, who helped create the Facebook Connect platform, left his position there to start Path, a startup that focused on micronetworking over macrobroadcasting. The *New York Times* described Path as "a reaction to Facebook, where people must both agree to be friends, but can have thousands of them, and Twitter, where anyone can choose to receive a user's posts."[9]

Path set out to connect individuals who are friends in the real world. The mobile app is essentially a social network for a close-knit group who wish to share experiences with one another without sharing with everyone in Facebook and Twitter. As Morin explained to the *New York Times,* Path will group just the people you'd invite to your birthday party, which is closer to between 40 and 60.

To repeat, information networks will be increasingly bound by experiences and prioritized by context and relevance.

As is, however, the reach of social networks is incredibly powerful. Simply catering to the most basic wants and needs of large networks is sometimes more than enough to trigger an impressive social effect. And sometimes reaching the masses is desirable, as long as interests serve as the ties that bind.

In 2010, Walmart introduced a new program that borrowed a chapter from the book of social commerce darling Groupon, a subject we dive more into later. Walmart's CrowdSaver program combined the benefits of group buying and Facebook's News Feed. Group buying is based on the premise that the more people who sign up for the deal, the better the deal becomes. For example, discount fashion retailer Nordstrom Rack offered Groupon users a straight deal of a $50 gift card for only $25. According to Groupon, over 57,000 people participated in the offer. Other offers require that a certain minimum of individuals sign up for the deal before it is unlocked, thus sparking word of mouth. Consumers are motivated to share the deal because there's a benefit in doing so, which is the ability to contribute toward the realization of the deal.

Like Groupon (pun intended), Walmart's CrowdSaver leverages the power of group buying to reward consumers with exclusive deals. However, the difference in this model is Walmart's wise integration into Facebook's social graph (Figure 7.5). The Walmart offer required

Figure 7.5   Walmart CrowdSaver Group Coupon on Facebook

5,000 Likes to unlock a deep discount on a plasma TV. This does two things. First, it heightens the demand for the deal, much like Black Friday and Cyber Monday does every year in the United States. Most notably however, CrowdSaver acts as a social object, meaning the act of Liking sparks actions and reactions. Most notably, it entices sharing within Facebook and across other social networks, each with a linkback encouraging an increase in Likes.

With each Like, the potential deal is spread to the news feeds of every corresponding social graph, thus increasing its reach, appeal, and visibility of the brand overall. Introducing elements of social graph theory, we can see just how far word of mouth travels in Facebook. With every Like, the average individual is reaching a fair number of their 130 contacts. As a result, the awareness increases within the social streams of everyone connected. As Likes extend from social graph to social graph, the audience for each action resides somewhere between 1 and 130. In the best-case scenario, 5,000 Likes can reach the news feeds of upwards of 650,000 people. If individuals decide to extend the link outside of Facebook to include Twitter, for example, each individual now has the capacity to reach the average Twitter user following of 140 followers.

Walmart hit the 5,000 Like mark almost instantly, proving the efficiency and reach of the social effect. The connected consumer activated her network to bring a desirable deal to life, and in this particular deal, Walmart earned a profit for each unit sold. The cost of the program was minimal in comparison to the costs of alternative media and marketing options to reach similarly qualified audiences.

Walmart learned a valuable lesson and in doing so shared priceless insights with the rest of us. Audiences with audiences are not only providing the ability to reach their peers en masse, these connected individuals are also increasing resonance and influencing actions that trigger outcomes. These networks and the resulting outcomes and overall experiences are yours to shape. The question is, what are you going to do about it?

Centers of Attention

➤ Individuals are compelled to share experiences with their social graph.

➤ With the combination of mobile and social networking, social graphs are weaving networks of audiences with audiences.

➤ What started as a backchannel for sophomoric chatter matured into a form of citizen journalism.

➤ People expect information to come to them and they expect it to appear personalized and contextualized.

➤   Individuals are motivated to share every reaction, Like, comment, and friend request that they earn.

➤   We learn how to improve what we share in order to improve the quality of reactions.

➤   Zuckerberg's Law suggests that the number of social objects we share in Facebook and online networks will double every year.

➤   Social graph theory suggests that connections will expand and contract based on the needs and long-term and short-term goals within each network.

➤   The social effect is far more efficient and cost-effective in reaching qualified audiences with audiences when compared to other paid and earned vehicles—assuming mutual benefits are woven into the construct.

Chapter 8

Convergence: The Intersection of Media and the Human Network

As you make your way through this book, you should find yourself identifying to connected consumerism. In different ways, you are learning about the behaviors of the very same connected consumers you are trying to reach.

Some of you may share passages from this book or your reactions with your very own network. Knowing this, I'm motivated to create meaningful and hopefully shareable touchpoints. If I can speak to you and through you at the same time, I reach a greater audience for my work just as you can reach a greater audience for your story. I suppose that's the point in all of this. The human network reveals new touchpoints that when unlocked, allow for deeper, more personal connections that inspire sharing and interaction.

This book is representative of an important form of convergence. You might be reading this in traditional book form, on a PC, a mobile phone, or perhaps a Kindle, Nook, iPad, or an Android-powered tablet. As you read, the content you share traverses the Internet from book form to social and mobile networks and services and eventually real-world conversations. And this list is merely a glimpse of the connected platforms where this work will reach.

We are at the convergence of platforms and people and this democratization of information is about to undergo incredible advancement.

Let's take a step back for a moment to look at the notion of convergence.

Convergence is an important concept in the world of technology and has been a fundamental part of all of the most recent technological advancements. Quite simply, convergence explains how two or more different technologies can and will converge into a single device. Two of the most familiar examples of this advancement are taking pictures with cell phones and surfing the Web on a television. But what if the device was you, your identity as well as your connections, and this powerful combination was portable across any platform and device, from phones to PCs to TVs to real-world locations? This is exactly where we are headed.

The connected consumer is giving way to something that is both revolutionary and evolutionary. Connections form the foundation for a global network that outperforms but also complements traditional print, digital, and broadcast media networks. At the center of this transformation are you and the experiences you choose to consume and share, regardless of medium. We are witnessing a powerful convergence of media, platforms, distribution channels, and human connections.

■ THE DIGITAL FOOTPRINT

The industrial revolution of the twenty-first century is the wiring of the human intellect and the creation of a real-time network that fosters nonconformity and progress. We are building networks of prominence and with each node we add to our social and interest graph, we gain strength as individuals and eventually as a society. Connected consumerism is far more powerful than simply pushing media or messages into it and expecting meaningful actions and connections. This is about co-creation and collaboration, where people have a say in what's shared and to what extent. With this new media comes great responsibility, however. We're learning how to use tools that are new to our teachers. We're learning how to communicate in ways that didn't exist when our mentors mastered the art of engagement.

This is our time to learn and teach.

As technology advances, we strive to master the services and the trends of the moment to stay connected. The connected consumer is constantly evolving his network to stay relevant within these defining digital societies. The convergence of individual networks and information distribution is quite compelling when we can portray its proportions. In early 2008, I took a moment to document the state of my information network. I simply wished to show the syndication channels I built over time and commemorate the moment in the form of a digital time capsule (Figure 8.1).

Looking back, it's painfully easy to recognize the information overload that was taking place as well as the overbearing sense of responsibility required to care for each network.

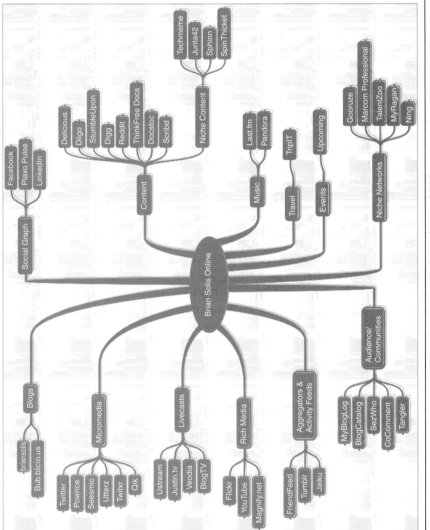

Figure 8.1   Brian Solis Online 2008

A few short years later, I revisited my personal media landscape to visualize the evolution of my online networking behavior. To no surprise, but with a little nostalgia, I found that my creation and distribution architecture had been transformed rather drastically. Not only had it contracted from 47 services down to 24, it matured with a focus on modernization and productivity (Figure 8.2).

To be fair, it's my job and my passion to experiment with every social service as they debut online. The truth is, though, I gain personal and professional value from each of the networks, and for the moment, they represent where I invest my time at least weekly, with several requiring daily attention.

In a few years, I'm sure my map will change again, but to what extent, I'm not sure. But this chapter, this book, is the reality of the connected consumer and the networks they weave. Once we understand their behavior, we can design our businesses, our processes, and our philosophies around them to become part of this vast and influential series of networks. This is about establishing and continually earning relevance within our customer's networks of relevance.

■ I WANT MY WEB TV. . . . BE CAREFUL WHAT YOU WISH FOR

This chapter will wind down our focus on the shifting behavior of new consumerism and transition to the role connected consumers play in the definition of this democratized information economy. In doing so, we will define our role in establishing presence and significance in these connected networks and set the stage for earned leadership.

On the train to enlightenment, an important stop is at the convergence of media and human networks.

One of the most debated aspects of convergence is the merging of TV and the Web. In reality, the computer-television convergence is already under way with players such as Apple and Google introducing platforms for web and TV programming. But even without these platforms and the devices that run them, you can already surf YouTube videos, follow your Twitter stream, and browse your Flickr photo albums on your TV while watching television programming. You can also update your social status through the remote at any time. The question is, however, whether or not you want to.

TV is a shared experience and the Web is often a personal activity that connects people through shared experiences. It's not uncommon now to find a family gathered around a TV with mobile phones or laptops channeling experiences between the big screen, the small screen, and the audiences of audiences.

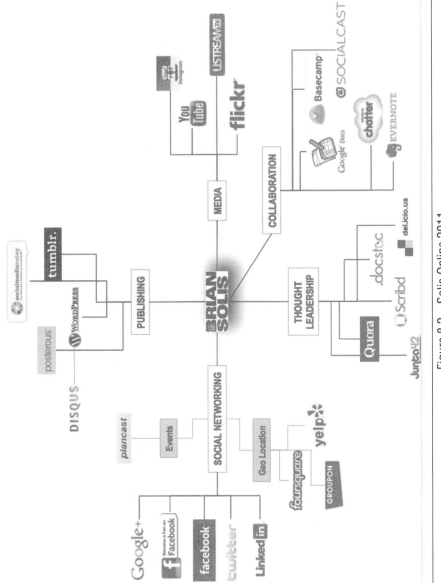

Figure 8.2 Solis Online 2011

cnnbrk: Citizens standing arm in arm alongside tanks to protect Egyptian **Museum**
http://on.cnn.com/gMUgpv

about 5 hours ago via *web* · Reply · View Tweet

200+ recent retweets

Figure 8.3   @CNNBRK Tweet Covering the Egyptian Revolution

In January 2011, two events within the same week dominated Twitter's Trending Topics, at some points simultaneously. The first were the now historic events hashtagged simply as *#Egypt* that chronicled the uprising of Egyptian citizens calling for the removal of President Hosni Mubarak from office. Twitter, YouTube, Facebook, and blogs arose as the social conduits that told the stories of rage, restlessness, and determination live from the streets of Cairo. (See Figure 8.3.) At one point, Egyptian officials severed access to the Internet, essentially shutting down the Web in an attempt to silence citizens and prevent them from organizing formative protests. Eventually, traditional news media caught up with the events and as these stories were aired and published, social networks extended their reach.

Once such story published on CNN trended on Twitter and earned thousands of tweets, Facebook shares, and reactions, placing CNN at the center of the breaking news for several hours.

I clicked through the link and immediately turned on my television. Naturally, I took to my social streams to share my reactions.

The human network connects shared experiences. This activity created a virtuous cycle that momentarily increased CNN ratings, traffic, and empathy for citizens of Egypt.

The audience of audiences were so moved by their experience that they naturally took to their social graph to share a deeply moving event the way they know how...tweets and status updates. Sharing adds a new dynamic that strengthens the bonds between the connected and it extends our experiences from our immediate proximity to a boundless landscape where relationships and meaningful interactions are forged.

■ CHANNELING A CONNECTED AUDIENCE

NewTeeVee Live is a conference organized by GigaOM, a popular technology blog network, and is dedicated to the exploration of the evolution of online and terrestrial video. In November 2010, MTV's Robin Sloan took the stage and shared that the network sees 90 million tweets every day and "a lot of those tweets are about TV Shows."[1]

Sloan added that this kind of "conversational choreography" will play a crucial role in any major TV event. It is the "new campfire," she said. It's also the new water cooler. Indeed, we're channeling experiences from the living room, the Web, print, and the real world to the social streams of the human network and back again.

The future of media is about steering experiences and that's how we need to think about it.

On January 29, 2011, Jesse Eisenberg, who played Facebook founder Mark Zuckerberg in the award-winning movie *The Social Network*, hosted Saturday Night Live.[2] During his opening monologue, the real Mark Zuckerberg surprised Eisenberg on stage and as you can imagine, tweets and Facebook status updates about the live event soared. Knowing it had a special moment within its grasp, NBC fueled conversations by releasing embeddable clips of the moment while the show was still airing across the country.[3] Conversations, tweets, blog posts, and status updates continued well into the next week. The event was worth sharing, but NBC's decision to proactively enable the sharing of that moment allowed them to relive the moment within the networks of relevance, growing its potential audience, even if it was just for that particular episode.

Individuals are the conduits for reach and relevance. Through their actions and words in digital networks, they reel in engagement. This activity sparks conversations, cultivates communities, and fortifies social and interest graphs. It is this behavior that will formally demand personalization and a defined role in the content experience to organize influential engagement to extend the concentric circles of reach and attraction.

It will change how content is produced and broadcast. Connected consumers and audiences with audiences can make or break programming.

■ THE LIVING ROOM IS ALIVE AND CLICKING

The living room is the epicenter of family, the hub of the household. Perhaps more so than the dining table, the living room hosts hours upon hours of family attention and interaction every week. Whether we are gripped by the music and voices being emitted from radios or entranced by the moving images illuminating our televisions, we celebrate togetherness and relaxation around a common centerpiece.

This once mighty magnet of attention, through its iterative forms, is learning to share its powers of attraction, forever changing the idea of the family cornerstone. Now attention is a battlefield and the laws of attraction are distributed.

Like passing ships in the night, the TV and the Internet have yet to intimately embrace one another. But that's changing. When Forrester Research published a report that, for the first time, marked equal time spent between TVs and the Internet,[4] it was and wasn't a surprise. It was inevitable. Depending on where you reside in the adoption bell curve, this news is either overdue or early. Either way, it's both a culture shift and shock. It's a moment when these two ships are frozen, floating across from each other without obstructing the respective courses. However, the wakes cast from each journey are felt on both sides.

If you are in the business of trying to reach consumers to earn attention, your world no longer rotates on its previous axis. Progressive brands are already experimenting with media and corresponding budgets to capture attention where and when it's focused. For example, Procter and Gamble is moving spend away from TV soaps and daytime dramas toward digital and social channels.[5] This move signals the beginning of the end of an era and is one of the many reasons why connected consumers and their audience of connected audiences represent the beginning of the end of business as usual.

■ NEW CONSUMERISM: FROM CLICKS TO CLIQUES

New media isn't going away. It's always new and that's the point. What's clear is that for the time being, attention is equally divided between TVs and the Internet. If we review the Pauli exclusion principle,[6] which states that no two identical particles can occupy the same space at the same time, we must believe that at some point, attention will be forced in one direction or another.

Quantum physics aside for the moment, let's apply social science to this equation to explore another possibility. Culturally, we already see the coalescence of these two activities. But attention might not prove to be what it was. Continuous partial attention,[7] while disputed, is something that is in play for the connected consumer. Regardless of their depth of comprehension and understanding, these digitally dexterous individuals can watch TV, live-tweet the experience, and discuss it with friends in real time.

But what if attention splits and continues to do so until a new series of applications surface? What if the living room becomes virtual, connected through individuals and linked by platform, time, and common interests? It's no longer a matter of what if; this is the new reality TV and we are inserting ourselves into the production through live commentary viewable and searchable by those audiences who have willfully connected to us.

The water cooler is already moving to the PC and social is emerging as the long fabled catalyst for the overdue convergence of TV and the Internet.

The future of broadcast is social. At the same time, the future of relevance and customer engagement is precipitated by shared experiences. As such, consumers will bring their mobile phones, tablets, and laptops to the digital living room or to any event to watch and share experiences and create a greater conversation and sense of belonging.

Producers will now need to create content that includes us in the event and the storyline. Architects of social and hardware platforms will need to rethink how TVs and the Internet converge to foster consumption and engagement. Those brands that subsidize content production will have to transcend the practice of following attention to captivating it through innovation and experimentation.

As we know, the audience is not the audience of old. That has dramatic ramifications for how messages are spread. The people who used to sit in front of a television and talk about their experiences later to friends, family, and co-workers are now empowered to do so right then, right now. Perhaps more importantly, however, people are building full-fledged networks around themselves, creating a distribution channel of audiences with audiences, and their reach is as influential as it is infinite.

Forrester published an important report in late 2010 that revealed the attributes of new consumerism, "Understanding the Changing Needs of the U.S. Online Consumer."[8] As part of its study, Forrester surveyed more than 40,000 people, and if nothing else, its findings serve as evidence that we must turn our wheel and change course.

Three short years ago, only one-third of Americans shopped online. Now, two-thirds rely on e-commerce to shop. Comparatively, 35 percent of respondents visit social networks today, up from 15 percent in 2007. Like e-commerce, we can make an educated guess as to where that number will climb to three years from now.

The proliferation of the Internet is far more disruptive than we realize. It seems as though decades, and in some cases, centuries, of media production and consumption, are becoming obsolete overnight. As a good friend of mine said in reaction to Forrester's controversial report, "I knew this would happen, but so soon . . . ?"

Traditional media properties, including newspapers, broadcast radio and TV, magazines, and others, were caught off guard when the new media revolution hit. Suddenly, everyone is turning to Facebook, Twitter, GoogleTV, and the iPad as the savior for the future of all traditional media. But this revolution didn't happen overnight. For many years, a quiet riot assembled until whispers amplified into cries for change. And when their pleas went unacknowledged, they, we, embraced the democracy of social media to ensure that their voices were heard.

Behavior is changing.

The balance of power between creation and consumption is moving toward the middle.

For businesses and media properties, unfortunately, social media, geolocation, and tablets aren't going to save you. Thoughtfulness and empathy are the keys to unlock the gates that will lead you onto a new path of awareness. It's the steps you take that reveal how to earn relevance within each medium that captivate your consumers.

■ AN AUDIENCE OF INFORMATION AMBASSADORS

We are fusing offline and online communication to nourish our thirst for connectedness.

With or without realization, we have become curators, carefully selecting the experiences that move us, colored with our thoughts and observations, to cater to our audiences of audiences and hopefully to those who, in turn, follow them. We are, in essence, live blogging and live-tweeting the world as we see it. For those businesses that master the art of storytelling and engagement and learn from the reactions of those who respond, they can invest in value-add experiences so that their consumers are both informed and inspired to take action.

The cultural impact of new media is profound as it weaves a new fabric for how we connect and communicate with one another. As a digital society, we are ushering in an era in which everyday people form a global network of self-empowered social intermediaries that accelerate and proliferate the reach and effect of information and experiences.

We are no longer just part of the information consumption or production process, we are transforming the system for learning and sharing through real-time signal repeaters that boost the reach of digitally transmitted messages—from your status update to the world in seconds.

Whether it's the sight of an open laptop, a live mobile phone or tablet in the audience, the living room, a café, or a train, connected consumers are sharing anything and everything that moves them in real life or virtually. They do, in fact, represent the channels that both broadcast and connect us. When the people formerly known as the audience are roused, they willfully share their experiences, and with enough momentum, content, information, and events extend the conversations across social graphs, introduce new opportunities for connection, and fuel online trends.

This is only the beginning, however, as consumers are also earning prominence within each of these networks. As their social graphs develop and mature, interest graphs take shape. As they invest time, resources, and insight into each, their social capital rises exponentially, commensurate with their contributions. The same is true for your business. Through every new connection we make, reinforced by how we contribute to online communities, we are establishing significance, and with it, our signal, its strength, and the resulting effect.

Centers of Attention

➤ New media opens up new touchpoints between consumers, brands, media, and audiences with audiences.

➤ Convergence is the integration of two or more disparate technologies in a single device.

➤ Connected consumers represent the convergence of information, technology, and distribution.

➤ The future of media and business is powered by collaboration and co-creation.

➤ Our personal information networks will evolve, mature, and focus over time.

➤ Time spent between TV and the Internet is now equal.

➤ Broadcast, and all media, encounter new life through the human network.

➤ Shared experiences are shared online, creating a new type of influential water cooler effect.

➤ Content must now include these networks in co-creation to steer experiences and earn relevance.

Chapter 9

Measures of Digital Influence and Social Capital: From Nobody to Somebody

In season 14, episode 4 of Comedy Central's *South Park*,[1] Eric Cartman's character taunts Kyle repeatedly by chanting, "I've got more friends than Kyle."

Kyle in turn responds, "How the h— do you have more friends than me?"

Cartman tries to justify the social hierarchy by linking the number of friends with social capital, "Because people think I'm cool, Dude."

Stan enters the room and expresses with a voice of disbelief, "Are you guys doing that stupid Facebook stuff again?"

Kyle, Cartman, and Kenny then present Stan with a gift, his own Facebook profile.

Stan expresses discontent and anger saying, "No, I told you guys that I don't want to be on Facebook."

Cartman replies, "Alright, fine, Dude. You don't have to add any friends. You could just be like Kip Drordy. He has no Facebook friends and he's been on Facebook for six months."

The entire episode plays out in a rapid-fire series of the struggles and challenges today's society faces when embracing social networks. The main premise, however, is the illusion of popularity and the need to increase the number of friends on Facebook so as to increase what Cartman refers to as social stock. In a particularly relevant segment of the episode, Cartman launches a podcast in which he debuts a show similar to Jim Cramer's *Mad Money* on CNBC. The analogies between financial stocks and social capital are brilliant as displayed in the context of the show.

Acting out of sympathy, Kyle befriends Kip Drordy, which of course dramatically elevates the self-confidence of the once sullen Facebook user. On the other hand, Kyle's stock plummets, as friends no longer wish to be associated with someone who is connected to Drordy. In the parody of *Mad Money,* Cartman tells his viewers that Kyle's stock is dropping and urges everyone to dump Kyle as a friend in order to keep their personal stock valuable.

The connected consumer is, at this very moment, scored and ranked based on her stature within the Social Web. Is the *South Park* parody of the reality of a hierarchal system within this social economy accurate? I'm afraid so. Connected consumers are directly or inadvertently contributing to a digital form of social capital by which their value is measured and factored into decisions outside of their knowledge.

■ THE HUMAN ALGORITHM

Early in the rise of social networking and social media, I observed how certain individuals elevated through the ranks of social hierarchies to garner greater attention and recognition than their peers. These individuals were rewarded with increased friend requests, follows, links to their online work and activity, clickthroughs, comments, and ultimately the most prized decoration of them all, conversations. I referred to this notion of attained stature in the social class system as *PeopleRank.*[2]

PeopleRank was a nod to Google's PageRank technology that helped improve search results by qualifying web pages based on a level of authority. Authority was established through a variety of complex algorithms, including the number and caliber of inbound links to any given page. Like PageRank, it was inevitable that software would eventually surface to track the activity of individuals and rank them on the basis of a variety of factors that include the rewards discussed earlier. PeopleRank was very apropos.

In the realm of influence and the services that attempt to track it, I officially categorized these measurement technologies as a Human Algorithm[3] of sorts.

■ DIGITAL INFLUENCE CREATES A NEW MEDIA WORLD ORDER

Influence is the latest buzzword that is sparking conversations, debates, and media attention—and with good reason. Services such as Klout, mBlast, Peer Index, and TweetLevel measure a person's level of digital influence on the basis of their activity within social networks, including Twitter, Facebook, and LinkedIn. By scoring influence, these services create a social hierarchy in which individuals are ranked against one another based on their capacity to influence the consumers who follow them in social networks.

Brands are starting to take notice as these services represent an opportunity to make contact with the connected customers who are beyond the reach of traditional media. These services offer the ability to identify candidates who were otherwise difficult to discover. Each social consumer receives a score based on what they do within social networks, who they know, and the activity that follows interaction. For brands, the ability to discover targets by individual scores *along* with the networks they touch provides an alluring opportunity to potentially influence the behavior of desirable consumers.

At the same time, social consumers see these services as an opportunity for reward. As a result, people seek to earn higher scores to gain stature, power, or recognition within their communities. Some also attempt to attract the attention of brands to earn free products, promotions, or deals.

■ DEFINING INFLUENCE

To begin, reviewing the standard definition of influence will help provide a clear picture for how it applies to the digital realm.

in·flu·ence \in'flü-əns, noun: 1. The power to change or affect someone or something. 2. A person or thing that affects someone or something in an important way

If influence is the ability to cause effect or change something, the measure of influence is then determined by the outcome or extent of change.

When striving to reach social customers through the peers that may influence their behavior or activity, the most direct route is thus through the social stream. This is why brands seek influencers. They potentially represent the holy grail of consumer marketing. When influence is activated successfully, it creates a domino effect that connects brands to digital consumers directly through their peers. I refer to this online phenomenon as *spheres of influence*. (See Figure 9.1.) Following engagement, brands can trigger desirable actions and reactions. By defining an intended clickpath, brands can evoke meaningful experiences that generate measurable business results and outcomes. Everything starts with the end in mind, requiring strategists to first establish the effect they wish to cause.

The ability to identify these new influentials presents an elusive but sought-after opportunity for businesses. With the ability to discover everyday, connected people who reach desirable audiences,

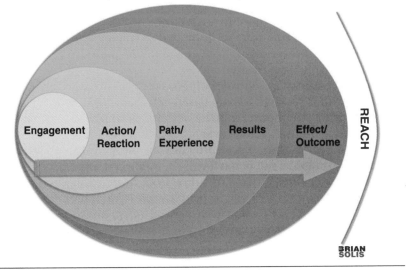

Figure 9.1 The Spheres of Influence

brands are closer than ever to arriving at a new frontier of customer engagement—the ability to reach people through an opt-in connection between trusted peers. At the heart of the matter, however, is the ability to identify these potentially influential individuals and understand what it is that makes them influencers.

■ SEEKING RELEVANCE: THE SOCIAL CONSUMER HIERARCHY

Brands can use search tools to find potentially influential targets for engagement, but that's not enough. Conversing with anyone and everyone may satisfy certain individuals, but the need to scale conversations to reach the appropriate audience around meaningful topics requires a more sophisticated approach. Businesses can no longer broadcast what they believe are desirable messages to the masses. They must instead survey the customer landscape to identify themes, opportunities, and understand how customers are forming and segmenting markets. Doing so surfaces customer wants and preferences, but perhaps most notably, the way they find and share information. And for those businesses that are paying attention, the connected customers and influential voices who influence customers will also materialize. By identifying and potentially aligning with these highly connected individuals, businesses can more effectively reach their customers. Rather than the traditional one-to-many approach of paid or earned media, influential individuals offer a one-to-one-to-many network within which brand reach is greatly amplified.

It's not just about reach, however. Because individuals are connecting with one another in personal networks, trust, authority, and relationships factor into how information is received and internalized. Needless to say, there's greater value in a message derived from someone held in high regard. These influential individuals can take the form of experts, tastemakers, peers, or topical authorities who are active within networks of relevance in which customers are engaged.

Certain brands are already realizing the benefits of engaging influencers and are creating influencer programs that reach desirable market segments. These programs are often used in advocacy or ambassador programs, new product launches, word of mouth campaigns, or noteworthy events. Many companies, as well, recruit connected customers into marketing programs because they're trusted. For example, Graco runs a long-time ambassador program called the Graco Nation, and Walmart continues to invest in its 11 Moms program through which highly connected customers within specific market segments, in this case, moms, are invited to represent the brand through an editorial campaign by way of blogs, tweets, social networking, and multimedia networks such as YouTube and Flickr to bring the brand promise to life through real-world experience.

These digital influencers carry the capacity to dramatically extend the reach of any brand and its value proposition. Similar to traditional celebrity endorsement models, these highly followed authorities serve as the voice of the brand within connected communities to attract friends, followers, and fans and convert them into prospects and customers.

Finding and then measuring influence is essential to introducing a sense of relevance and permanence into the vastness of the social graph and the billions of exchanges that take place every month in connected ecosystems. While traditional search tools may help you find a few influencers here and there, new services are emerging to help organizations identify authorities within desired market segments.

■ THE SOCIAL STOCK MARKET

As connected consumers live in public by sharing their moves, experiences, and thoughts online, this activity is measured by an emerging class of customer relationship management systems (CRM) that are changing the dynamics of business to customer engagement. This new breed of technologies helps businesses identify would-be influencers by indexing and scoring them based on various criteria. Klout, PeerIndex, and Twitalyzer are some of the leading tools that attempt to score influence by using sophisticated algorithms that measure what individuals say, what happens after they say it, how many people they potentially reach, and the stature of the individuals who also follow them. Services such as mPact by mBlast, Appinions, and Traackr focus on leverage according to topical relevance, reach, and resonance, measuring the authority of individuals tied to specific subject matter.

If a prestigious brand such as Rolex sought to find all of the authoritative voices on luxury goods, men's style, or business travel, the ability to surface *influencers* by topical relevance becomes paramount.

Influence is a complex subject and not one that is computed by a standard formula to reveal an absolute score. Companies that promise to measure influence are in fact measuring various sociological elements that may contribute to the capacity to cause effect or change something. While the score these new services produce is not indicative of decided influence, it is still telling. Starting with popularity and authority, influence becomes a product of a recipe. That recipe and its end result differ from person to person. Corresponding scores represent the potential to trigger an outcome or reaction, but they mostly symbolize the state of one's social capital within social media. The scores are nonetheless valuable to your organization. The weight you place on them is directly related to your intentions and goals.

The question is, what is the effect you want to cause or what is the behavior you wish to change? Once you have the answers, work backward to find the right people and then develop a mutually beneficial engagement program that activates communities to achieve the desired result.

As influence is rooted in cause and effect, businesses must begin by understanding the nature of how information travels, the dynamics of relationships and social hierarchy, and the measures new services analyze. By understanding the dynamics of social capital and its relationship to influence, organizations learn how to identify connected individuals who reach ideal communities and offer the ability to amplify reach, build relationships, and drive beneficial outcomes.

■ THE SQUARE ROOT OF INFLUENCE IS SOCIAL CAPITAL

As connected consumers live in public, their activities are captured and measured. These actions, reactions, and the relationships that expand and contract as a result contribute to the state of an individual's social capital within each network. This capital is a reflection of the size, quality, and scope of their social or interest graph and is measured by the sentiment and leverage that comes to life in each exchange.

Robert Putnam, a political scientist and professor of public policy at the Harvard University John F. Kennedy School of Government, explored social capital in his essay "Bowling Alone: America's Declining Social Capital," published in the *Journal of Democracy*.[4] In it, he defines *social capital* as "The collective value of all 'social networks' and the inclinations that arise from these networks to do things for each other."

Putnam believed that social capital "can be measured by the amount of trust and 'reciprocity' in a community or between individuals."

If we apply Putnam's definition of social capital to the greater discussion of influence, we draw an important parallel. Our actions and words in social networks represent a form of social currency. As such, what we say online, who we know, and the ensuing activity accumulates into an implied value that either adds or subtracts from our social bank accounts. The resulting balance is then reflective of our stature within the social economy.

As influence is a measure of social capital, social capital is then a product of pillars of digital influence, seven characteristics that equate to an individual's perceived value. Some of these pillars are measurable, others are extrapolated, and not all are required to influence behavior or action. Any combination of these pillars will most likely trigger an effect to varying degrees.

➤ *Relevance*—Topical relevance is the glue of the interest graph. The closer an individual is aligned with a subject, the greater the likelihood of topical association.

➤ *Authority*—As an individual invests in the subject of topical relevance, they naturally earn a level of authority on the subject matter. Authority levels also prompt respect, which is a reward for expertise or specialty.

➤ *Affinity*—A natural liking or sympathy for someone or something. Connected consumers establish affinity within their communities and it buoys their position.

➤ *Proximity*—The location of an individual is taken into consideration when effect is necessary within a particular setting or environment.

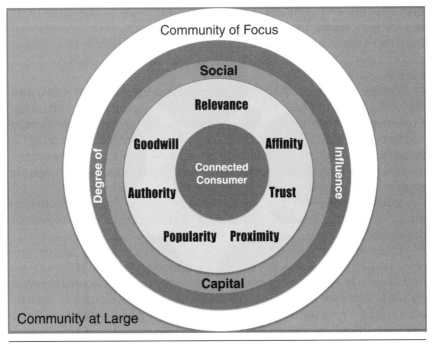

Figure 9.2   Pillars of Digital Influence

➤ *Trust*—Difficult to measure, trust is the source of most meaningful relationships. It's also a word that's difficult to describe. We all know what it is. Here, trust is the firm belief in the reliability, truth, ability, or strength of someone.

➤ *Popularity*—The state of being liked, admired, or supported by many people.

➤ *Goodwill*—If you remember, Putnam described social capital as "the collective value of all 'social networks' and the inclinations that arise from these networks to do things for each other." Investing goodwill into one's community increases appreciation and the probability for collaboration and action.

The hub in Figure 9.2 depicts the connected customer as a center of influence (COI). Let's assume that there is a score associated with the COI and that that number is a derivative of pillars or attributes of influence. The pillars surrounding an individual are enlivened by actions and words, and its effect changes over time. For brands, these centers of influence represent the ability to promote advocacy, endorse products, and build ambassadorships.

The pillars of influence also symbolize a series of concentric circles in which the capacity to influence is commensurate with the various levels of investment made in each. This is referred to as the degree of influence. The sum of these investments equate to social capital and the capacity to influence peers and peers of peers. As social capital is expended, influence affects behavior or has some effect among peers who form immediate communities of focus (connected interest graphs), and as influence travels, it ultimately extends its reach to touch larger market segments that form communities at large (interconnected social graphs).

The net worth of an individual's stature within society, the value of the networked relationships, and the balance of the digital pillars in total equate to overall social capital. Social capital also commands a price. Individuals who boast the capacity to influence possess the capital to spend, but they do so only when it is advantageous.

Influence happens when someone spends social capital that yields a measurable effect and earns a return for the effort. The trick for organizations is to not only identify relevant individuals who possess valuable social capital, but to also encourage them to spend it on the organization's behalf.

■ THE NEW ERA OF ENDORSEMENTS: WHEN NOBODIES BECOME SOMEBODIES

Brands experimenting with these services are opening up entirely new channels for marketing with the hopes of unlocking new customer touchpoints. Much like loyalty programs in which customers are rewarded for their repeat business, brands can now reach connected customers to build relationships, recruit into ambassador programs, or reward them with products and prizes as recognition for their social stature. The goal is to encourage, directly or indirectly, positive word of mouth across social and interest graphs. Think of it as a celebrity endorsement program in which the celebrities are now extraordinary and highly connected everyday people.

To test this idea, Klout debuted a perks program that connected brands with users who possess notable clout. It is advertised as a way to help businesses "find and engage these influencers and they can become evangelists for your brand." The program is already host to hundreds of campaigns that offer connected individuals discounts, free products, access to special events, and opportunities to meet celebrities and VIPs.

Klout

Hi unbrelievable,

Virgin America, one of the coolest airlines in the skies, is coming to Toronto. They want to share their excitement with the top influencers in their latest location.

You have so much Klout that Virgin America has asked us to give you a free roundtrip flight to San Francisco or LA. They're flying from YYZ (Toronto Pearson) to SFO and LAX. Virgin would like to offer you a free roundtrip flight*, free on-flight Wifi (because they know how you rock the internet), and a special invitation to their star-studded inaugural party on the evening of June 29th (which you're welcome to go to even if you don't go on the flight).

Unfortunately we haven't been able to get the government to recognize your influence yet so you will have to pay the tax on the flight, but we think it's totally worth it!

Please know, you are under no obligation to accept this offer, and none of your information has been, or ever will be, shared or sold . For your convenience we have included our Klout Perks Code of Conduct below. We think this is a great chance for you to be one of the first to experience this route and share the experience with your network.

For more information on travel dates, destinations, and booking just head here. But do it soon -- this is on a first come, first served basis and supplies are limited.

Feel free to let your friends know how influential you are

Thank you,
Joe Fernandez
Klout Founder and CEO

Figure 9.3   The Klout Virgin America Promotion

Klout Perks was officially introduced through a joint promotion with Starbucks. Klout influencers were offered a free sample of Pike Place Roast. The promotion was unique in that it targeted individuals who were ranked as top influencers on "the topic of coffee."[5]

In 2010, Virgin America partnered with Klout to commemorate the debut of its new routes between San Francisco and Los Angeles to Toronto. Klout identified influencers, and through the Perks program offered individuals free round-trip airfare, Wi-Fi included, along with an invitation to Virgin America's Toronto Launch event (Figure 9.3).

Klout explained the advantages of an influencer program versus traditional endorsement advertising in a blog post[6] announcing the partnership, "We do not want to 'buy' your tweets. You are receiving the product because you are influential and have authority on topics related to the product. This is a more targeted form of receiving a sample while shopping at the grocery store. You are welcome to tell the world you love the product, you hate the product or say nothing at all."

Those who participated did tweet, blog, vlog, and share their experience with those who follow them in social networks and in the real world.

Shortly thereafter, the Palms Casino and Resort in Las Vegas partnered with Klout to introduce a special perks program. In 2010, the program launched with a simple mission: to offer upgrades, complimentary drinks or food, special offers, and discounts to those who provided their Klout scores upon check-in to the resort.

By 2011, Palms launched an official Social Rewards program.[7] Points are awarded to anyone who tweets about the hotel. Each tweet earns 10 points. For offers that friends purchase, 250 points are awarded. As points accumulate, they can be redeemed for free rooms, dinners, free drinks, and more.

Audi has also experimented with Klout on several programs. When the automaker introduced its 2011 A8, influencers were invited to test drive it in San Francisco. A few special influencers were given the car to drive off to a luxurious weekend getaway. In June 2011, Klout, along with Involver, introduced a new product that allows brands to integrate Klout scores into Facebook brand pages. Audi was the first brand to embrace the platform and rolled out a customized brand experience, tailored to visitors based on their Klout score.[8] (See Figure 9.4.)

The *Wall Street Journal* explored the topic of new influence.[9] In the article, reporter Jessica Vascellaro interviewed Casie Stewart, a 28-year-old social media consultant from Toronto. She was part of the program with Virgin America and Klout that earned her a free flight to Canada because of her Klout score. Her Klout score is a gift that keeps on giving, as it also yielded a shopping splurge at Mark's Work Wearhouse and an all-expenses-paid trip to New Zealand during fashion week. These perks are the result of her social stature earned by tweeting and blogging about her life. According to Klout, Stewart is a networker and boasts a Klout score of 74 (out of 100). According to the article, she tweets to build her personal brand, and receiving these lucrative gifts serves as a form of recognition and validation for the effort.

▨ INFLUENCE IS NOT POPULARITY AND POPULARITY IS NOT INFLUENCE

In each of the preceding examples, popularity, reach, and stature were important factors in campaign engagement. What's unclear is whether the individuals included in each promotion were selected because they genuinely earned clout around subjects such as coffee, travel, cars, and so on, or was reach the primary factor. Either way, the

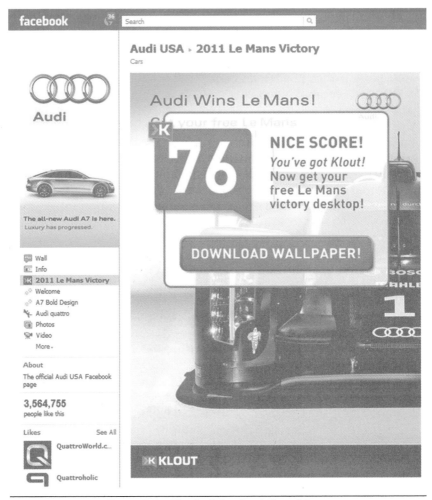

Figure 9.4   The Audi Facebook Brand Page

distinction between subject matter authority and popularity is important for brands to evaluate before rolling out influencer programs.

If we revisit the earlier example, an important question to ask
is did Casie Stewart influence her social graph to purchase a ticket
for a flight on Virgin America? The possibility is very good that Klout
influencers who participated in the Virgin America program increase
brand lift for Virgin and perhaps sold a few tickets in the process.
One can also make an educated guess that those selected as part of
the program were now loyal to Virgin America and perhaps other
Virgin brands.

Embracing connected consumers allows brands to borrow the social capital of those who can potentially steer activity or change behavior. In the Klout examples mentioned earlier, participants were more than willing to spend social capital in exchange for branded rewards. Like celebrity endorsements, there's a strong aspirational and affiliation bond associated with the act of aligning the brand with the brand of a famous and adored personality.

Essentially, the brand borrows the social capital of that individual to appear approachable and desirable to the individual's followers. Depending on the personality, the brand either strives for reach through popularity or that of relevance whereby spokespersons are viewed as subject matter experts. In some instances, a combination of popularity and authority may offer an exponential increase in both awareness and outcomes.

■ THE TOOLS OF THE TRADE

Up to this point, we've discussed only a handful of vendors that measure various elements of influence. Analyzing platform features and organizing these tools by their design and focus helps to identify strengths in the design of any influence program.

To organize vendors, we need to revisit the pillars of influence, relevance, affinity, trust, proximity, popularity, authority, and goodwill. These factors will serve as the classification for how each platform is categorized, based on the elements of influence they quantify. As you'll see, each service offers a unique approach to how it ranks influence and attempts to identify influencers. While judging the output is not the goal of this report, understanding its significance helps in campaign development.

As we examined earlier, influence is the ability to cause effect or change behavior. In several of the examples we reviewed, authority and popularity, as well as other pillars of influence, contribute to a score, which indicates the capacity to cause effect. When measuring influence, authority is referred to as relevance, and popularity is described as reach. Each time social capital is spent or earned, the events that follow are traceable and measurable. These proceedings are referred to as *resonance,* the distance information travels, how long it stays alive online, and to what extent it triggers actions and reactions.

To simplify the measurement of the influence, the pillars of influence arrange into three groups: reach, relevance, and resonance, or the 3Rs for short.

Reach and relevance define the potential resonance that an individual possesses. Resonance is a reflection of one's standing online and represents the goodwill and overall social capital one banks as a result of social networking behavior. This balance is representative of the score that is assigned through today's influence ranking systems. As each vendor scores reach and relevance differently, the value of the score is commensurate with its usefulness. Or said another way, value is in the eye of the beholder.

Worth is determined by the resulting actions that occur based on an individual's activities within that person's communities of focus (interest graph) and the communities at large (societal graph). True influence is not measured by a score but instead by the outcome produced when social capital is spent. At the moment, this is not an element currently measured by any vendor but instead by those organizations that experiment with influencer engagement. By intentionally designing outcomes into the campaign, businesses can measure activity and how it converts into desirable outcomes to gauge influence.

Looking at Figure 9.5, we can see that influence is neither clear nor is it decisive. The capacity to influence behavior can follow two parallel paths. First, information can travel across an interest graph through to the social graph to trigger potential outcomes. Secondly, information can travel directly through the social graph with or without ever passing through interest graphs to cause effect.

To help make sense of how influence takes shape, we must understand how reach and relevance feed into resonance. Based on the

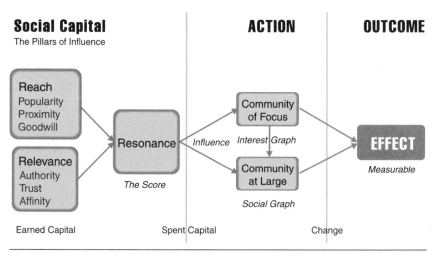

Figure 9.5 Charting a Course for Influence

extent each pillar plays into mix, resonance feeds either into the interest or social graph or both. As a result, the activity that follows then contributes to a measurable effect. The effect is measured by outcomes. But, in order to measure outcomes as a brand, they must first be designed to trigger desired outcomes and defined through integrated metrics. What we learn here is that influence isn't inherent in an absolute score, it's measured through actions and words. Brands that get it will design, measure, pilot, learn, and repeat.

By evaluating and charting tools that attempt to measure influence, we can visualize the value and differentiation of many of today's players. The influence quad organizes each of the platforms based on the essence of the service, not how the company positions itself. It's important to note that this is not a scoring or ranking system in and of itself. Figure 9.6 is designed to help organizations evaluate which services will best help them connect with those who define their markets.

You'll notice immediately that influence as a category does not yet exist. But there is tremendous value in focusing research on identifying the right people and networks of people for the right reasons based on the social capital these services measure in addition to reach and relevance. Brands can greatly benefit by studying the offerings of

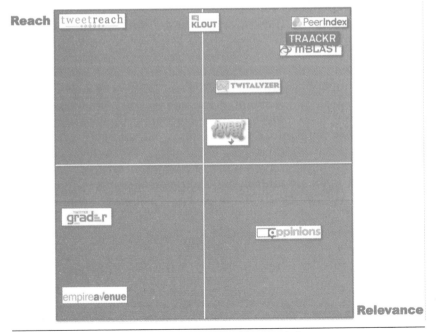

Figure 9.6   Vendors That Measure Influence

each company and experimenting through a variety of focused campaigns that combine reach, authority, and relevance to benchmark performance against one another as well as the existing programs running today. For detailed descriptions of each service, please visit TheEndofBusiness.com to download the full report on influence.

■ INFLUENCING THE INFLUENCER

Influence scores serve as indicators that may represent the capacity to change behavior or cause a desirable effect. As such, businesses can benefit by identifying high-ranking individuals and groups and understanding the role they play in digital markets. Doing so provides businesses with an opportunity to build relationships with highly connected consumers, authorities, and their networks.

There is no magic bullet to hit target markets with one shot. Understanding what these services measure and how the scores align marketing goals with intended audiences is key to experimentation. Through practice, however, brands can use these services to identify potential tastemakers and learn how information travels among consumers in relevant networks.

It's important to remember that these individuals are not traditional market makers and therefore do not respond to traditional marketing programs. They have earned a strong standing in their social networks and they do not spend their social capital foolishly. Businesses must look beyond ordinary pitches or generic incentive programs to entice topical authorities that make sense for the brand and the customers they're trying to reach. Borrowing social capital is a steep request and it is not to be taken lightly. To succeed now and over time, brands must design engagement programs that consider the value of an individual's social capital and offer incentives, rewards, or a form of reciprocity commensurate with the ask.

Brands that design measurable actions and outcomes into engagement programs establish the ability to measure the effects of individual social capital and its impact on business metrics. Measurable effects might include brand lift, sales, lead generation, sentiment shifts, and share of voice. But without designing desirable outcomes into these programs, brands are unable to measure the performance that actually defines influence. As a result, social capital is spent without an understanding of meaningful returns. Studying the effects of influencer engagement helps brands enhance interaction, improve clickpaths, and optimize overall experiences and outcomes through the spheres of influence.

In the end, the true measure of influence is effect. While scores can indicate social capital or popularity, it is up to the brand to measure the effect of connected individuals based on the design, execution, and corresponding activity of any customer engagement program. If in the real world, actions speak louder than words, in the realm of digital influence, actions speak louder than scores.

Centers of Attention

➤ Popularity is not influence and influence is not popularity.

➤ New tools are hitting the market that rank the stature of connected consumers to help brands identify possible ambassadors and spokespersons.

➤ These same tools are introducing connected consumers to a new reality that what they share online can and will be used for and against them.

➤ Consumers must now invest in their social capital just as they do with their traditional credit scores.

➤ This measured status is closer in alignment to social capital than true influence.

➤ Other forms of measurement focus on reputation, popularity, and topical relevance or authority.

➤ Brands must consider what they wish to accomplish through these relationships to help identify advantageous relationships and outcomes.

➤ In the end, brands become the ultimate judge of influence by benchmarking the performance of the consumer voices they align with in new marketing.

To help better understand how to activate influencers in a brand marketing campaign, please download a copy of the report I published on the subject. You can find it at AltimeterGroup.com and TheEndofBusiness .com.

Chapter 10

The Dawn of Connected Consumerism

In the last chapter, we discussed the phenomenon of everyday people becoming influencers, tastemakers, and market makers. This is at the heart of the matter and, channeling my inner Don Henley, the end of the innocence of social media. This type of evolution within media doesn't evolve without personal recognition of this new stature. Simply said, consumers are learning the benefits of establishing vibrant networks and nicheworks.

As cast mates, we are playing a significant role in a great production of change. It is you, me, and others like us who are leading this culture shift and culture shock, changing everything this (r)evolution touches.

The stairway that leads to the future of business and culture is shaped by each step. This chapter is a looking glass into some of the steps we're taking today. These steps not only define a path, but also represent a blueprint you can use to shift your role from that of follower to leader; student to teacher.

Andy Warhol once famously observed, "In the future everybody will be world-famous for 15 minutes."[1]

Warhol exhibited his first international retrospective exhibition at the Moderna Museet gallery in Stockholm in February 1968. It was in the exhibition catalog that we were introduced to these famous words. In 1979, Warhol repeated his line to address the unceasing questions from journalists about its meaning. His statement read, "My prediction from the sixties finally came true: In the future everyone will be famous for 15 minutes."

Now with reality television, YouTube, and social networks, Warhol's words have never been truer. And for the first time, we are in control of how long we wish to be in the spotlight. It may be a different type of spotlight, but it is significant nonetheless.

Going back to the days of Web 1.0 and through every social network that has risen throughout the years, we were introduced to remarkable individuals who networked their way to Internet popularity, with many crossing the borders from online fame to real-world celebrity.

In social media, we are the stars of our own reality show and our audience, like any audience, must be cultivated. As such, your "15 minutes" are yours to define.

While some individuals strive for stardom, others seek relevance, while many more simply meander through their social networking experiences not thinking about the past, future, or the present; they just simply network in the moment—without pretense or objectives. This is less about a new generation of fame and fame seekers. In our own way, we are all remarkable. This is more about you and your investment in signal over noise.

Focusing on the signal and investing in relevance reinforces this new era of social consumerism. Doing so improves the network, your place within it, and the reach and velocity of your role in the greater network effect.

■ YOU ARE NOW ENTERING THE TRUST ZONE

When we examine the evolution of the social and interest graphs, we can see that at the center of each connection is trust. Remember, connected consumers define their online experience, and the information that finds them is based on whom they connect with. At the same time, these networks develop into trust-based networks in which experiences form common bonds. Connected consumers proactively take to their streams for guidance on decisions, especially purchasing decisions (Figure 10.1).

Businesses seeking to gain the attention of connected consumers need to grasp the dynamics of what I call the *trust zone* to one day

 @alexklevine
Alex Levine

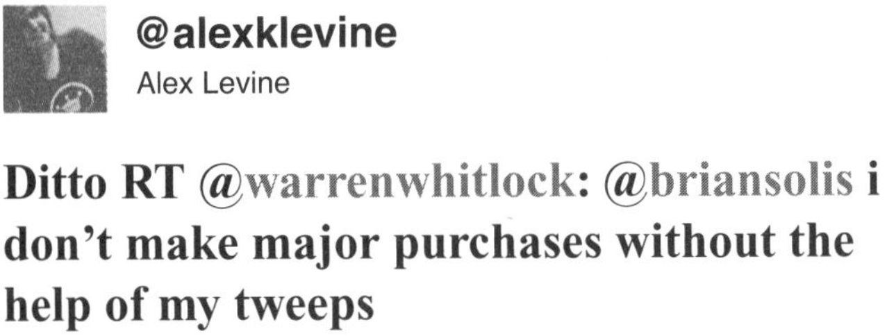

Ditto RT @warrenwhitlock: @briansolis i don't make major purchases without the help of my tweeps

Figure 10.1 Social Shopping: Making Decisions in Public

earn a place within it. Entering the trust zone requires work, but it is through this process that relationships are established. As such, there are only two ways to enter the trust zone: through someone who is already connected to your business or because a direct relationship is already established. Direct and indirect connectivity provide the scale to eventually reach the trust zone of other customers through the individuals who represent you within extended networks of trust. Scale is achieved through community.

From the outside in, reviews and experiences from trusted peers, experts, and influencers form the foundation of the network. The information that flows into the stream from multiple networks sparks conversation and triggers clicks, while shaping perception and steering decisions in the process. From the inside out, experiences are shared through networks of relevance that affect the perceptions and activities of those who follow them. Social customers are highly connected and trust networks are affecting outcomes with or without the businesses they affect. (See Figure 10.2.)

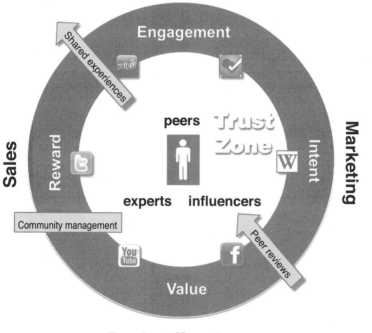

Figure 10.2   Entering the Trust Zone

Businesses that can earn the attention of the connected consumer and more importantly, a connection, find themselves in the advantageous position of being trusted to deliver information directly to the consumers they are trying to reach. But as in any relationship, trust must be earned now and over time. This is done through a form of engagement and community management stemming from not just one (although it's a start), but from various departments within business, including:

➤ Customer service

➤ Marketing

➤ Sales

➤ Products and services and the experiences they engender

Customer touchpoints are unlocked through triggers that answer the prevailing question of the connected consumer, "What's in it for me?" There has to be value in the equation not just for the business, but also for the individual and his network. And while everything starts with recognition, social consumers are looking for incentive objects that are not just worthy of consuming, but also sharing.

Defining the following attributes and executing counts for everything here:

➤ Value

➤ Rewards

➤ Intentions (May I have your intention please? What's your mission and purpose?)

➤ Engagement (Why should I engage and what do I do after the engagement?)

■ A DAY IN THE LIFE OF THE CONNECTED CONSUMER

Consumers are becoming increasingly sophisticated. Their daily habits extend beyond social networking, watching videos on YouTube, and texting. It's how they make purchase decisions, offer referrals, and share experiences that require an open mind.

What I'm about to explain should not be discounted. This isn't a fad. This is what connected consumers know. Their behaviors are also leading to changes in behavior in others around them and it is only going to continue to progress.

To understand the mindset of the connected consumer, one must realize that everything begins with search and intent. When a traditional or online consumer approaches a decision, she may take to

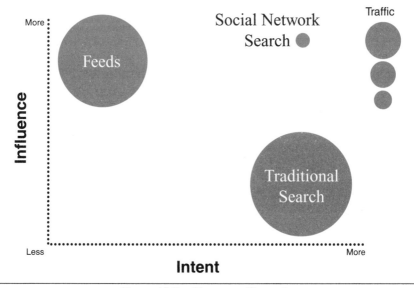

Figure 10.3   Discovery Channels

a search engine such as Google. As GIGYA, a software platform designed to make websites social, discovered in its report "Open Graph
Today,"[2] connected consumers first look to their social stream or to
the search box within their social network to see what others are saying about a particular topic or how they're interacting around it. (See
Figure 10.3.)

The distinction between search conduct and the objects that return is profound. Typically, in a Google search, results mostly feature
web pages, news sites, or blogs. In the case of a social search, the
results are conversations or interaction around social objects. Such
social objects include links to web pages, videos, images, commentary, and status updates, as well as the Likes, comments, favorites,
bookmarks, and so on associated with each object.

While writing this chapter, I was simultaneously monitoring my
social stream. Just a few minutes before reaching this point, I noticed
the following tweet (see Figure 10.4).

 @SteveSchuitt
Steve Schuitt

Does Anyone Know the Best Juicer to Get?
I'm pretty sold on the Omega 8005, but if
you know a better one let me know!

Figure 10.4   Connected Consumers Need a Little Help from Their Tweeps

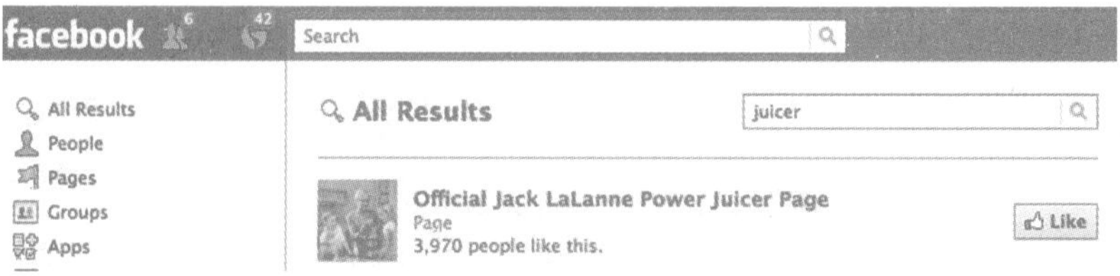

Figure 10.5   Jack LaLanne Power Juicer Page on Facebook

@SteveSchuitt did his research, possibly using a combination of Google and social search to make a short list. But when it came time to make his decision, he cut right to the chase and asked his social graph for direction.

Just trying a quick search in Facebook, it appears that my social graph may prefer the Jack LaLanne Power Juicer (Figure 10.5).

At this point, I decided to run a variety of keyword searches around "What should I buy," "Which should I buy," and "Thinking about buying." I was not disappointed in the sheer volume of conversation on Twitter, where consumers were looking for real-time input on purchase decisions, with many happening at the point of purchase (Figure 10.6).

To bridge the gap between the needs of traditional, online, and social consumers, Google has modified its search algorithm to include results from social networking platforms, including real-time Twitter

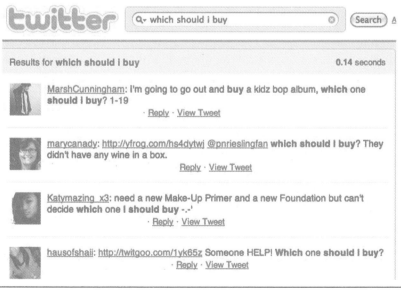

Figure 10.6   Buying Decisions Go Public to Get Advice

search as well as the social graph, into its search results page. For example, typing "best juicer" into Google will show top websites; below that are real-time conversations about "best juicers" in Twitter. At the bottom are a series of social objects produced by people in one's social graph, including pictures on Flickr, videos on YouTube, or posts created by my friends on the subject.

But it's not just Google and Twitter. Locally, social consumers take to Yelp, Trusted Opinion, or Foursquare to find out what the experiences of their friends and peers are at local businesses. Many of them have never used the Yellow Pages, Yellowpages.com, or CitySearch. It's a different culture now and it's our job to not ignore it, but to find how to embrace and steer it.

This activity will only become more widespread. The opinions of those in the social and interest graph are sacred, trusted, and more importantly, curated. Remember, people connect with those in the majority because their perspective is valued.

Using Twitter, Facebook, YouTube, and blogs, individuals are earning prominence through the tireless acts of interaction, content creation, and establishing goodwill by contributing to the experiences of others.

■ CHECKING IN TO THE NEW REALITY OF GEOLOCATION

Are you playing Foursquare? Have you found your *place* in Facebook?

Increasing visibility in the real world, on the traditional Web, and on the Social Web, is essential when competing for attention where your audience's focus is. Foot traffic, Yellow Pages, Google, and Yahoo! Search are losing favor to new forms of research and referrals. Yelp paved the way for social reviews and referrals, but Foursquare and the like are introducing trusted opinions and real-life networking into the mix that reward exploration and experimentation. Businesses can only benefit by playing along.

Location-based services are changing the face of social networking. When relationships were once at the center of user experience, in the golden triangle of mobile, social, and real-time interaction, places now take center stage and corresponding activities and rewards become the cast and crew of the production.

Foursquare and Facebook Places, among many others, are ushering in a new form of networking that use smartphones to fuse the social graph, game theory, real locations, businesses, and brands into one mobile experience. They married the online and offline, and introduced people to the gems of their locale as championed by their friends who frequently check in.

What started as a way to literally see and be seen has now transformed into a universe in which physical and online activity merge to improve experiences and relationships between people and between people and businesses, services, and locales. Connected consumers are lured into checking in through gaming and game theory. They earn points and badges as rewards for adding locations, checking in to them, and adding tips for other related activities worth consideration.

For those who are not familiar with checking in, here's how it works. Social consumers launch their favorite app, such as Foursquare, when arriving at a particular destination to check in. Doing so sends an update to their network that they have quite literally arrived. In many cases, these networks are also designed to simultaneously send updates to other networks such as Twitter and Facebook. Most importantly, the check-in serves as a social object, which may spark reactions within each network while also serving as a powerful form of personal endorsement. In line with the theme of this entire book, sharing experiences triggers a network effect across a highly qualified and extensive audience of audiences.

Geolocation apps offer various platforms for connected individuals to not only check in, but also share tips about the business or the area. Indeed, the social consumer is steering the experiences of those in his social graph and as such, any business not at least monitoring activity to glean insight is missing a powerful outlet into digital relevance.

Connected consumers expect to be rewarded, however, and they're showing that electronic badges just aren't enough. They're demanding discounts, special offers, and freebies to continue serving their personal endorsements across their social graphs. After all, the activity is mutually beneficial. Businesses attract customers who help spread the word and consumers feel that their presence and network are appreciated.

ReadWriteWeb, an online blog network that examines the technology behind emerging trends, published an interesting study that explored the psychology of why connected consumers check in.[3]

The study found that motivation for using a location-based app was driven by:

➤ Finding people

➤ Chance meetups

➤ Badges/points/gifts

➤ Special offers and coupons

➤ Local tips/discovery

➤ People tracking

➤ Personal history/diary

I would add one more—social currency. Whether it's said or simply a subconscious motivation, this is the essence of social networking universally. People check in as a form of social currency and the resulting capital is different network by network. It governs how we interact with objects and one another and also defines our net worth based on how we earn, spend, lose, and build capital.

In 2010, I wrote the cover story[4] for *Entrepreneur* magazine on innovation in entrepreneurship. In the story, I had an opportunity to interview Foursquare founder Dennis Crowley. We discussed how Foursquare redefined the role of the patron and the relationship between businesses and customers.

"The network started to take on a life of its own," Crowley said in the interview. "Foursquare gave everyday people, venues and local merchants a voice. It opened the doors for businesses to see a whole new way of seeing their customer."

Geolocation represents an important role in the future of connected consumerism. SNL Kagan reported that in 2010 the number of location-based users tripled, reaching 33.2 million.[5] In early 2011, *eMarketer* published projections for the number of mobile social network users who will check in, showing adoption to double between 2010 and 2015. (See Figure 10.7.)[6]

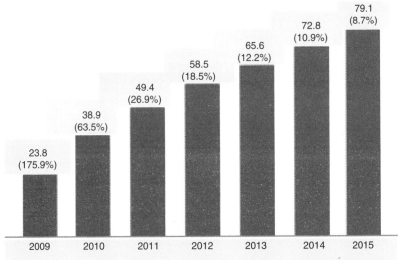

Note: mobile phone users who have a profile and access social networks from a mobile browser or an installed application at least once per month

Figure 10.7   U.S. Mobile Social Network Users, 2009 to 2015 (millions and % change)

Source: eMarketer, December 2010.

In a study published in *ReadWriteWeb,* Foursquare and Gowalla shared a ranking of some of the top businesses that reported check-ins:

➤ Starbucks

➤ McDonald's

➤ Burger King

➤ Walgreen's

Not only do businesses need to compete for the moment, they must also compete for the future. And with limited resources, identifying where to focus time and energy is paramount. What took Twitter some time to formally embrace, Foursquare, Facebook Places, and others are realizing that businesses, in addition to everyday users, are the beneficiaries of check-ins. For example, Foursquare is concentrating marketing and development resources to helping businesses compete for check-ins.

Foursquare encourages businesses to claim their location to increase traffic, customer base, and use of the geolocation app as a next-generation loyalty program.[7] These offers carry across the mobile and social experience, using iPhones, Androids, and BlackBerrys as the bridge between social graphs in each respective geolocation network in addition to Facebook and Twitter.

Foursquare specifically recommends offering:

➤ Mayor specials

➤ Check-in specials

➤ Frequency-based specials

➤ Wildcard specials

➤ Loyalty programs

➤ Variable ranges for nearby offers

➤ Tips

Using Foursquare as an example, business owners can gather insight into their connected customers to spark creativity in campaigns and service programs. At the time this chapter was written, available information included:

➤ Most recent visitors

➤ Most frequent visitors

➤ Times of day for check-ins

➤ Number of unique visitors

➤ Histogram of daily check-ins

➤ Gender

➤ Check-ins also broadcast to Twitter and Facebook

Foursquare provides window clings, as does Yelp, Facebook, and other localized services, to attract passersby. For example, Hampton Inn and Suites and Whole Foods are among the many businesses proudly displaying the ability to check in "here."

While effective, this is only one of the ways a business can leverage location-based social networks for customer acquisition and retention.

The following are a few other examples of how businesses are competing for the attention and patronage of the connected customer.

The San Francisco Bay Area Rapid Transit (BART) system partnered with Foursquare to encourage transit ridership. BART encouraged people to check in to their usual stations and routes through Foursquare in the attempt to tap into the mobile networks of its passengers while rewarding them with dedicated badges for doing so.

Starbucks offered $1 off any size Frappuccino for mayors, and as a result, observed a 50 percent increase in check-ins at its locations.

Monique's Chocolates in Palo Alto, California, acquired more than 50 new customers and earned more than 100 redemptions for its special of "buy one, get one free" for truffles. Each redemption also equated to a 25 percent return ratio. In comparison, the chocolate shop ran an ad in a local paper and acquired only one new customer, at a cost of $300.

AJ Bombers, a popular burger joint in Milwaukee, increased menu item purchases by 30 percent through its special promotions of free burgers for mayors and free cookies for adding tips. And demonstrating creativity, AJ Bombers also hosted the equivalent of a tweetup for customers to help them earn coveted Foursquare "Swarm" and "I'm on a Boat" badges while increasing loyalty and sales.

Using Gowalla, the New York Nets hid free pairs of virtual game tickets throughout sports-related check-in spots. These tickets could be exchanged for real game tickets as well as other prizes.

Through Gowalla, the *Courier-Journal,* Kentucky's largest newspaper, hosted a city tour and bar crawl during the Kentucky Derby from which visitors earned special badges for following the guided tour.

While these examples represent only a few of the many ingenious and viral ways to attract and reward customers, the true promise of these portable social networks is the ability to bring to life online and offline relationships. Business owners, the question for you is: Have you checked into the future of local business?

■ STEERING ACTION THROUGH INCENTIVES

Both brilliant and absurd, Gap garnered attention when it introduced its new logo (see Figure 10.8). For better or for worse, people reacted and social networks become their stage. On Twitter, a fake account (@GapLogo) was created to mock the new logo and encourage Gap to rethink its approach. The account, in addition to the concentration of negative feedback within social networks, inspired blog posts and coverage in traditional press, which Gap harnessed into momentum for what later appeared to be a campaign intended to crowdsource a new logo.

Regardless of outcome, Gap tempted fate by casting lines to the networks of connected consumers to reel in engagement. From online to offline to online again, Gap understood that connected customers are checking in to businesses, fusing virtual and real-world engagement and influencing behavior and decisions in the process. These increasingly important acts of social exchanges are gaining in value and delivering benefits for both sides.

In 2010, Gap offered visitors 25 percent off purchases in store, simply for checking in through Foursquare. A separate offer titled the Black Magic Event offered Facebook and Twitter users 25 percent off as well as a free pair of jeans to the first 50 people who showed up in each location.

Gap executives realized that offering a discount on merchandise represented a tiny investment in comparison to other traditional means. Activating this emerging form of social advertising through word of mouth extended the special offer from Foursquare to Twitter to Facebook to blogs and eventually traditional media. It was a

Gap + Others **Just Gap** Just Others

Gap Thanks for everyone's input on the new logo! We've had the same logo for 20+ years, and this is just one of the things we're changing. We know this logo created a lot of buzz and we're thrilled to see passionate debates unfolding! So much so we're asking you to share your designs. We love our version, but we'd like to see other ideas. Stay tuned for details in the next few days on this crowd sourcing project.
12 hours ago

👍 319 people like this.

💬 View all 305 comments

Gap Want to recycle your style? Bring in some old denim and we'll start

Figure 10.8   The New Logo: A Discussion on Gap's Facebook Brand Page

lesson in earning relevance, which for all intents and purposes, is now a daily ritual all businesses must undergo. For without relevance or presence, businesses cannot engage nor attract connected consumers. Out of sight does equal out of mind. Brands, too, need to extend their 15 minutes.

At a minimum, progressive businesses are starting to realize that checking in, tweeting, +1's Liking, and sharing are forms of social currency as well as a personal endorsement. Recognition is the least that a business can do to attract and incentivize connected consumers to eventually earn a spot within the trust network. Introducing special offers and rewards is how we amplify these lucrative endorsements, extend brand reach, and transform businesses into social objects whereby everyday people contribute to increased presence in social streams. The benefits are not only mutual, they are empowering.

■ WHEN PURCHASES BECOME SOCIAL OBJECTS

Experiences shape experiences. In many ways, what we purchase is symbolic of who we are and who we want to be. When we combine the allure of social media, it seems almost natural to share our purchases and experiences with friends who define our social graph online and in real life.

Not only are consumers broadcasting their location through geo-location services, but new tools also invite them to share their purchases as well.

Blippy is described as a network in which "consumers obsessively write reviews about everything they buy." Here, the purchase is the social object and each transaction is the catalyst for conversation. Services like Blippy introduce you to an even more liberal form of shared consumer behavior. Blippy users readily connect payment accounts such as iTunes, Amazon, Sephora, Starbucks, Target, and Walmart, among many others, to automatically trigger an update upon purchase into the Blippy stream. Like most other nicheworks, Blippy can also connect to other major networks to broadcast purchases to the social graph.

For example, if I purchase a new book on Amazon, that transaction is then introduced into the Blippy stream, where my followers can comment, interact, and share experiences. If I send the update to Twitter and Facebook, friends within other networks are now introduced to the extended conversation.

Shared purchases and product reviews do a few very important things. First, shared purchases contribute to the digital persona of the individual. Second, in-stream product reviews invite responses

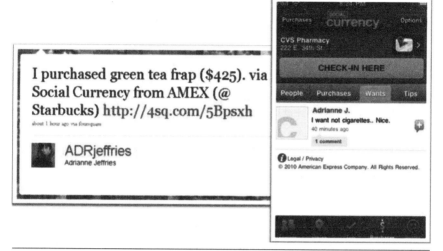

Figure 10.9   Social Currency Purchase Becomes a Social Object

and, ultimately, conversations. And third, reviews, conversations, and resulting exposure potentially influence buying decisions.

But it isn't just emerging companies that are facilitating the syndication of transactions in streams, major financial organizations are experimenting with social influence and commerce as well.

Social Currency by American Express socializes transactions using an iPhone app built on the Foursquare platform (Figure 10.9). Social Currency lets users check in to locations, build wish lists, broadcast purchases, share photos of purchases, and comment on friends' activities. Like Blippy, these transactions can also be syndicated to outside networks, including Foursquare, Twitter, and Facebook. Launched as a complement to Currency, its portal for providing financial advice for young professionals, American Express is placing transactions and intentions at the center of social networking, encouraging interaction and, ultimately, action through the social effect.

These are but two of many apps and services that exist and will soon exist. The future of commerce will be socialized!

■ IT'S NOT HOW YOU SEE ME, IT'S HOW I WANT YOU TO SEE ME

Why would someone broadcast their purchases to the Social Web, you ask?

I have a working theory to address at least part of it.

When a brand does its job right, it creates hooks to establish an emotional bond. The affinity it engenders contributes to who we are as individuals and how others perceive us online and in the real world. As discussed earlier, sharing our purchases and experiences serve as social objects, which are catalysts for sparking conversations and creating perceptions. At the center of this discussion is the product. Experiences, impressions, and perceptions cast bridges that link us together. As the conversation unfolds, the hub connects the product to individuals who not only respond, but also consume, where information influences behavior, opinion, and experiences. According to some new research, this form of subconscious empowerment seemingly builds confidence.

The *Journal of Consumer Research* published a study conducted by the University of Minnesota, "Got to Get You Into My Life: Do Brand Personalities Rub Off on Consumers?"[8] The study sheds light onto a subject that sociologists have long believed: Our favorite brands contribute to who we are.

Authors Ji Kyung Park and Deborah Roedder John of the University of Minnesota set out to answer the critical question that is actually paramount in social media, "Why are brands such as Cartier, Harley-Davidson, and Nike so well-liked by consumers? One of the reasons is that they have appealing personalities."

As part of their research, women were given bags to carry around a local mall for an hour. Several were given Victoria's Secret bags, while others toted plain pink shopping bags. The experiment surfaced an interesting connection. Those women who carried Victoria's Secret bags felt more feminine, glamorous, and good-looking. On the contrary, those with the pink shopping bags felt indifferent.

These studies represent a harbinger of the importance of personal relationships and how they're fostered in brand experiences. Businesses must bring their brand and products to life as consumers are looking for the attributes that facilitate alignment and embodiment.

As such, services like Blippy or Social Currency may actually contribute to the cycle of social maturation and lend to the idea that brands not only rub off on self-perception, but sharing these transactions helps to fortify the vision we have of ourselves. This makes a strong case for investing in the shift from the intangible relationship a brand may have with its consumer to a more tangible, steerable, and measurable relationship.

As social capital factors into the equation, these conversations represent touchpoints in which positive experiences take the shape of endorsements and, ultimately, contribute to the overall branding process. At the same time, brands also assist in shaping the personal brands of its customers. Psychologically, this can also boost the confidence of connected consumers, encouraging greater levels of sharing, amplifying the reach of potential brands, and eventually boosting the likelihood of influence within the social graph. Over time, this connected behavior carries the latent capacity to establish the role of the connected consumer as the definitive taste and market maker. And as these networks proliferate markets online and offline, their stature within the overall economy is forged with every question, shared purchase, reaction, and outcome.

In the end, experiences are increasingly socialized, and the ability to forge emotional connections is instrumental in forging bonds and cultivating community development, loyalty, and advocacy.

Everything starts with intentions. Brands must now define the pillars of character, mission, purpose, and persona so as to foster desired engagements and outcomes. No brand is an island and we must now build bridges to better connect our value proposition to customers and the people who influence them. The grail of any business is the trust zone.

The rise of the connected consumer gives rise to a genre of connected commerce. Everything begins with recognition of this new consumer and a heartfelt understanding of what inspires them. It's then our responsibility to earn attention and establish relevance within their communities to make them our own.

Centers of Attention

➤ Connected consumers are extending their 15 minutes of fame.

➤ This new level of presence is escalating the role of the connected consumer in the emerging genre of social commerce.

➤ Consumers build a trust zone around themselves to learn, help, and interact with trusted connections to make and steer decisions.

➤ Businesses must earn their way into the trust zone of social customers.

➤ Rather than disregard behavior unlike your own, understand how consumers interact and learn from it to participate in it.

➤ Decisions may start in traditional search engines, but connected consumers take to social networks for insight and direction.

➤ Connected consumers are checking in to locations to share activity with peers and also earn rewards and recognition from the businesses they frequent.

➤ Check-ins are a form of social currency.

➤   Businesses can encourage favorable activity by monitoring, learning, and investing in the activation of desirable and mutually beneficial experiences.

➤   Social customers are now broadcasting their purchases to engender responses.

➤   Syndicated purchase experiences contribute to the personal branding and social stature of each consumer.

Chapter 11

The Rise of Collective Commerce

> When a hundred people stand together, each of them loses their mind and gets another one.
>
> —*Friedrich Nietzsche (Adapted)*

Across the generational divides, technology builds the bridges that connect us, creating a greater society of informed and connected individuals. Within this new digital sovereign, like in the real world, not one person knows everything, but everyone knows something. Unlike in the physical world, however, this emerging utopia is connected to a repository of collective intelligence (CI) that serves as the intellectual database for the human network. Access to information is a commodity, but the significance of the network is as valuable as the insights poured into it and the creativity it inspires.

Collective intelligence might sound like it's out of a James Cameron movie or a novel by Isaac Asimov. It is however, a reality. For those who realize the value of information, the deafening noise created by the chatter of connected customers can be filtered down to themes, trends, and opportunities for a triaged approach.

Collective intelligence was originally coined by French philosopher Pierre Levy in 1994.[1] Levy used the term to describe the impact of the Internet on the cultural production and consumption of knowledge. Levy recognized that because the Internet facilitates a rapid, open, and global exchange of data and ideas, eventually the *human* network would "mobilize and coordinate the intelligence, experience, skills, wisdom, and imagination of humanity."[2] As a result, he made a profound prediction, "... we are passing from a Cartesian model of thought based upon the singular idea of *cogito* (I think) to a collective or plural *cogitamus* (we think)."[3]

117

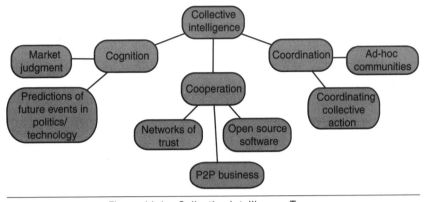

Figure 11.1   Collective Intelligence Types

Figure 11.1, created by Olga Generozova,[4] illustrates that collective intelligence touches everything. And in the realm of influence, engaging with connected individuals and earning their attention can directly shape behavior and outcomes.

Collective intelligence is empowering and it inspires individuality, freedom, and innovation. In the context of this book, CI also accelerates informed decisions and does so through the smartphones, laptops, tablets, and other extensions of the digital lifestyle—creating an on-demand knowledge network wherever and whenever information is needed. But for the connected customer, this knowledge isn't relegated solely to the crowd-sourced encyclopedic content that populates Wikipedia; this CI network is also rich with everyday experiences of our peers. It's open for consultation all day, every day, and this connected society leans on it for the most complex as well as the simplest decisions in life. It's how this genre communicates and learns. And it's how they influence and are influenced when making purchase decisions.

■ ON THE WEB, ONE IS A LONELY NUMBER: SOCIALIZING COMMERCE

Shopping is a social experience. Nearly two-thirds of Millennials report that they shop for groceries, electronics, and clothing with someone else. Now that experience is moving online as well, creating a genre of shopping that is not just the next big thing, it is the new reality.

If we had to simplify the differences between Web 1.0 and Web 2.0, it would come down to one thing: people. And, while the industry is hesitant to talk about the idea of Web 3.0, what it represents is how technology and people can work together to create more productive experiences. The Social Web introduced us to real-time collaboration, not just for work, but for everything we do. Perhaps one of the most fascinating aspects of this, however, is that connected customers no longer need a traditional PC to access or publish information or experiences or reach out to one another. Mobile is the portal to connecting online and offline, bringing to life a new reality that blurs the line between the virtual and actual worlds. The results are immediacy and influence, and it is at the heart of how people make decisions and share experiences.

Connected customers make purchases in the presence of their human network and specifically with reliance on the people and experiences within their trusted nicheworks.

The connected customer is a hybrid individual, someone who, like any consumer, purchases goods and services for any given reason. The difference, however, is in how she chooses to do so. As introduced in the last chapter, individuals are taking to their streams for direction as well as to share experiences. These streams are highly intertwined, and this information feeds the nucleus of collective intelligence. It is how this information is brought to life that starts to exemplify the future of commerce.

Picture if you will the science fiction characters the Terminator or the Predator. In the movies, there are several occasions when we, as the audience, are given the ability to see the world through their eyes. Rather than merely seeing landscapes and objects in plain view, these characters benefit from an additional layer that translates objects into information. Similarly, connected customers see the world differently, whether online or in the real world.

Products become social objects. Suddenly, everything is worthy of sharing with friends on Twitter, Facebook, or Google. And each time something is shared in the stream, it invites reactions and thus sparks real-time threads around the moment. Decisions are considered, made, or abandoned based on what happens next.

For example, everything begins with the price as it becomes a point of contention and comparison. The connected customer will use a mobile app such as RedLaser to scan the UPC or QR code of a product to compare prices and features or get more information. This is done without feedback of a frontline representative. Onsite service now comes from online information or friends who are at the ready via mobile devices. Savvy retailers will recognize that a new type of onsite service will be required to not lose the deal. If a lower price or more attractive deal is available at another store or online, store managers will need a process to respond. Additionally, brands sold through retail stores will need to assist retailers in recognizing and assisting with these opportunities virtually. The scan can reveal more than price; it can reveal wonderful experiences, extras, or other information vital to a decision. This is something brands can assemble and push to the right places. But, it can't resemble marketing content designed for the general consumer. It must be additive. It must be remarkable.

Discerning consumers not only expect immediate access to information, they expect closure. Regardless of outcome, these individuals will share the experience. In-store representatives and the products that sit on shelves now have the potential to reach hundreds or thousands of individuals through one engagement, through one scan, through one shared experience.

Through check-ins, places come to life. Through RFID (radio frequency identification) locations can now broadcast themselves through customer devices. Through QR codes and Microsoft Tags, customers are scanning objects to unlock hidden content or special offers. And through augmented reality, device screens transform what the eye sees into something much more useful and engaging.

In this new reality, experiences are shared and consumed as a matter of fact, a routine that extends and enlivens noteworthy moments.

To bring this idea to life, Figure 11.2 is a representation of what a connected customer may visualize in a retail setting.

Figure 11.2   A View of the Retail World Through the Eyes of the Connected Consumer

This change in behavior is the result of technology's impact on society, led by the youth as well as everyday early adopters who realize the benefits of their experimentation. Eventually, all consumers will expect a layer of interactivity that spans online and offline igniting connections with every step.

To activate these new experiences, businesses will have to adapt. To adapt, however, requires a culture that recognizes new opportunities, innovates against them, and changes processes and systems to execute. But make no mistake. Change is not an option. Businesses will need to evolve to prove relevance, to garner attention, and in turn, lead. You are the key to this transformation. What you read here and everything you learn requires documentation and presentation to the decision makers around you. And if you are the decision maker, let's get to work.

■ THE FIFTH C OF COMMUNITY = SOCIAL COMMERCE

In the social realm, brands are racing to create a social presence on the hottest social and mobile networks of the moment. They are the new websites, so why not? The initial goals, of course, are to increase brand awareness and build community. To do so, however, takes a holistic approach that extends beyond the regimen of broadcasting messages to audiences. Clearly brands must establish a social equilibrium whereby the 4 C's of community[5] drive measurable and mutually beneficial activity and engagement through the thoughtful introduction of:

1. Content (We'll add creation and curation)
2. Conversation
3. Context
4. Continuity

More importantly, however, brands must now find creative means to recognize the role of a more informed and connected customer and the varying influence they wield in the social ecosystem.

Recognition and empowerment represent the social sparks that can help businesses not only socialize their brands but also activate consumer behavior. While editorial programming and meaningful engagement unlock the spirit of community, they ultimately set the stage for more useful conversations, beneficial connections, and monetary transactions. Connected consumers do not want to leave

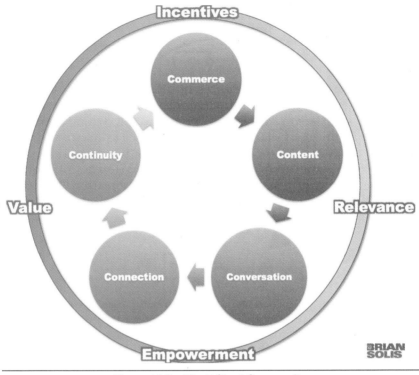

Figure 11.3   The 5 C's of Community

their network of relevance; they would prefer to make a purchase on the spot.

As social media matures, brands must introduce new social sparks that convert decisions and intentions into outcomes where and when attention is focused. Doing so introduces us to potentially viral opportunities that trigger a social effect propelled by a new "C" in the 4 C's of community . . . social commerce (Figure 11.3).

The rise of the socially connected consumer warrants much more than attention; it requires an understanding of what motivates them to click, act, and share. Unlike traditional and perhaps to some extent, the digital consumers that followed, they are not motivated by clever gimmicks nor are they inspired to seek out your presence within these networks. Attention is a precious commodity and these individuals require direct engagement that recognizes their interests as well as their stature in the Social Web. Businesses have to make it worth their time.

Why?

We've already established that the connected consumer is just that—connected—and their actions reverberate across social graphs to spark conversations and, ultimately, clicks to action. It is when they're motivated or inspired that businesses can trigger a desired effect to convert conversations into outcomes.

Integrating social commerce as the fifth C of Community unlocks much more than a new channel to sell; it surfaces the ability to shift social media from a cost center to a profit center. From Delta Airlines and Disney to Nike and Starbucks to Max Factor and Lady Gaga, F-Commerce (Facebook-based e-commerce stores) is becoming an everyday extension to e-tail strategies. The more we experiment, the more we learn. Ultimately, the discussion of return on investment (ROI) becomes a matter of process as we're able to measure investment and return as well as improve conversions to escalate ROI overall. By heightening value and delivering personal experiences, we empower and reward social consumers and as such, improve the online experiences for our community. If we are not competing for tomorrow today, we lose critical opportunities to capture attention now and in the future. It's a matter of digital Darwinism, through which if we are out of sight, we are indeed out of mind.

From here henceforth, the new formula for social commerce = personalized + collaborative + shareable shopping experiences.

■ BUY WITH FRIENDS! THE SAVINGS OF THE CROWDS

In the United States, there are two shopping days each year that generate the most revenue for retail outlets. The health of the retail industry and the economy overall are largely weighted on Black Friday, the day after Thanksgiving, and Cyber Monday, the first day at work following the Thanksgiving weekend. But with social consumers and connected customers, every day is a day to save and share in the saving.

When you ask a connected consumer why they usually connect with brands in social networks, among the top reasons given is access to special offers and promotions—either exclusively or first. It makes sense, of course. Coupons, promotions, and sales are a natural part of the commerce ecosystem. The difference here, however, is that connected consumers do not respond to just any offer. They want to feel like they're part of something bigger. Group buying has emerged as a vital artery in the flow of social commerce.

In Chapter 7, we reviewed an example of group buying. In each case, a Groupon-like experience demonstrated the extent of the

@benasmith
Ben Smith

Good Groupon today for #Lawrence - $10 for $20 of food @MirthCafe groupon.com/?utm_campaign=...

53 seconds ago via Tweet Button   ☆ Favorite ↻ Retweet ↩ Reply

Figure 11.4   Sharing the Savings: A Tweet about a Groupon Deal

network effect. In those cases, opportunities for desirable deals sparked activity, drove sales, and triggered word of mouth, all by design. Social commerce is a function of all of that.

Groupon, LivingSocial, and Facebook Deals are services that connect connected consumers through special deals limited by time, locale, and platform. Whether it's in email, through a mobile app, or through online, individuals unlock the power of savings through bulk. When enough people show interest, the deal unlocks. Other deals are driven by time, encouraging people to act on the basis of time or number of deals remaining.

Sharing is of course encouraged, giving people incentives when recipients act on the basis of your referral. In any relationship in which people are bound by friendship, or at least interest, sharing specials increases the capital of that individual in the relationship. Saving money for something valuable is almost as valuable as giving money. At the time this chapter was written, total Groupons purchased hit 30 million, with a total of $1.3 million saved.

What Groupon unlocked was the power of the "savings of the crowds." The network effect is unlike that of email in which you may send something special to your inner circle or even a special list of contacts. In a social graph, your sharing is tied to the reach of your network. It's far more potent. (See Figure 11.4.) As a result, new services are erupting to compete for the attention and dollars of the connected consumers.

In December 2010, Amazon.com invested $175 million in a similar service, LivingSocial.[6] This might seem like a lot of money to invest in a daily deal provider, but 2011 revenue was estimated at well over $500 million. Groupon's annual revenue was estimated at $1.5 billion.

I remember walking into my local Target and Safeway stores one day to find Facebook gift cards amidst the other retail cards available for purchase. I thought about the prospect that one day Facebook would become a bank not unlike how eBay's PayPal facilitates payments across the entire Web. Initially designed for the purchase of virtual goods, Facebook Credits represents its own economy that removes the fear of integrated personal finances into the social network. Users deposit credits instead in an individual Facebook bank account for the purchase of desirable items as needed. Of course, there's the element of social commerce that comes into play, another reason why the connected customer is already thinking differently about how, when, and where they make decisions or affect the decisions of others.

As the premier social network in the world, Facebook also aimed at activating social commerce, outside of F-commerce, by introducing Facebook Deals into the location game. Through the mobile Facebook app, people could uncover special offers nearby to help them explore their city through incentives. Like Foursquare, these deals are intended to trigger the social effect, showing friends and friends of friends the opportunities you're discovering in real time.

In the Facebook economy, Facebook Deals are only the beginning. Facebook also introduced "Buy with Friends"[7] to increase group purchases through the sharing of deals and transactions in the Facebook update stream. The key differentiator here is empowerment. One user can unlock a deal and then share it with friends once unlocked. In this case, the individual becomes the hero.

In tests, Facebook's head of commerce product marketing, Deb Liu, claimed that more than 50 percent of users chose to share with their social graph a purchase they had made—a number that will only continue to grow.

The Facebook and even the social economy is vast and its expansion is practically unlimited. At the center of everything is the individual egosystem; the information network acts as a micro exchange that connects goods, services, and brands. Currency is also the next frontier, a universe that's already under development, designed with value in mind and driven by intended outcomes.

Social commerce is unlike any online behavior we've seen to date. However, it's not unlike the activity we've long known in the real world. People affect the decisions and impressions of others. Without attention or acknowledgment, it goes unnoticed and ultimately moves further and further away from you. Businesses are in control of relevance in these new markets. How they activate deals and ignite word of mouth across these expansive social and interest graphs determine their value in the social economy. Ignore at your own peril.

■ BUILD IT AND THEY (WON'T) COME

Merchants have little choice than to cater to the connected consumer. But how is not so simple a question to answer.

In late 2010, Gigya published a report that revealed the importance of fusing the social and online shopping experience. The report documented a milestone. Over one-half of the retail sites that responded reported that they had either implemented social commerce as a way to shop or planned to add it in the near future.

Web retailers are integrating social sign-on services such as Facebook and Twitter into the shopping platform, allowing people to connect their social graphs into the shopping experience at the moment of interest. This act displaces the existing process of requiring visitors to create yet another profile for every e-commerce site they visit.

The benefits in doing so are as revealing as they are promising.

Loyalty: 84 percent of businesses reported an increase in loyalty and the ability to engage users and build engagement.

Targeting: 80 percent received richer profile information to inspire personalized product recommendations, emails, promotions, and coupons.

Word of Mouth: 77 percent found that customers shared and promoted the site to their social graph.

Revenue: 75 percent reported an increase in revenue, directly affecting the bottom line.

What we learn from this Gigya report is that integrating social login is Part 1 of a multipart engagement strategy. Part 2 is squarely aimed at delivering the commerce experience directly to consumers in the networks or in the style and format they expect. Some brands experiment with the creation of microsites or dedicated landing pages, others with F-commerce, and a few with a combination of all of these and more. Also, loyalty programs can take on an entirely new form of personalization and as a result, relevance. Facebook, for example, offers businesses the ability to extract the name, email, photo, profile URL, birthday, gender, locations, social graph, and additional insights. Twitter is similar, minus email, birthday, and gender, although there are a series of third-party apps that could help fill in the blanks based on each user name. The takeaway is invaluable. If businesses wish to get closer to their customers, they now have access to information that tells them who their customer is, whom they're connected to, and what's important to them.

When we look at the evolution of social commerce and the touchpoints that trigger activity, we need look no further than F-commerce as a natural example of the future of social shopping. Whether it's in Facebook or integrating the Facebook login into the dot-com, the social effect is built into the system. The advantages to capturing attention where and when it's focused should not go unsaid. We stated earlier that, on average, individuals on Facebook are connected to 130 people. But there are many with thousands of connections. Liking, commenting, purchasing, reviewing products, or creating commerce applications that invite new forms of engagement, allow individuals to transmit transactions, purchase considerations, or experiences into the streams of their peers.

If you didn't see the Facebook logo in the upper left-hand corner of the site, you would forget that you were actually shopping within the social network. 1-800-Flowers.com developed early on a shoplet within Facebook as an extension to its brand page through which consumers could browse through arrangements and order directly without leaving Facebook. In 2010, I worked with the Austria-based team of Swarovski Elements to develop the first luxury goods store within Facebook. Delta Airlines launched the first Facebook Ticket Counter, which triggered promotional updates back into the news feeds of its customers, "I used Delta's Ticket Window to book a flight from . . . to . . ." Diapers.com opened an entire store for parents within Facebook, complete with a "deal of the day." The list goes on and on until it just simply becomes a "must have," rather than a "nice to have." Consumers are already saying that they prefer to buy in their network. They don't want to leave.

■ THE LAWS OF ATTRACTION AND AFFINITY

Social commerce, as any new medium such as mobile or social media, requires a great shift in methodology. It starts with letting go of the dot-com as the sole hub for customer traffic and engagement.

The basic focus of any online business strategy is to increase traffic and conversions. This is all well and good unless the focus of the business strategy also includes, as it should be, the emerging share of social consumers. Here, the idea of destination traffic flirts with extinction. The digerati are not going to your website, and attempting to lure them to do so is becoming a pointless game of "catch me if you can." This is a game businesses cannot win, and trying to force this contingent of influential consumers is nothing short of trying to change the behavior of the market. Good luck with that.

Traffic at the website is only one side of what is now a multifaceted approach. Unless you're in the business of monetizing traffic at your website, then forcing people through a funnel is as unnatural as it is unlikely. This is a topic we discuss in depth later, but for now, the first

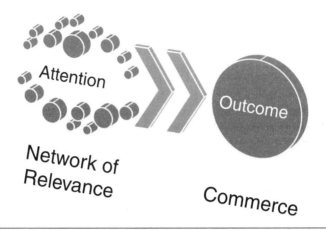

Figure 11.5   Converting Attention Where It's Focused into Clicks to Action (C2A)

lesson we learn is that the traditional funnel of customer activity and the associated touchpoints are different among this new customer delegation, hence the title of this book. Here, the laws of attraction and the laws of affinity are vital to engagement and conversion. The funnel is less linear than it is elliptical. (See Figures 11.5 and 11.6.)

The more progressive business will develop instead an online and offline business strategy that captivates the attention of desirable consumers on their terms, but does so in a way that converts eyeballs into clicks to action (C2A). The old adage is truer here than ever before:

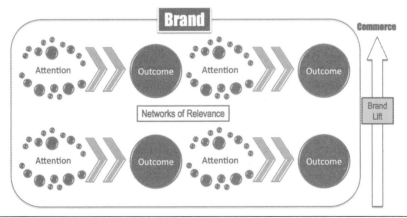

Figure 11.6   Distributed Networks of Relevance and Microsites Contribute to Overall Brand Lift and Outcomes

Fish where the fish are. While this is nothing new, it is imperative nonetheless.

This activity goes against what we were taught in website marketing 101, but it still operates within the realm of common sense. Just because we show up doesn't mean we attract attention or drive meaningful engagement or outcomes. I've long maintained that engaging in social networks and attracting attention is an earned privilege.

So what is the magnet for attention and the glue to hold it?

Enter the laws of attraction and affinity. And here, we have to travel back in time to see the future.

Empedocles was a Greek philosopher who lived between 495 and 435 B.C. His work in human chemistry is still highly regarded today, especially his philosophy on social groups. Empedocles' explanation of the mixing of social groups was based on the model of chemical solubility of liquids.[8] He believed that philia (love) and neikos (strife), or love and hate, were the two ruling passions in human life and the motion of the universe.

People who love each other mix like water and wine; people who hate each other segregate like water and oil.

Later, Greek philosopher Plato based his laws of affinity on the work of Empedocles. Plato postulated that the first law of affinity was that "likes tend toward likes." Or said another way, likes attract. Here, we discuss attraction in the same vein as magnetism. While there are other working interpretations of laws of attraction (LoA) as a form of positive thinking to cause desirable change, in this illustration, I use it quite literally . . . attraction.

In this connected society, in which digital and virtual worlds not only coexist, they collide, likes are more than coincidental; they are essential in attraction. It is what we introduce after the attraction, then, and over time, which shapes affinity, and eventually, loyalty.

Here, we're catering to a connected customer because it is beneficial to the consumer and the brand. We come to them, and if the proposition is compelling, we convert one exchange into the potential for many exchanges.

The difference between traditional pull-and-push models, those through which we push our message through channeled media and pull prospects through the funnel, is in its designs and intentions. Indeed, we address from the onset the skepticism of the connected consumer by proactively answering the question, "May I have your intention, please." In the design of a direct-to-consumer model (D2C) we set up shop within their realm and identify ways to push relevance through their channels in the hopes of pulling them into a value proposition that's mutually beneficial. It's a quid pro quo of sorts, advantage granted in return for something.

It is in this direct connectivity that we are addressing the first points in a new set of laws of attraction and affinity for connected consumers: location (localization) and interest (context). Reviewing the additional laws and integrating them into the business plan, or as friend Hugh MacLeod refers to it, our *evil plan,* we set out on a quest for relevance.[9] The upside of this path is that we earn relevance with every step. At the same time, we also earn irrelevance with every step away from our mission and intention.

The laws of attraction and affinity guide us in our quest for attention magnetism, affinity, loyalty, and ultimately an improved bottom line. Everything comes down to establishing relevance in the greater aspiration of earning allegiance.

To that end, Karen Karbo published a fascinating study on the attributes of friendship as tied to the laws of attraction.[10] She also assembled the elusive nuances that escalate friendship to best friend status (or in the language of social consumers, BFFs). I share this excerpt with you to help us get in the right frame of mind:

> *New research shows the dance of friendship is nuanced—far more complex than commonly thought. With intriguing accuracy, sociologists and psychologists have delineated the forces that attract and bind friends to each other, beginning with the transition from acquaintanceship to friendship. They've traced the patterns of intimacy that emerge between friends and deduced the once ineffable "something" that elevates a friend to the vaunted status of "best." These interactions are minute but profound; they are the dark matter of friendship.*

The laws of attraction and affinity are designed to keep us on the right path (Figure 11.7). They were inspired by my research as well as the everyday dynamics of relationships. They serve as a foundation for D2C engagement and commerce, but are also effective in community building just the same.

The Laws of Attraction and Affinity

➤ Identify where the attention of the connected consumer is focused.

➤ Define a higher purpose along with genuine intentions. Also, establish a sense of value to attract connected consumers, giving them something to align with.

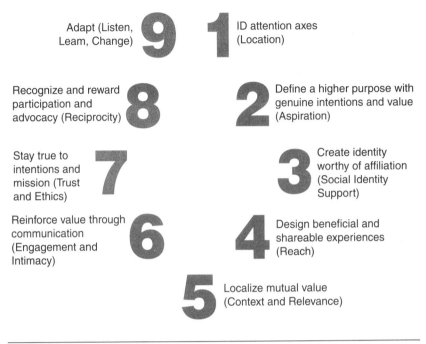

Figure 11.7   Laws of Attraction and Affinity

➤ Establish an identity and a presence worthy of affiliation. Give people something to believe in and something exciting to be a part of.

➤ Design the presence and engagement strategies and all that fuels interaction to be beneficial and shareable—this is, after all, about shared experiences.

➤ Based on the presence of each D2C community, localize the value, content, storefront, and engagement program to match the culture and activity within.

➤ This isn't a power switch; stay consistent and dedicated through meaningful interaction.

➤ Remain true to the original mission and intention. Do not be swayed on the basis of short-term temptations.

➤ Recognize and reward community participants—reciprocity is a strong pillar of community and relationships.

➤ The adaptive business will listen, learn, and change based on the needs of the connected, and all other consumers to stay relevant, indispensable, and valuable.

In the era of new business, it pays to always #payitforward.

■ ABC: ALWAYS BE CLOSING

In 1992, Alec Baldwin starred in the cult classic film *Glengarry Glen Ross* along with all-star powerhouses Al Pacino, Kevin Spacey, Jack Lemmon, and Ed Harris. Baldwin plays Blake, a high-powered executive sent from corporate headquarters to motivate, or more accurately, intimidate, a team of underperforming real estate salesmen. The scene is dark and tense as Blake spells out the future of failure that awaits each person in the room if they can't determine how to reverse declining sales.

Blake sets the tone for the discussion, painting a grim picture for everyone in the room:

> *The good news is you're fired. The bad news is you've got—all you've got—just one week to regain your job, starting with tonight. Oh, have I got your attention now? Good. 'Cause we're adding a little something to this month's sales contest. As you all know, first prize is a Cadillac El Dorado. Anybody want to see second prize? Second prize is a set of steak knives. Third prize is you're fired. You get the picture? You laughing now?*

Blake then takes to a chalkboard and writes three letters, A, B, and C. He then explains the importance of these letters and the role they play in their futures:

> "A, *Always*; B, *Be*; C, *Closing*. Always be closing. Always be closing!!!"

While it is melodramatic, it isn't far from the truth.

In this era of what is nothing short of digital Darwinism, businesses face change. While we can each appreciate the difficulties inherent in any form of change, the Internet has unfortunately (or fortunately depending on your role in all of this) already claimed many institutional businesses, ones that appeared invincible to any market condition.

The list of terminally ill or deceased businesses is humbling:

➤ Tower Records
➤ Blockbuster Video
➤ Hollywood Video
➤ The Wherehouse
➤ Borders Books and Music

➤ Hummer

➤ Oldsmobile

➤ Ann Arbor News

Bob Dylan was indeed a soothsayer in his prediction, "The times, they are a-changin'." Not only has society continued to transform, the empowerment of everyday people is equally forcing a revolution in business.

In 2002, Arie De Geus shared in his book, *The Living Company,* that the average life expectancy of a multinational corporation—Fortune 500 or its equivalent—is between 40 and 50 years.[11] He based this on the surveys of corporate births and deaths. He observed, however, that a full one-third of the companies listed in the 1970 Fortune 500 had disappeared by 1983. De Geus and his team studied businesses around the world, some of which were 200 years old or older, to identify the common traits. In the book, we are introduced to four key factors in business survival:[12]

Long-lived companies were...

1. *Sensitive to their environment.* "Societal considerations were rarely given prominence in the deliberations of company boards. Yet they managed to react in timely fashion to the conditions of society around them."

2. *Cohesive, with a strong sense of identity.* "This cohesion around the idea of 'community' meant that managers were typically chosen for advancement from within; they succeeded through the generational flow of members and considered themselves stewards of the longstanding enterprise. Each management generation was only a link in a long chain."

3. *Tolerant.* As observed, "These companies were particularly tolerant of activities on the margin: outliers, experiments, and eccentricities within the boundaries of the cohesive firm, which kept stretching their understanding of possibilities."

4. *Conservative in financing.* "They were frugal and did not risk their capital gratuitously. Having money in hand gave them flexibility and independence of action. They could pursue options that their competitors could not."

Adaptive companies are indeed living and they can learn from these observations, as they're eerily pertinent to these times and the times that lay ahead. The democratization of information is both a revolution and an evolution, introducing blatant and also inconspicuous signs of change. Companies are forced to compete aggressively beyond profitability. They must first compete for attention through the hearts, minds, words, and clicks of the social consumer. Doing so establishes reach and relevance for a new generation of consumerism.

Think about all we've learned thus far in this book and compare what we know now to the list de Geus presented in *The Living Company*.

Society is changing. A day in the life of the connected customer is unlike that of traditional or online consumers.

Brand identity is not necessarily established within these new egosystems. Businesses are living off of the fumes of the carryover effect of what consumers know and share based on offline interactions and experiences. Unless they're renewed and reinforced here, the shelf life of the brand now carries an expiration date.

Tolerance is necessary. It is through open-mindedness that businesses can recognize the need for change and the leadership to change course.

Money talks and spending it without a plan is unfortunately what many businesses attempt to do in times of uncertainty...they just try to buy their way out of a problem. As Winston Churchill said during World War II, "He who fails to plan is planning to fail." However, understanding when, where, and how to build bridges between connected consumers and your business creates a road to relevance and success.

The ABCs of business now moves beyond the notion of Always Be Closing to Always Be Changing!

Concentrating effort here is the key to unlocking the commerce gates to the future of your business. Engaging where attention is focused, when, where, and how is the root of any adaptive business.

We are competing for the moment.

We are competing for the future.

We are competing for relevance.

Centers of Attention

➤ Collective intelligence is at the center of the information democracy and influences all it touches.

➤ Connected consumers purchase in public, and as such, they influence the decisions of others through the public stream.

➤ Social consumers see the world differently, looking for opportunities to share any and all experiences through their networks of relevance.

➤ Social consumers marry the online and offline worlds through shared experiences, bringing to life businesses, brands, products, and opportunities with every click.

➤ Social commerce is the fifth C of community.

➤ Buying with crowds unlocks deals and empowerment among connected consumers—they want to share in the good fortune.

➤ By socializing the shopping experience, businesses increase loyalty, targeting, word of mouth, and revenue.

➤ The laws of attraction and affinity start with capturing attention where it is focused, and through the combination of location, aspiration, identity support, reach, context, intimacy, trust, reciprocity, and change, businesses can build communities, drive activity, and earn relevance.

➤ ABC has moved from "Always be closing" to "Always be changing."

Chapter 12

Creating Magical Experiences

I see the world through two lenses, my way and through the eyes of my social graph. I share both experiences equally to express individuality and compassion.

Shared experiences and relationships are at the heart of online inter-action. Connected customers capture moments and experiences from the real and online worlds as they live them and share everything nonstop. These exchanges represent the currency that funds relation-ships and establishes the net worth of an individual's social capital within each network. The same is true for businesses. If we were to visualize this activity to convey the incredible proportions of trans-actions, it might look a bit like the trading room floor in any high volume stock market. What is your stock worth today?

This connected behavior is a real-life act of pinging, an underly-ing procedure of testing relationships in the world of networking. Packet Internet Gopher (PING) is a utility used to query another computer on a TCP/IP network to determine whether there is a con-nection to it. Similarly, these seemingly random acts of altruism sym-bolize pings to the network to verify connections. The difference is that instead of solely seeking a successful ping response, connected consumers invest in the value and shape of their network of relation-ships and relations. By including their peers in important moments, these small but important forms of social pings result in continuous communication.

In this chapter, we are approaching the final stages of immer-sion in our journey to understanding the traits and impact of con-nected customers. The new world of consumerism is activated through empowerment. Introducing shareable moments into the routines of connected consumers helps them curate interesting and personalized moments, spark threads of interaction, and collaborate in decisions. When shareable experiences are designed into products and services, the stage is set for advocacy and loyalty.

Understanding the unique behavior of those we need to reach is equally empowering. By marrying the elements of "what's in it for me" with the tools and services that connect customer networks, we can eventually steer activities, extend our reach, and stay on the top of the minds of desirable consumers. This is about encouraging meaningful, shared experiences through the social and interest graphs that link audiences with audiences of audiences.

But it is not the last discussion of shared experiences. Just ahead, we review how these experiences join together to not only steer the experiences of others, but also how brands are ultimately affected by the concentration of shared sentiment.

Aberdeen Group released a report stating that more than half of retailers felt that they were pushed into using social media because of its role in the shopping cycle[1]—a subject we review in greater depths later in this book.

In the study, 53 percent reported entering social media because of customer demand. Forty-seven percent did so because of competitive pressure to do so. Twenty-eight percent cited the rapidly changing affinities of consumers. Nineteen percent jumped into social media because consumer response to existing marketing campaigns was on the decline. All signs point to a reality that the era of business as usual is shifting. Businesses must now find comfort outside of their comfort zones.

■ m-COMMERCE: THE SMARTPHONE MAKES SHOPPERS SMARTER

The balance of power is shifting from brand and retailer to consumer. As we saw earlier, the mobile phone is a window to an improved decision-making process. Connected consumers are seizing this position to find relevant information their way, and, brands and retailers aren't necessarily in a position to change the dynamic. Everything begins with an admission . . . an admission that they are not in control. That is the first step in bringing order back into the balance. Consumers wield this power through their smartphones. iPhones and Droids place product information and peer reviews at their fingertips and makes or breaks buying decisions at the point of purchase. This behavior affects e-tailers as well. Connected consumers simply fire open a new tab to compare prices, learn more, and also find related reviews that detail experience.

Welcome to an era of mobile commerce, or m-commerce, for short.

Booz and Company surveyed U.S. consumer usage and attitudes toward mobile commerce and found that between 15 and 20 percent use their cell phones for price discovery and product comparison.[2] Twenty-five percent expect to do so in the near future (which is already here). In 2011, it was expected that 10 to 15 percent of retail revenues were influenced by mobile applications, which could account for as much as $340 billion in total retail sales across the United States and the EU 3 (Germany, France, and the United Kingdom).

Many retailers are already immersed in m-commerce.

Retailers such as Target and Best Buy are creating mobile apps that help customers navigate stores, look up prices, and find special offers and promotions. Target's iPhone app, for example, uses the phone's camera as a bar code scanner for in-store product lookups, whether items are in stock, and where they reside in the store. Daily deals are also presented upon entering the door as a friendly reward for visiting the store and using the app.

Electronics retailer Best Buy uses QR codes, which are similar to bar codes, but presented in a small, square format designed to unlock specialized information on the mobile phone. Customers hold their phone's camera over the QR code to reveal additional information and sometimes hidden specials. The app aids the decision-making process by allowing customers to compare features side by side. Also a plus, Best Buy's app provides customer reviews for a peer-to-peer perspective.

An online consumer finds value in the product reviews that underscore products and services. AMP Agency released a study in reference to consumer shopping behavior that found 72 percent rely on general consumer reviews for feedback on product performance. This is almost twice the amount (42 percent) of consumers who place decision value on expert durability or functionality reviews. With the connected consumer, however, the key difference that separates a review seen as relevant from just any review is the relationships. It's opinion versus trusted opinions. For example, if I base my purchase on reviews on Amazon.com, I am making an assumption that the reviewers' tastes, interests, and expectations of a particular product are in line with mine. We all know what happens when we assume, right? The connected consumer uses his social networks to surface reviews of peers. At the core of those connections are shared interests, and that perspective is far more valuable than that of a stranger.

Recognizing the significance of the shared experience is critical to embracing the opportunity. It's not a stretch to improve apps to fundamentally improve the brand and in-store experience. For example, TrustedOpinion and Trusted Reviews are networks where reviews are just that, trusted. Based on connections and product relevance, consumers are presented with relevant reviews of products, services, and establishments. If reviews don't exist through first-degree relationships, the reviews of people like them are presented. This is based on interests and relationships. While the future of shared experiences are the future of online interaction, we know trusted opinions and relationships guide the decision-making process of the connected customer.

■ REALITY BYTES

Retailers are experimenting with augmented reality, QR codes, and Microsoft Tags to trigger a variety of outcomes and new in-store experiences.

In 2010, world-famous ice cream maker Ben & Jerry's introduced an iPhone app that gave us the gift of sight in the form of Moo Vision. Consumers could hold their phone up to a lid of Ben & Jerry's ice cream to bring to life a series of virtual 3D dioramas. These digital landscapes displayed scenes from small family farms where ingredients were sourced. If they unlocked four dioramas, consumers were given a special set of wallpaper as a reward.[3]

When the Ben & Jerry's app was stirring up new ideas, I was tasked to create a series of blueprints for an upscale grocery chain that would give customers a reason to use their smartphones as part of the experience. Using both QR codes and also augmented reality (AR) technology, the plan was to provide product insight and also introduce specials based on behavior. If a consumer held up the custom-branded app to a particular product, using AR, a 3D landscape would materialize to visualize the nutritional facts of the in-store product versus the popular brands found at other stores. Also, based on scanning activity using QR codes, specials, additional product information, and discounts were presented. The schematic also introduced game theory into the mix to encourage greater adoption and usage of the in-store app. The more that was scanned, the greater the likelihood of earning rewards and discounts.

Macy's department store bolstered designer sales using QR codes through a special promotion during the release of spring fashions in 2011.[4] As part of its Backstage Pass program, Macy's scattered red star-shaped codes that could be scanned by any QR code reader to unlock mobile content, while watching in-store videos from favorite designers, including Bobbi Brown, Sean "Diddy" Combs, and Tommy Hilfiger. Customers could also scan codes for fashion tips and advice.

The applications for QR codes are far and wide. Their use in magazines and in-mail ads are becoming increasingly popular as well. Target introduced QR codes in its print ads to entice consumers to learn more about featured products. In one such campaign, readers were introduced to style expert Sabrina Soto, who demonstrated how Target furnishings and products can liven up home décor.

In an interview with *Mobile Marketer,* bar code expert Laura Marriott commented on Target's creative mobile ad strategy: "By including mobile bar codes in print advertising, a smaller area of advertising inventory space is utilized, allowing brands to pack more information in and gain better value for their advertising initiatives."[5]

■ PRICE COMPARISON APPS LEAD TO PURCHASES OR COMPETITIVE PURCHASES

The *Wall Street Journal* tells the story of a connected consumer in an article that was titled to do exactly what it was attempting to report, "Phone-Wielding Shoppers Strike Fear Into Retailers."[6] In the story, we learn about Tri Tang, a 25-year-old marketer who walked into a Best Buy one weekend to find the perfect gift for his girlfriend. As he was thinking about spending $184.85, he consulted his Android phone by scanning the product barcode into TheFind, a popular price comparison app. Lo and behold, Mr. Tang was presented with an instant alternative: Amazon.com offered the same product for only $106.75, with no tax and free shipping.

This is but one example in a drove of countless scenarios that may indeed strike fear into the pockets of retailers. In new media, everything is transparent, including prices. And while price isn't always the sole factor in a purchase decision, it is important. What was once an advantage of the retailer, through sales, clever point-of-purchase displays, and savvy salespersons, the mobile phone has, as Greg Girard of IDC Retail Insights told the *Journal,* "eroded" the retailer's advantage.

IDC published interesting data that reveals up to 45 percent of connected consumers, in this case, consumers with smartphones, are already performing due diligence on prices.

Best Buy is well aware of the rise of the connected consumer and is actively exploring solutions to steer this activity within Best Buy or in other retailer's locations to its advantage. For example, Best Buy now partners with TheFind to trigger advertisements when the app is used to compare prices at the location of competitors.

The *Wall Street Journal* shared particulars of the partnership:

> If shoppers use TheFind's free app to compare prices on TVs at Wal-Mart, for example, the phone gleans the particulars from their recent search and shows them ads of similar electronics for sale at Best Buy. The items aren't always identical, and the prices aren't always better, but it is an attempt by Best Buy to enter the competition, similar to the way that marketers now target special offers to consumers based on what they are searching for on home computers.

Best Buy CMO Barry Judge captured it best in his quote, "That is an opportunity to steal a sale right when someone is in the throes of making a decision. That is what makes mobile so powerful."

Apps such as TheFind allow for competitive shopping. Ads show price comparisons and alternatives. Savvy marketers will embrace these apps to introduce value into the deal so that it becomes more than just about a product, but an opportunity to increase the value of the deal. A solution could be as simple as a price match. After all, the customer is already in the store, why would any reasonable manager let her leave. An additional solution could also include throwing in extras or special treatment.

Even Amazon.com released an app that encourages consumers to scan codes, take pictures of items on shelves or describe products to see if Amazon.com can beat the price.

Countless apps exist today with more on the way. Google is also a player with Google Shopper for Android and iPhone. Shortly after the *Wall Street Journal* story was published, Google introduced a version for iPhone, and in its announcement, the team boasted that millions are already actively using the product on their Droids to learn about products, read reviews, compare prices, and save and share products.[7] As this chapter goes on, you'll learn more about the tug of war between retailers, e-tailers, and connected customers.

Hundreds of millions of connected customers are demanding that retailers use social media in addition to point-of-purchase apps.

■ DISCOUNTING PRICES, BUT NOT LOYALTY

Price comparisons are an important factor in the immediate future of in-store and online commerce. Mobile couponing is one solution to keep customers entranced and hopefully loyal. Is it a magical experience? It's *an* experience, and a new and personalized one at that. Mobile geolocation networks and services such as Groupon,

LivingSocial, and others are contributing to the in-store allure of shops as a derivative of relationships and specials. Once in the store, however, marketers are always going to experiment with conversion.

New services such as Shopkick introduce real-world incentives to recognize and encourage checking in and might well represent the future for location-based marketing overall. Using mobile phones, consumers can check in to a store to initially earn Kickbucks. Consumers are also urged to scan bar codes to increase points and learn about special deals. The service uses special audio transmitters, costing less than $100 and about the size of a novel to determine where in the store a consumer is at any moment. Knowing this critical information, which is not at all close to accurate using GPS, allows marketers to encourage engagement as well as lure consumers toward exclusive offers and promotions simply by walking around. Kickbucks are bankable and redeemable at any partner store or converted into gift cards, discounts, song downloads, movie tickets, Facebook Credits and also charitable donations.[8] As of late 2010, Shopkick was already running in 1,100 U.S. retail outlets and 100 shopping centers with partners such as Best Buy, Macy's, Target, Sports Authority, Crate and Barrel, and mall operator Simon Property Group.

When asked to compare the demographics of connected consumers using Foursquare and Shopkick, Shopkick founder Cyriac Roeding explained, "Eighty percent of Foursquare users are male and 70 percent are between the ages of 19 and 35. [In contrast,] 55 percent of our users are female. Forty-nine percent of all users are aged 25 to 39, and 13 percent are 40 or older. Only 6.5 percent are 13 to 17. It's the perfect shopper demographic."[9]

Perhaps it's not the "perfect" demographic, but it is a *different* demographic and that's the point. Any retailer seeking to connect with the great variety of connected customers will cater to how they network and share experiences.

Reward and loyalty are also instrumental in nurturing relationships with connected customers. As part of the Booz and Company survey referred to earlier, 54 percent of connected consumers would join a mobile loyalty account if it offered credit, points, and promotions online and offline.

Loyalty is a precious commodity in a day and age when attention is focused everywhere else but on you. Acknowledging the end of the destination and the beginning of co-created experiences, SNAP introduced a platform in early 2011 that transformed online social and real-world activity already taking place on Foursquare, Twitter, and Facebook into tangible rewards. The platform provided retailers with a net to catch, reward, and encourage digital word of mouth through check-ins, status updates, Tweets, and posts.

Tasti D-Lite, a Franklin, Tennessee–based frozen dessert chain, tasted a sample of SNAP throughout more than 30 U.S. locations. The experiment upgraded existing members of the TastiRewards loyalty program to earn greater benefits in exchange for online social interaction.

In an interview with QSRWeb.com, B. J. Emerson, Tasti D-Lite vice president of technology, shared the flavors behind the campaign and why it tasted so delightful: "This [SNAP] allows us to acknowledge and reward our customers for their brand loyalty and for spreading the word about Tasti D-Lite with their friends and followers within the most popular social networking communities. The SNAP platform now offers us greater flexibility and functionality, where the potential for our success is limited only by our ability to creatively engage our customers and execute effective loyalty campaigns for our franchise network."[10]

The campaign won multiple industry awards, including the Retail Solutions Providers Association (RSPA) Innovative Solutions Award and the Quick Service Restaurants Applied Technology Award.

Stella Artois introduced La Société in 2010 as an online loyalty program designed to recognize and reward social aficionados who shared interesting experiences that involved their favorite beer on Twitter, blogs, and Facebook (Figure 12.1). The program originally debuted in Canada and New York and tracked the activity of its members and awarded points for each instance. These points were then redeemable for luxury goods and events. Stella Artois combined shared experiences to activate online networks around its brand, enticing people to join with every update. Indeed, Stella could toast to a connected form of branding and loyalty, as every update would reach hundreds and even thousands in exchange for points.

Again, the key here is that those activities were shareable, and while customers were rewarded for their activity, each update was crafted as part of the campaign to also market an aspirational lifestyle. People *also* share experiences because it paints a picture of not only who they are, but who they aspire to be. When they Like a brand or tweet a purchase, it's not just an update, it's a form of self-expression.

Cheers!

La Société Stella Artois

The Film Independent Spirit Awards are tonight, and one of our Elite connoisseurs is enjoying the glitz & glamour of Santa Monica first-hand. Watch Joel McHale host the ceremony on IFC at 10 PM ET/PT.

Figure 12.1   La Société Rewards Go Social

■ VIRTUAL MIRRORS REFLECT THE TRUE PERSONA OF THE CONNECTED CUSTOMER

Mirror, mirror, on the screen, who's the most connected one of all?

The clear and constant presence of technology, coalesced with a lifestyle of living in public, is in fact the enabler for a new era of connected consumerism. Add a few extra ingredients such as personalization, ego (in a nice way), and the social and interest graphs, and we now have a recipe for commerce, reach, and influence.

Virtual mirrors and augmented reality dressing rooms allow consumers to virtually try on clothes and merchandise without actually stepping into the dressing room or having to leave the comfort of their home or office. (See Figure 12.2.) Combining augmented reality, not unlike the example in the Ben & Jerry's discussion earlier in the chapter, connected consumers can stand in front of their computer, turn on the webcam, and the screen reflects a mirror image of the person wearing the merchandise.

Sunglass manufacturer Ray-Ban experimented with the idea by launching an AR sunglass mirror with which consumers could see themselves wearing the sunglasses without leaving the PC. In late 2010, fashion retailer JCPenney partnered with Hearst digital media

Figure 12.2   Virtual Dressing Room

and Metaio to introduce a virtual dressing room that incorporated AR, motion capture, and e-commerce.[11] Consumers can try on clothes using their web cam to capture their frame and from there, they can browse through options by moving their hands to the corresponding button floating on their screen. Different sizes are available by waving their hand in a different spot. Most importantly, however, they can take a snapshot and broadcast the new look across their social networks for feedback or simply to share. And, of course, customers can purchase the item on the spot. Social commerce isn't just alive, it's alive and clicking!

This technology isn't limited to in-home shopping either. Imagine virtual mirrors adorning the walls of your favorite retails shops, trying on clothes that you can see virtually and in real life, without having to stand in line and go through the hassles of the dreaded dressing room! And imagine sharing it with friends in real time to make a sound decision on the spot.

◼ EXCUSE ME WHILE I CHECK OUT

It's one thing to feel anxious in the dressing room line; it's something altogether different, however, when a social customer needs to check out from a retail endeavor. While it's easier to entice a social customer to check in, many check out without actually checking out. Their time is precious. They're VIPs. They don't wait in line. Everything comes to them, so why should checking out be any different.

Retailers realize the importance of time and the incredibly thinning state of attention and patience. If the connected customer won't go to the cash register, bring the cash register to them. Not only is it helpful, it creates a magical experience, which is also shareable depending on its design. When you walk into an Apple store, you get a unique view of a brand that has designed its retail environment around connecting brand essence with individualism, personality, and personal aspirations. Most notably however, is that the cash registers come to you when you're ready to pay and here, the cash registers are merely modified iPhones that every salesperson has that can accept payments no matter where in the store you are. Ka-ching! But Apple didn't stop there. The company invested in radio-frequency identification (RFID) and near field communication (NFC) technology to fund future payment frameworks whereby consumers could use their iPhones to pay for goods and services.[12]

Online content producers, service providers, and merchants, however, are now presented with an array of options to cash out. Jack Dorsey, the man behind the original idea for Twitter, parlayed his vision into a new system for the payments industry with Square. His gift for vision is uncanny and I had an opportunity to sit with him for an interview for an *Entrepreneur* cover story.[13] Jack looked to Apple's in-store payment network when designing the Square experience. Rather than forcing people to stand in line behind a cash register, he appreciated the process of swiping a card right at the moment of decision. Thus, he set out to extend that "magical" experience to everyone.

Square was the merging of several important elements: technology, mobile, social, and financial.

Ninety percent of the world uses plastic cards to pay, but only about 2 percent of merchants accept them. Since a sweeping majority of consumers rely on cards, Square was faced with the challenge of replicating the simplicity on the receiving end. In our discussion, Dorsey candidly shared the inception of Square, a sugar cube–sized credit and debit card reader that plugs into the headphone jack of an iPhone or Android. The team set out to transform payments to create, as Dorsey describes it, "A magical experience around payments and what it means to pay people. Innovation could impact everything, making payments faster, richer, and more information-dense as well as actionable and memorable."

Accepting payments is just the beginning, however, as Dorsey and the Square team envision payments as catalysts for social and actionable interactions. Every transaction involves a receipt. Print receipts aren't actionable. Such is true with electronic receipts. Square believes that there is life after the transaction, as Dorsey asks, "What if you could actually browse the receipts?"

The examples he shares are as interesting as they are practical. "When you get home, the receipt could serve as an ingredient list to discover the blends that went into your espresso, to see how many times you've been to that particular location, used a loyalty or rewards system, click into a merchant's Twitter or website, forward the receipt for expenses, and see, through a beautiful visual, where the transaction took place."

His point is that the receipt will move beyond a static record. It becomes a platform for extending experiences and facilitating the exchange of information and communications during and after the sale between the people on each side of the transaction. The acts of paying or receiving payments are just the beginning. Square seeks to improve the dynamics and relationships between businesses and their customers.

This vision of simplified and portable payment systems is on its way to standardization. Starbucks introduced its Starbucks Card Mobile App throughout 7,000 stores and 1,000 locations in Targets as a micropayment system to allow customers with iPhones, iPod Touches, Droids, and BlackBerrys to pay for their necessities and pick-me-ups at the swipe of, not a card, but a finger.[14] The app turns the phone into a digital card that can then be scanned using the standard 2D scanner at the register. Like Square, the app is designed to track purchases, manage the account, and also earn and monitor rewards. Clever. Clever indeed. Starbucks is a modernized business and is always experimenting with technology. This is just the beginning of what's sure to be shared commerce.

Thinking back to the examples of Blippy and American Express's Social Currency, transactions become social and shareable objects and, as a result, conversations ensue, aspirations become influential, and commerce becomes social.

■ DESIGNING SHAREABLE EXPERIENCES

Undoubtedly, mobile phones are becoming a critical factor in the decision-making cycle. While the preceding examples are meant to convey new functionality and behavior, I'd like to take a moment to remind you of one key behavioral trait of connected customers—their willingness to capture and share experiences across their network of hundreds or thousands of contacts. Catering to mobile consumers and enchanting connected customers require two very different methodologies. The latter involves the idea that experiences are designed to be shared.

Forward-thinking retailers are experimenting with NFC and RFID technology beyond just payments. They're actually designing shared experiences directly into point-of-purchase displays and in-store hotspots to trigger everything from check-ins to unlocking specials.

Fashion group WeAretheSuperlativeConspiracy uses RFID in distribution and tracking processes. With Hyper Island, a concept platform was introduced to bring NFC technology to their line of footwear.[15] Shoes featuring RFID chips could store opt-in information about the consumer wearing them, basically a record of integrated preferences. (See Figure 12.3.) Simply by stepping on specialized mats, the shoes trigger a series of interactions on any number of social networks, including:

➤ A real-time photo booth that snaps a picture and automatically uploads it to Flickr.

➤ Turning two strangers into friends when they both step on the mat.

➤ Update predefined status updates on Facebook and Twitter.

Figure 12.3   These Shoes Were Made for Walking and Connecting Connected Customers to Information

The options are limited only to the imagination. The technology and the human network are already here.

The future of business is about connecting to a connected consumer and promoting interactivity within their networks. A genre of consumers is connected to their social graph and their devices equally and they're plugged in simply because it's in their DNA. Laptops, PCs, tablets, and smartphones represent extensions of their identity. To close this chapter with a short, but telling anecdote, think of the smartphone as a digital appendage. Attention is absolutely distracted or focused, depending on your perspective in this matter. Communicating with one's social graph is so important that connected consumers are mastering a new talent, typing and walking or driving at the same time. People are just that connected and it's painful when they're forced to stray away from their stream, even if for but a moment. Driving? Walking? Why not do both? It's dangerous, yes. But it is what it is. To help, app developers are releasing new solutions that activate the phone's camera so that texting and typing can be done with full view in front of them while they move forward. (See Figure 12.4.)

Simply hold the phone up and now the view of the connected consumer is complete. Virtual and real worlds collide, well, hopefully not collide in a way that hurts.

Centers of Attention

➤   Shared experiences are forms of social currency. People share things to show their friends that they're investing in the conversation.

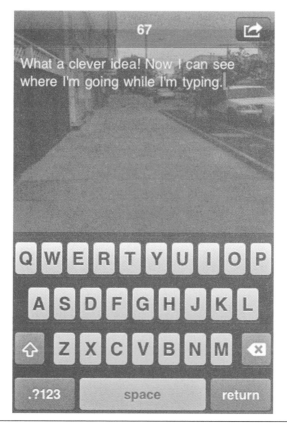

Figure 12.4   Email N'Walk for iPhone

➤ Shared experiences can be shaped and steered.

➤ Smartphones and mobile devices connect shared experiences from the real world to online friends.

➤ The balance of power is shifting from retailer to the connected consumer.

➤ Customers compare while shopping, making sure that they're getting the best deal even if it means leaving the store or the transaction.

➤ Price matching, relevant reviews, and value-added transactions are now expected by connected consumers.

➤ To compete for the attention of the connected consumer requires that you first acknowledge that consumer behavior is for the time being out of your hands and off of your balance sheet.

➤ Mobile opens up a new era of loyalty and reward programs.

➤ Retailers are bringing experiences to the connected consumer from virtual dressing rooms to cash registers, letting them shop, share, and pay on their terms.

➤ Shared experiences must be designed into the shopping experience to officially shape the next generation of social commerce.

Chapter

Brands Are No Longer Created, They're Co-Created

Value is in the eye of the beholder. No matter what we say about our company or products, it's ultimately the customer experience and the collective customer perspective that define value and ultimately the state of the brand in the new democratized marketplaces.

If the future of business is filtered through shared experiences, we need to prioritize the phases of transformation by recognizing the array of dimensions and the part each play in decision making. In the previous chapter, we learned how new technology combined with new business methodologies can activate touchpoints to trigger decisions and sharing. Creating magical experiences can help bring businesses into the trust zone of desirable and connected customers. In this chapter, we tackle two sides: reactive experiences and alternatively, how to proactively engineer positive and shareable encounters.

Everything discussed up until now requires change. Change is never easy. Whether it's innovation or adaptation, it's still change, and each step carries diverse challenges making transformation possible at different points in time, if at all. It takes a fighter and a champion to convince others of the need, and a relentless leader and visionary to see it through.

■ BRANDING THE CUSTOMER RELATIONSHIP

Let's examine the role that the customer plays in the dilution or reinforcement of brand identity, equity, and brand value. One of the primary reasons why this is a difficult endeavor is that we fundamentally clash with brand managers, marketers, and customer service executives on this front. Questions and territorial rights serve as blockades. Who owns the brand? Who owns this new connected engagement? Is this exclusively a marketing or sales function?

Focusing on those conversations is done so in vain. The real questions we need to ask are: Who owns the customer relationship and who owns the customer experience?

When asked this way, it is clear that no single individual or department owns these relationships from beginning to end. The customer doesn't see the brand as a series of departments; it sees the brand as a single, unified entity. Therefore, as a business structures itself for outside engagement, it must function as one, seamlessly externally and internally. However, this is not how businesses are structured today. Many are fashioned around the traditional sales funnel and in the realm of the connected customer, that's a problem.

Some brand experts believe that the act of branding is top down and that the desired impressions consumers form are givens in any good branding campaign. While it starts that way, over time, it is up to the company to define and reinforce it. How it's done, however, requires ongoing investment and commitment to a more rigorous set of determination and intention than ever before. You already know that attention is scarce among the connected consumers and brand messages and visuals wash away from their hearts and minds like wet snow. Most of the time it melts before it can even stick.

While we talk about customers and service in this chapter, this is not about traditional customer service. This is about creating a memorable and shareable brand, improving brand strength and integrity, and steering positive experiences. Knowing that brand encounters trigger exchanges naturally, companies are now gifted with an unprecedented ability to discover, learn, and participate in the evolution of the brand and its value in these developing economic landscapes.

In these interactive online colonies, brands are not only created, brand stature and strength are co-created. The new social landscape is rich with emotion. Updates, posts, and other forms of digital self-expression are the platforms for shared experiences. Sentiment is served through temperamental overtones and undertones.

■ IF IGNORANCE IS BLISS, AWARENESS IS AWAKENING

I'm not listening to you . . .

Perhaps if we say this over and over, we'll either chant ourselves into a perpetual state of unawareness and irrelevance or we'll realize just how silly it sounds.

Up to this point, we've discussed the importance of shared experiences and how they disseminate through the social and mobile networks of the connected customer.

The reality is that online conversations do not fall into a black hole never to be heard from again. There is no event horizon preventing their escape.

The social effect is more powerful than we realize. The truth is that if one voice finds the right audience, not only can businesses realize that conversations are taking place, they can find the power to listen. And rather than merely reacting, they'll be initiating interactions and opportunities. The conversations taking place are growing from sporadic mumblings to thunderous roars. Businesses are finding that their secrets that were once protected in semiprivate phone calls, emails, and filed complaints from customers now exist in the public view of prospective consumers and the people who influence their decisions. This means your brand is defined by the collective experiences of your connected customers.

For a few of the top businesses, a quick search uncovered what seemed to be an infinite loop of customer commentary online:

This airline sucks. When I check in, I was told, "I'm sorry, there's nothing we can do about bumping you off this flight or losing your luggage." Really, well not only did you just lose a customer, I'm going to go out of my way to ensure that no one I know flies with you again.

Why do I have this phone if I can't make phone calls. I don't care if you're on Twitter or Facebook. Fix the service. I don't need to hear, "experiencing dropped calls? We're working on that . . . but it's quite normal. What? Your neighbor received a complementary MicroCell because they're a valued user and you're not? We have no idea who sent that unit. We are not aware of such a program." Yeah . . . I googled it and guess what I found? Now I'm pissed.

These experiences are not solely expressed in social networks; experiences are shared everywhere, online and offline. In the realm of transactions and commerce, shared experiences connect consumers in a variety of ways. And these experiences, both good and bad, live in different domains acting as guides for other customers seeking input and direction from peers and experts. This information affects the decisions of individuals when they're most open to impressions. Your brand is affected with or without your engagement. Designing experiences and strengthening them based on what's learned through customer sharing sets the stage for adaption and improvement.

Online reviews aren't new, of course. Amazon, epinions, and others have given customers a platform to voice their impressions. Now these insights are becoming social and searchable, and as such, their reach and effects are exponentially greater. In point of fact, when we factor in the social effect, the reviews of the linked in inevitably affect the bottom line of any business. What is new is how this collective intelligence is recognized and embraced by affected organizations, people, and establishments.

Shared reviews affect everything and everybody. For example, local businesses will find that customers are willfully, and often aggressively, sharing and rating their encounters and impressions on Yelp, Trusted Opinion, Angie's List, and blogs, to name a few. Brands with fan pages on Facebook or Google+ will find that customers are sharing reviews on the main wall. They're also taking to Twitter to broadcast their views and opinions to a greater community. As this feedback accumulates, the hope for a global delete button becomes not only a fantasy, but less important. Change, improvement, and innovation become as paramount. Now the connected consumer is validated, empowered, and contributing to your brand and how it is perceived by others. But, they are open to forming a strategic alliance to improve the experiences of others by contributing to improved service and innovation.

Are you ready?

■ IN THE HUMAN NETWORK, BRANDS BECOME THE CULMINATION OF SHARED EXPERIENCES

As connected consumers climb the ranks of social hierarchy, they do so by earning prominence with every new connection they make. Suddenly, the connections people have made become a powerful force of nature that holds the potential to transform markets and define (or redefine) the stature of brands. All it takes is for enough of these conversations to pool and index in traditional and social search to overtake traditional marketing messages during a decision-making cycle. While both affect decision making, it boils down to either an *aha* or *uh-oh* moment. The corresponding actions, however, hopefully lead businesses to right their course and begin to connect with those who feel disconnected from them.

To this social consumer, the culmination of these experiences reveals the true value of a product, service, person, or company when their attention is most receptive. Conversely, this online activity is, at any point in time, a reflection of the perceived state of a brand. But here, a brand, its symbolism, and its essence are felt and reborn from

Figure 13.1   Consumer Experiences Collectively Define Brands: An Example of Conversations about an Airline

the consumer perspective. It is in this tug-of-war over brand strength and valuation that consumers have a stronghold. Understanding this, however, is the beginning of a new path for branding.

A simple search of a particular product in any social or dedicated network of relevance will produce the state of a product or company as told by the people who know best . . . customers. Here, company messages and creative marketing might help prep a customer for consideration, but connected customers rely upon one another to help make more informed decisions. The particular word cloud in Figure 13.1 is the visualization of customer sentiment tied to a leading airline in the United States. The company positions itself as customer-centric, but it's clear that the very people paying for its services do not agree. And they're not biting their tongues, either. They want hundreds, thousands, and more to hear their wrath and react accordingly. The balance of power is shifting and en masse; this communal condemnation strikes at the jugular of the brand to impart the anger, pain, or displeasure they feel. For some, it's therapeutic. For others, it's a mission. They want change. The difference between business now and business as usual is that customer voices and opinions were largely ignored unless extraordinary circumstances made them impossible to snub. Here, those who are connected to individuals who share this sentiment or those who simply search these networks will come to an unfavorable conclusion without the benefit of the airline having a say in the matter.

In each network and in their connections, the sum is in fact greater than its parts, but its parts are still great. In its own way, the truth, or the truth as we know it, comes alive. The dirty laundry that businesses didn't want you to see is finally airing and it's going viral.

Running a word cloud of brand perception among the connected is a simple demonstration of what is frankly a complex subject. New services are emerging that analyze customer language and sentiment to index satisfaction. Services like Klout and PeerIndex are ranking the social stature of consumers. Services such as Groubal index customer satisfaction. By design, Groubal is a platform for consumer advocacy and consumer rights. Similar to how consumers search online and in social networks for peer insights, Groubal collects public conversations, reviews, and associated sentiment, and in turn, generates a Groubal customer service index (GCSI) that measures satisfaction or dissatisfaction.

As described by Groubal, the company mission is to *"Responsibly and credibly report the true sentiment and opinions of how customers feel they are being treated by the businesses that sell to them."*[1]

The GCSI index is based on a scoring system between 1 and 1,000. Higher scores indicate a greater level of in-the-moment dissatisfaction. The index is updated hourly, but at the time this chapter was written, Groubal had tracked more than 300 brands with the following companies indexing the highest level of dissatisfaction:

➤ Time Warner – 991
➤ US Airways – 983
➤ Blue Cross – 914
➤ U.S. Postal Service – 890
➤ Nextel – 872
➤ Aetna – 869
➤ Telus – 863
➤ United Airlines – 862
➤ Bell – 861

I ran the scores several times over several days and the number one spot didn't change much, so I decided to share the collective customer sentiment around Time Warner and see how a finely tuned, prestigious brand is deflated in an influential conversational landscape.

A quick search on Twitter at the time this chapter was written revealed a firehose of customer anger:

➤ Okay, Time Warner, your customer service has been spectacular but this terrible Internet service has got to go. LA alternatives, anybody?

➤ I hate you so much, Time Warner. #itrainsandtheinternetbreaks #thatsridiculous

➤ Avoid Time Warner Cable in NYC at ALL COST! When will FIOS be available on our block? TWCNY lies, cheats, and has stupid policies. #AWFUL

Twitter isn't the only network in town, so I also searched a bit on Facebook, only to find similar sentiment:

➤ Time Warner Cable is so horrible

➤ my cable is being weird... i hate time warner

➤ Time warner cable is the f***ing worst! 220/month for services that don't work more than half the time! Wtf

Similar to the airline example, I ran a word cloud to explore shared sentiment. Each of the highlighted words represents a firehose of discontent. (See Figure 13.2.)

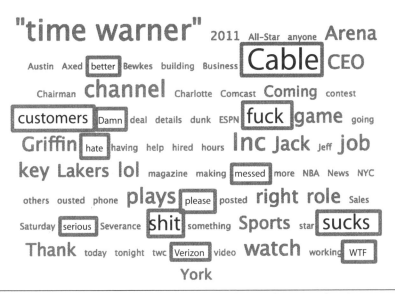

Figure 13.2   Time Warner Word Cloud of Shared Customer Sentiment

After 30 to 45 minutes of exploration, I gave up. It was clear how connected consumers felt about Time Warner at that moment. But before I moved on, I also examined "lol" out of curiosity. Turns out that it was its own meme where people were sharing in laughter at the expense of Time Warner.

➤ Damn Time Warner lines r busy lol this is hilarious I got an error when I called lol

➤ Clearly...They are pissed! Lol RT @richb_qc: Damn Time Warner doing a lot of my #followers wrong LOL

➤ But we just got TVOne in HD!! LOL RT @SeigeOTC Time Warner Cable is like the MetroPCS version of cable.

➤ LMAFFFAOOOO y'all better go in on Time Warner lol thank God my house has DirecTV

Clearly, this isn't the brand or the experience Time Warner has meticulously designed. To be sure, I checked the company's website to see if this is indeed the experience it wishes to impart. To my surprise, it wasn't. Okay, I wasn't really surprised, but you get my point. Running a rough word cloud on how the company describes itself online, a potential customer would view it as (work with me here, as I strung it together based on the cloud), "An innovative cable company that is committed to customers and its community, providing entertainment and business services and support to people who want access to diverse programs and products." Compare Figure 13.3 to the previous word cloud.

adjust believe bill business **cable** careers
challenge committed **community**
company control corporate **customers**
digital **diversity** employees entertainment
events give highlights home inc information
innovations **investor** latest **learn**
looking media meet **news** overview pay
people policy power privacy products **program**
relations sales **services** setting site
support tap terms tv **warner** ways

Figure 13.3   The Time Warner Brand as Defined by the Words on Its Website

If you were considering either company for service, what conclusions would you draw from the consumer-generated airline or Time Warner word clouds? Would your search results affect your decision? Would the negative reactions to either company as responses to your public questions sway you?

Is it fair to businesses? No. But it is what it is.

▩ THE AWAKENING FLIPS THE SWITCH

Surveying the landscape for converging brand impressions can't help but engender empathy. Listening, reading, feeling customer sentiment is a difficult, but necessary step in earning relevance as a business in these personal networks. That's where this begins. That's the switch.

The distance between a brand and its customers is measured by shared experiences. This gap is what I refer to as the empathy divide (Figure 13.4). And the extent of this division is revealed through insight and realization.

Acknowledgment is just the beginning in what represents nothing short of an exhaustive renovation in business values, structure, and innovation. It's not easy, but then again, if it were, anyone could do it. Right now, customer focus is a competitive advantage. While this position will inevitably become standard, it is a chance to earn a position of prominence in a rapidly shifting landscape in which attention is precious and the need for solutions is endemic.

Shared experiences that matter to businesses are either negative or positive. They are shared with or without you. Rather than balk at the existence of collective sentiment, take the wheel and steer

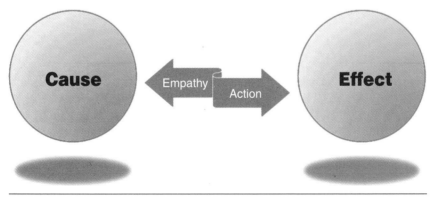

Figure 13.4   The Empathy Divide

experiences and resulting dialogue in your favor. Defiance in this case, is pointless. Redesigning experiences before, during, and after transactions is how we start to shift collective sentiment in our favor. Listening is all about empathy, and empathy lies in the words people use. The expressions, the questions, the answers that never come, the experiences that go unguided, the problems that never get fixed. This is where the real listening happens and serves as the beginning of bridging the empathy divide.

Businesses can learn from the very same publicly available data and resources that connected customers rely upon to express views and base their decisions. They can move from a point of weakness through disregard to a position of strength through engagement and adaptation. This is the beginning of a much greater transformation process en route to the more desired stage of adaptive business.

These conversations, regardless of how mundane, crass, or elementary, are essential to learning and advancement. Businesses learn where they rank in the hearts and minds of the connected consumer. Insights directly point to what they're doing right and what they could do better. Conversations also highlight disconnects between brand elements, brand essence, and consumer perception.

The first step in a course of action is listening. And by listening I don't mean monitoring conversations for keyword mentions. Someone within the organization must be charged with listening, tasking, and learning. This collective intelligence gives way to a new genre of business intelligence. This is not an administrative position left to a recent college graduate because they get social media. This is a senior function that reports into management that possesses authority to make decisions about change or feed it into the groups that can respond to improve experiences and strengthen the brand. It requires nothing less than an advocate who will fight for change and unification every step of the way.

The three areas of focus for this function include:

1. Helping the organization learn and adapt by forming an internal coalition of affected departments or roles to establish workflow and governance.

2. Conveying consumer recognition and empathy through direct communication and engagement.

3. Collaborating internally to innovate on the basis of insights and creativity to continually demonstrate leadership and appreciation.

You cannot pretend to be a customer-centric brand, nor can you simply state this is your mission if the company doesn't practice what it preaches. Actions speak as loud as words in the egosystem and as such, we enter a new era of new customer centricity, in which the customer is at the center of everything!

The requisite challenge facing any organization today is how to blend the need to compete for the moment at every moment into the mix of business dynamics. You cannot compete for the future if you cannot compete for attention and relevance today. Perception, attention, and desired reactions are earned through design, reinforcement, and engagement.

Understanding customer concerns, challenges, and opportunities and responding to them directly through engagement or indirectly through evolution or innovation, bridges the empathy divide to form a tighter bond between connected customers and adaptive businesses. Accordingly, the concentration of sentiment expressed through conversations and shared experiences begin to sway toward the positive, thus influencing and inciting advantageous behavior and outcomes. These engagements steer the brand in a direction in which its design and intentions are fortified and believable (Figure 13.5).

We observed earlier that the @ sign is the universal sign for engagement. @ is a two-way endeavor that demonstrates that a brand is listening and is also engaging. When combined with support that not only recognizes individual and collective concern, but also boasts the wherewithal to change products, processes, and outlooks internally, customer sentiment shifts positively now and over time.

Darren McDermott, deputy managing editor of the *Wall Street Journal* online, and I hosted an intimate discussion during which we explored the future of media and journalism at Creative Artists Agency's headquarters in Los Angeles. At one point in the evening,

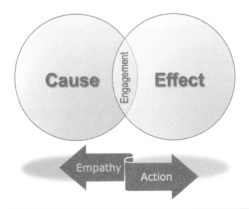

Figure 13.5   Bridging the Empathy Divide through Informed Engagement

Figure 13.6 The *Wall Street Journal* Demonstrates Engagement

McDermott discussed the importance of engagement and its impact on reader sentiment and, ultimately, relevance for a media brand that was founded in 1882. He shared two examples where @wsj engaged to shift perception and as a result flipped negative sentiment to positive and at the same time, walked away with greater social capital and relevance (Figure 13.6). While just an elementary example, it demonstrates the opportunity to spark positive experiences that contribute to a more engaged brand. Imagine what a deeper engagement program might yield.

The *Wall Street Journal* is not alone in its initial endeavors to directly engage. In February 2011, worldwide communications agency Burson-Marsteller published an encouraging study on the rise of D2C engagement among Fortune Global 100 companies.[2] Of the 100 companies studied, 67 percent are actively using the "@symbol" to directly engage with or mention other users. This number represents an astounding 76 percent increase over the previous report the year before. On Facebook, the report demonstrates that businesses are embracing openness, with 74 percent allowing user-generated posts on Facebook brand pages and 57 percent responding to these posts and comments.

As evidenced in this report, companies are learning to engage. As such, both ends of the new business spectrum are working their way toward the middle. Social consumers have made greater progress in their journey, but businesses will follow suit, especially if this book has something to say about it. It's important to understand that even though companies are engaging through social networks, this is merely the beginning in what will amount to nothing short of organization transformation. We'll discuss models for organization transformation before you reach the last pages of this book.

The truth is that simply engaging customers who experience problems or those who have shared negative experiences without the capacity to change within is merely lip service and placation. Staffing organizations to scale to the demands of activity in social networks is less important than scaling organizations to more effectively meet customer needs by creating products, services, and processes that produce favorable experiences. Then, by default, customers become the social extensions to an organization's new media team by actively sharing positive experiences from network to network and social graph to social graph. Eventually, businesses will shift from a role of reactive learning and responses to a position of leadership.

■ THE POETRY OF LANGUAGE AND MEDIA

As we'll see in the next chapter, emotions serve as the framework for enchanting customers. As I say over and over in this book, it's not what we say about us that counts; it's what customers say that accounts for everything. To define this a bit more clearly, it's what we say, what they hear and experience, and in turn, what they share that defines the brand and brand value in the connected egosystems of our customers and prospects.

Business language is operationalized with important value propositions, missions, and benefit statements written by committee through a top-down process. The ambition of what mission statements were intended to convey is lost in translation. No longer do mission statements represent mission. They're factory-churned statements designed to appease executives, stakeholders, investors.

But, what are words for if not to inspire the hearts, minds, and actions of our employees and customers? Words are the very likeness of the brand and the manifestation of the brand essence. Yet, businesses use words to convey industry position or marketing rather than building bridges. Cleverly designed to convey benefit, they are dastardly selfish in their very nature.

The vocabulary of any business these days seems limited to the following glossary:

➤ Industry leading
➤ Paradigm shifting
➤ Disruptive
➤ Innovative
➤ Groundbreaking
➤ Gamification
➤ Market-leading
➤ Customer-focused
➤ Best practice
➤ Focus on excellence
➤ User
➤ User experience
➤ User-friendly
➤ Turnkey
➤ Mission-critical
➤ Differentiate
➤ Out of the box approach
➤ Win-win

Businesses lean on these words as crutches for characterless engagement (Figure 13.7). It's also this view that is indicative of

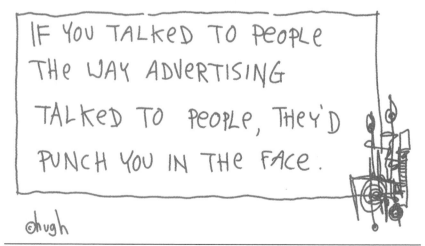

Figure 13.7   Hugh MacLeod on Marketing Speak

how businesses see (or don't see) employees and customers. How words are used today are the source of the *not so* apparent disconnect between the brand and the wants, needs, and aspirations of desirable stakeholders.

A business's mission must be communicated in a way that touches someone personally, as opposed to firing words as darts and hoping that some eventually stick or hit the bullseye. The language used is the pavement that lays the foundation for the last mile of engagement. The distance between a connected customer and a brand is measured by that engagement. The distance between connected customers and their peers is measured by shared experiences. Language is the artistry of meaningful engagement and shared experiences.

Language represents the constructs for enlivening the brand and reaching customers. We either speak to their hearts and minds, or we're speaking over their heads (Figure 13.8).

Language brings to life intention, the brand essence, story, personal value, and company culture. It must be defined.

Take the company mission statement, for example. It's supposed to represent the very fabric of the company charter, its purpose for being, and its promise to employees and customers alike.

When's the last time you read your company's mission statement? You probably haven't in a long time. If you have reviewed it recently, would you tweet it?

Let's review a few examples of mission statements published by Fortune 500 companies:[3]

Advance Auto Parts, Inc.

It is the Mission of Advance Auto Parts to provide personal vehicle owners and enthusiasts with the vehicle-related products and knowledge that fulfill their wants and needs at the right

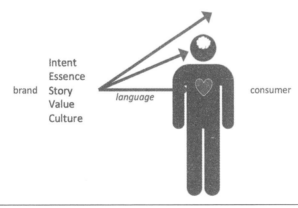

Figure 13.8　The Last Mile of Engagement

price. Our friendly, knowledgeable and professional staff will help inspire, educate and problem-solve for our customers.

Aflac

To combine aggressive strategic marketing with quality products and services at competitive prices to provide the best insurance value for consumers.

The Walt Disney Company

The mission of The Walt Disney Company is to be one of the world's leading producers and providers of entertainment and information. Using our portfolio of brands to differentiate our content, services and consumer products, we seek to develop the most creative, innovative, and profitable entertainment experiences and related products in the world.

These statements are as complex as they are meaningless. They speak over the heads of customers. Disney, a company that was built on imagineering and bringing dreams to life, is especially disappointing.

Nike on the other hand focuses on elegance and simplicity:

Nike Inc.

To bring inspiration and innovation to every athlete in the world.

A company is only as valuable as the promises it keeps. A mission statement is much like a brand promise. A brand promise[4] is a statement of the enduring, relevant and distinctive benefits employees and customers associate with a product, service, or company. As companies move toward the recognition and eventual engagement of connected customers, revisiting the mission statement and the language that enriches the last mile of engagement is pivotal to future relevance.

This is an opportunity to renew the brand promise and its vows to traditional, online, and connected customers alike. This is a chance to empower the front line of engagement . . . your employees.

Take a moment to answer the following questions:

➤ What is the call to action?
➤ What is your true purpose and mission?
➤ What benefits do you offer that real people want?
➤ Does your mission fit in a tweet (140 characters or less)?

At PopTech, a conference in Maine that spotlights world-changing people, projects, and ideas, Kevin Starr, executive director of the Mulago Foundation, shared invaluable wisdom for companies to rethink how they speak and how they define their place in our society. Mulago is an investment organization that focuses on socially minded businesses. Starr and his team base investments on mission statements. He believes that companies should express their mission statement in fewer than eight words.[5] His format includes:

- ➤ Verb
- ➤ Target
- ➤ Outcome

Examples he shared include, "Save endangered species from extinction" and "Improve African children's health." These are not unlike the example we see from Nike. All are tweetable and each leave room for retweets, which is the ultimate test of relevance!

In brevity there's clarity.

The connected consumer sees through marketing-speak and hones in on the individual and collective intelligence that stems from direct awareness and exposure. Ignoring it doesn't make it go away. As such, those brands that move away from an era of "hear no evil, see no evil . . ." to a genre of engagement will reverse the reckoning.

In the highly connected ecosystem of influential consumers, whom will you believe when it comes time to make a decision about your next flight, product purchase, dining endeavor, or which service provider to hire: the customer collective or the business itself? Hopefully, one day they'll be one and the same.

This is not a fad, and for those who hold their breath waiting for these days of customer influence to pass, their legacy will live on in the museum of businesses claimed by digital Darwinism. Those that engage, learn, and adapt unlock an era of collaborative business and, ultimately, relevance.

Centers of Attention

➤ Connected customers define the value and equity of a brand within social networks.

➤ No one division owns the customer relationship. Everyone affected by outside customer activity is responsible for introducing and shaping positive experiences.

➤ Top-down branding goes only so far; in social networks, brands are almost starting from ground zero.

➤ Compare the brand stature according to connected customers versus how a brand describes itself to identify the empathy divide.

➤ Your mission is to bridge the empathy divide to trigger a desirable series of cause and effect.

➤ Brands are not created, they are co-created, as such businesses will have to redesign processes and structure to enliven those words.

➤ Ignore customer complaints and negative experiences at your own peril.

➤ Learning from these experiences must inspire change and innovation.

➤ Engagement demonstrates listening, as does product and service enhancement.

➤ Customers see every business as one, not as a series of departments.

➤ Language plays a critical role in engagement.

➤ Brands are presented with a new chance to prove their worth to people who are focused everywhere else but the brand.

➤ Take this moment to revise your mission statement, and your mission!

Chapter

14

Reinventing the Brand and Sales Cycle for a New Genre of Connected Commerce

The steps we take from this point forward are either toward a new era of relevance or irrelevance, everything else matters elsewhere, but not here.

Problems emerge for resolution.

Opportunities emerge for establishing leadership.

In the last two chapters we transitioned from immersion to leadership. The switch from learning to guiding is how we change the organization from the inside out. The switch from reacting to participating is how we earn trust among connected consumers.

The world of influence is shifting, and like information, the capacity to cause effect is equally democratizing. We are not without hope, but this changing environment needs a leader who can see and feel the transformation unfolding before us. It takes a leader to recognize a calling to take this boulder of change and begin the long and mighty push uphill. While you may start alone, you will reach the top surrounded by everyone. It just takes someone to believe, to take the first steps for everyone else to follow.

The language of change is yours to define, but it starts here. It starts now.

We spent time redefining our mission. Understanding how we speak and how to connect our story to those who are looking for meaning and personalization. We should by now appreciate how investing time and resources here carries the capacity to travel well beyond our reach, influencing decisions along the way. In this chapter, we dive even deeper, understanding how the laws of emotion apply to decision making and sharing. Understanding this opens up new doors to reach connected consumers in ways that we are not currently structured to grasp today. It starts with not only revising the mission, but also stripping down the brand to its very essence to reinvigorate its meaning for a new world of connected consumerism and to galvanize everyone who will champion it moving forward. That's where you come in. Someone has to walk through the door first.

■ PLUG INTO THE GRID OF DECISION MAKING

At the center of every shared experience is human reaction. In fact, that is the focus of some fascinating research taking place at the University of Akron, led by Vicki Chisholm, marketing research manager at Suarez Applied Marketing Research Labs and the Taylor Institute for Direct Marketing.[1] Vicki's team is studying the brain in relation to online advertising and marketing using an innovative approach. Subjects strap on a sophisticated series of sensors mounted to what resembles a shower cap. The Neuronet, as it's called, creates a brain heatmap as individuals are viewing various forms of online marketing. This is only one part of a multifaceted study that also includes 256 visual and physiological measures that capture eye movement, EKG, heart rate, and electrical impulses from the scalp.

The study uses four cameras to track the focus of an individual's attention. As the brain responds, researchers then analyze stimuli heatmaps to connect activity to different potential sources in the brain. As Chisholm told Nate Riggs during an online video interview, "We can't read minds, but we can tell when your brain lights up."

The body reacts to marketing just like it does everything else. Physical response isn't the only thing we can measure, however. Sentiment, emotion, experience . . . these are the constructs of the human network and as such, it's time to understand the effects of our presence in the market to eventually improve our place within it.

It is sentiment that fuels emotion and deliberate acts of connected participation. Because emotions are in play and serve as a common thread in social linkages, alternative touchpoints for consumer engagement and influence materialize. These discussions tend to draw either curiosity or indifference, as consumer emotions are largely left out of the discussion. Emotion is a big part of what moves us to share and consume. Humans are emotional creatures, and our actions and decisions are driven by a combination of experience, education, instinct, and emotional intelligence. Sophisticated marketers and brand managers certainly understand that there are emotional levers to pull to get a customer to take decisive action. But what happens when the emotions we trigger turn on us? While we're good at igniting emotions that work to our advantage, we're not designed to acknowledge them systematically. This story begins with an understanding of how brands must figuratively wear their hearts on their sleeves to best connect with connected customers.

■ ONCE MORE, THIS TIME WITH FEELING

While the culture and corresponding mechanics of social networks remain elusive to many executives and marketers, their promise is far more profound than we realize. To identify and define the methodologies that equate to new relevance, we must remove our marketing caps and instead remember who we are as individuals.

Before we are marketers, sales or service professionals, executives, employees, or leaders, we are human beings. Everything in social networks and online for that matter, begins with us as individuals. We define our own experiences. We decide who we follow and who follows us. We choose which stories we read and those we share. And it is only those experiences that we connect with emotionally that we push across our social and interest graphs.

To connect with the connected consumer, we must be part of the community. We must approach business and the business of marketing and engagement with the same resolve that we approach our own social networking. We must become the very people we're trying to reach, because ultimately, we are consumers and we are stakeholders in the evolution of our relationships and experiences online and in real life.

What this effort shows at the very least is that in a complex emotional webwork, we cannot brand, market, or message our way to relevance. As detailed in our discussion around the trust zone, it must be earned.

Adam Penenberg, a contributing writer to *Fast Company*, volunteered as a test subject in Dr. Paul J. Zak's neuroeconomics research, an emerging field that combines economics with biology, neuroscience, and psychology.[2] The studies seek to "gauge the relationship between empathy and generosity."

In a series of studies spanning nine years, Zak found that Oxytocin (aka the cuddle drug, not the pain killer Oxycontin) is not only the hormone that forms the bond between mothers and their babies, it is, as Zak says, "the social glue that binds families, communities, and societies," and therefore acts as an economic lubricant to engage day-to-day transactions. Zak's work has essentially recognized oxytocin as the human stimulant of empathy, generosity, and trust, among other important social attributes.

Penenberg connected with Zak to learn if Zak's research on oxytocin is applicable to social media research. I, too, have long theorized that social media *is* driven by emotion, and therefore, our interactions and relationships are indeed rooted in biology. As such, we can learn from the behavior that ensues through not only biology, but other social sciences as well, such as anthropology, sociology, ethnography, and psychology.

In Penenberg's telling post in *Fast Company*, he summarizes the findings that could have massive implications for the future of socialized media, "...all of this research reinforces the idea that we are biologically driven to commingle, and suggests that online relationships can be just as real as those conducted offline." He continues, "...social networking may increase a person's oxytocin levels, thereby heightening feelings of trust, empathy, and generosity."

In fact, in a series of three experiments in social networking, specifically with Twitter, Penenberg's oxytocin levels jumped 13.2 percent while hormones related to stress waned. Zak concluded that Penenberg's brain, "interpreted tweeting as if you were directly interacting with people you cared about or had empathy for."

Empathy is a powerful catalyst for sparking meaningful interactions and relationships in social media. Individuals online are empowered and as a result, their attention focuses on those who can demonstrate an awareness and understanding of their interests, challenges, and options. Empathy is detectable and contagious.

To garner empathy, we must feel what moves our communities and markets to unlock affinity, communicate value, and create a sense of belonging. To do so, we must transcend listening and monitoring into a form of kinesthetic analysis to truly become the people we're trying to reach.

▣ I'M NOT JUST LISTENING TO YOU, I HEAR YOU; I SEE AND FEEL WHAT YOU'RE SAYING

If we look to forms of interpersonal, sensory, and experiential marketing, the cornerstone of connectivity is built upon meaning, relevance, belonging, and purpose. As such trust becomes a measure to weigh our participation efforts. Emotional marketing value (EMV) ranks our ability to demonstrate empathy and earn attention, support, and affinity. This insight should absolutely change how you approach consumers in their social realms. This includes, but is not limited to, re-imaging your brand so that its essence connects beyond the moment to anchor itself in the hearts and minds of connected consumers. From design and imagery to intent and communication to the pillars of influence, people align themselves with particular brands or communities for a reason. It's usually because they don't have to make huge leaps toward affinity. Elements are inviting, alluring, and in harmony with their personal values and aspirations.

This requires understanding and defining yourself in landscapes in which you are not anywhere close to realizing the potential or promise of what your work can lead to.

■ BRING THE ESSENCE OF BRAND TO LIFE

A brand is recognized as the unique identity of a product, service, or company. Its elements and incarnations distinguish it from competitors. Brand essence, however, is felt. (See Figure 14.1.) It's not something easily recognizable such as a logo, trademark, or design. It is something that people think and feel. Brands live in our hearts and minds, and for those we support, we see ourselves differently because of their inclusion in our lives. It is part of a consumer's persona.

In the human network, brands that incorporate emotional hooks stand a far greater chance of connecting during engagement in critical touchpoints than those that rely on brand legacy. Experience is the

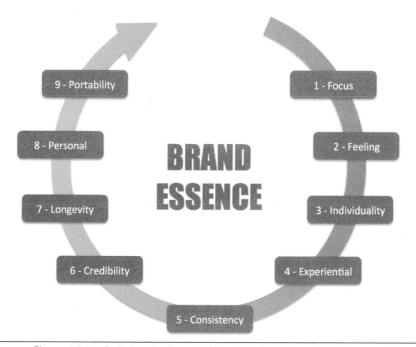

Figure 14.1   Defining the Brand's Essence of Connected Consumers

common denominator and the more seeds planted in the trust zones of connected consumers ensure that brand essence scales through word of mouth.

Brand essence is something that either requires definition or re-examination to establish a relationship with connected dignitaries. No matter how much money and time you've invested in traditional media, every medium in which engagement is accelerating requires a new investment in understanding, adapting , and cultivating relationships between customers and brand representatives. Without doing so, you leave brand and brand essence as user-defined, a topic we discuss at great length in the next chapter. The following exercise is for brand managers to complete before they invest in networked presences. It was inspired through experience navigating businesses through similar landscapes and it includes input from brandSTOKE's "9 Criteria for Brand Essence."[3]

■ BRAND ESSENCE EXERCISE

Focus: Find one or two words that define the brand. Deliver a unique experience and document what it is you want to evoke. Apple really nailed this approach with its "Think Different" campaign.

Feeling: Describe what it is you want a consumer to feel when he comes into contact with your brand. Harley-Davidson is a lifestyle people buy into because it makes them feel independent, free, and nothing less than a badass that everyone else admires.

Individuality: In these communities, brands are people, too, and they require a persona, character, mannerisms, and everything necessary to stand alone. The key here is uniqueness and charm. As my good friend Guy Kawasaki says, we want to be enchanting! Ben & Jerry's and Starbucks certainly convey a strong sense of personality and as such, we're enchanted.

Experiential: When a consumer experiences a product or service, what is that encounter eliciting? For example, driving a Volvo feels safe. Driving a Jeep feels adventurous. Running while wearing Nikes makes me feel faster.

Consistency: Dependability is a brand attribute and is not what this stage requires. Here, consistency is what a brand conveys now and every day. That's only part of the story, however, as it is just as important to reinforce the brand essence through representative engagement. Consistency is also a call to ensure that the brand team is structured in a way that allows it to deliver as promised. I believe that Oakley glasses protect my eyes, but in a way that enhances performance and appearance. Almost every product that Oakley releases reinforces this innovation and style.

Credibility: This is a big part of the next chapter on collective brand experiences, but it comes down to aligning the brand essence with experiences and righting the course through engagement and transformation when necessary. If people don't feel the way they did, there's a reason and they'll tell you. Pay attention.

Longevity: Is the essence designed to last, something that can stand the test of time and patience regardless of medium? Zappos's unique culture and its focus on customers thrives, even now as a part of the Amazon.com family.

Personal: Brand essence must carry meaning, something personal that people aspire to embrace and be part of, something that speaks to them. Swatch screams individualism, style, and self-expression without compromise and remains true to that image since its debut in 1983.

Portable: In new media, brand essence requires scalability to permeate brand extensions as the opportunity grows. Essence also requires portability across media where context comes at a premium. This step requires a strong understanding of how emotion is transferable across networks. Starbucks, Red Bull, Skittles, and Oreo maintain their essence across new media networks in which the company hosts profiles and this holds true in consumer mentions.

Everything that we do, the words we choose, and the imagery we use are all instrumental in the definition of brand essence and brand animation. Thus, our words, and actions, contribute to the last mile of customer engagement.

■ A MODEL FOR EMOTIVE ENGAGEMENT

The Advanced Marketing Institute divides language into three segments: intellectual, empathetic, and spiritual.[4] (See Figure 14.2.)

Intellectual
These words are especially effective when offering products and services that require reasoning or careful evolution.
Empathetic
Words that resonate with empathetic impact often bring out profound and strong positive emotional reactions in people.

Spiritual

Words that have the strongest potential for influence and often appeal to people at a very deep emotional level.

Traditional marketing focused on one-to-many mass broadcast communication using rational, left brain–directed persuasion. By contrast, experiential engagement makes personalized connections using emotional, right brain–directed involvement, validation, and empowerment. Outbound strategies will require an understanding of digital sociology and psychology and how it applies to desirable networked customers. Once understood, the next step is to bring the brand to life consistently through experiential engagement. The formula for experiential engagement[5] connects audiences through the authentic essence of a brand through participation in personally

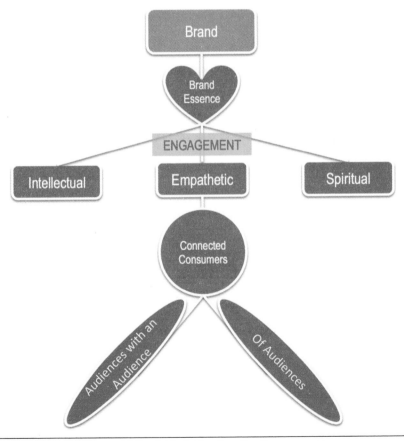

Figure 14.2   A Model for Emotive Engagement

relevant, credible, and memorable encounters. These encounters are hosted by the brand, delivered through its product, or shared by connected customers in their domains.

Engagement is an emotive endeavor. Emotional landscapes are just that, they're emotionally charged. Brand essence is subject to interpretation and as such, it requires thoughtful crafting and genuine human embodiment. This isn't traditional media in which it is defined and published. In the egosystem, brand essence requires reinforcement through proactive and reactive engagement.

■ FUNNELING THROUGH TIME

The difference between average and effective forms of marketing, advertising, and selling is measured in persuasion and outcomes. It is persuasion that fosters desirable actions and effects. Over the last century, the pursuit of mastering persuasion as an art and science has spawned several models to help businesses influence consumer decisions. Most of the leading theories fall under a hierarchy of effects[6] to explain how advertising works, while also exposing the steps customers take in making their purchase decisions.

Returning to *Glengarry Glen Ross*, Alec Baldwin's character Blake makes a reference to A-I-D-A, which in the movie represents Attention, Interest, Decision, Action. Blake uses this model to motivate the sales team to sell, "A-I-D-A. Get out there!!"

The AIDA model was developed over 100 years ago by American advertising and sales pioneer E. St. Elmo Lewis in 1898.[7] Lewis aimed to develop a practical sales tool based on customer studies in the U.S. life insurance market to identify the mechanics of personal selling. Just as a refresher, the AIDA model, also referred to as the AIDA funnel or the sales funnel, defines the basic process by which people are motivated to take action toward a purchase. (See Figure 14.3.) As described in the model, AIDA represents:

Awareness of a product or service

Interest in the product's value proposition and benefits

Desire for the product

Action, the natural result of moving through the first three stages, addressing

Are you talking to me and why?

Do I really need it?

What will I have to do to get it?

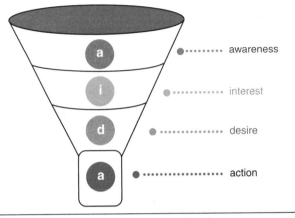

Figure 14.3   AIDA Model

In his book *The Art of Selling*, published in 1911, Arthur Frederick Sheldon introduced a fifth step to the sales funnel…satisfaction.[8] His idea of permanent satisfaction stressed the importance of repeat sales.

Russell H. Colley revisited AIDA in 1961 and introduced the advertising world to his idea of DAGMAR,[9] an acronym for Defining Advertising Goals for Measured Advertising Results. According to DAGMAR, marketing and advertising must lead a prospect through four basic steps (also referred to as ACCA):

1. *Awareness*—The consumer must be aware of the brand or company
2. *Comprehension*—The consumer must have a comprehension of what the product is and its benefits
3. *Conviction*—Requires that the customer must arrive at the mental disposition or conviction to buy
4. *Action*—Did the consumer make the purchase?

Colley focused his work and discoveries on establishing solid objectives so as to refine campaigns and improve outcomes. He categorized objectives into five characteristics:[10]

1. *Concrete and measurable*—Document the communications task as a precise statement to convey the intentional appeal or message to a target audience.
2. *Target audience*—Clearly define the target audience, who they are, and what they want and don't want.

3. *Benchmark and degree of change sought*—Before any campaign introduction, a clear definition of where the audience stands allows for the establishment of metrics to track progress across ACCA. To be successful, marketers must establish the degree of change or movement desired, such as an increase in awareness levels, development of favorable attitudes and sentiment, or the number of intentions to purchase, and so forth, as well as outcomes.

4. *Specified time period*—Set a specific timeline for the objective to be accomplished.

5. *Written goal*—Goals should be clearly written, so that any shortcomings and misunderstandings can be exposed and it's easy to determine whether the goal fits into the DAGMAR approach.

The stages of the funnel matured over the years to include important steps and potential influences in the purchase cycle such as opinion, consideration, preference, and purchase.

Also in 1961, marketing experts Robert Lavidge and Gary Steiner published their contribution to the hierarchy of effects in a *Journal of Marketing* article titled "A Model for Predictive Measurements of Advertising Effectiveness." Lavidge and Steiner assumed a level of high involvement and believed that consumers are active thinkers and participants in the gathering of information in decision-making cycles. As such, consumers (think) about a product, company, or service of interest, and, in turn, form an opinion or sentiment about it (feel). Based on these two steps, they either take action (do) or they don't.[11] This model explores three categories in the hierarchy of effects, cognition (mental or rational), affection (emotion), and behavior (decision or action).

Think, Cognitive Stage:

Awareness—Introduced to a brand/product.

Knowledge—Customers gain knowledge of the potential features, benefits, and uses of a product (a variant of comprehension).

Feel, Affective Stage:

Liking—The customer develops a favorable attitude toward the product or brand.

Preference—A key milestone for any brand is persuading customers to develop a preference for their brand over that of the competition.

Do, Cognitive (Impulse or Directed Effort) Stage:

Conviction—Evokes desire to buy and is convinced in their decision to do so.

Purchase—The action of buying the product.

Using the example of purchasing a car, a consumer may have an awareness of several brands she is considering based on a combination of ads, marketing campaigns, and perhaps personal experiences, for example driving by a dealership or seeing a particular series in the wild. Once a consumer is ready to move toward the next phase, she pares down his choices based on knowledge and preference with a strong dose of reality added for good measure. A consumer typically sees himself in the car, evoking emotion and triggering a sense of desire and aspiration. At this point, she would receive input from trusted advisors, resulting in a lean toward a particular brand. Preference and conviction are established. The next step is a visit to a local dealer, where it is the job of the salesperson to reel in the customer and close the sale. At that point, the consumer decision to either purchase or not purchase that vehicle comes down to engagement and experience. Following the transaction, however, the buyer's relationship with the dealer isn't complete. Service reinforces the brand over time and contributes to either positive or negative referrals in the future.

■ THE COLLAPSE OF THE FUNNEL AND EMERGENCE OF NEW CONSUMER TOUCHPOINTS

In the face of an empowered and connected customer, the various models for the funnel are quickly becoming antiquated. Many of these models were created in an era when information and sources were limited.

The psychology of consumer behavior is far more complex and dynamic as a result of the Web and now the Social Web. These linear assumptions place the brand in control of the interaction, and as such, tools of persuasion boast specific roles and timing to influence desirable behavior through potential touchpoints.

The goal of any business is to connect with a potential customer and lead them in a positive direction. Consumer behavior was presumed to react to brand marketing and sales campaigns at varying steps. Decisions, as a result, were based on information presented, resulting research, and most likely solidified through input from a focused group of peers with trusted opinions.

Following these models too strictly impairs influence among connected customers as they no longer follow sequential steps in the decision-making process.

Real-time streams have disrupted the flow of the decision making and sales processes, and buyers are now empowered in a social economy in which information and influence are democratized. The funnel is morphing from a linear sequence to an elliptical journey in which steps follow a spiraled path, exposing new opportunities to shape and steer decisions before and during a sale, as well as influencing experiences and engendering loyalty after the sale.

Through informal, but telling experiments over the years, I learned that by using everyday social tools, we could explode views of consumer touchpoints that affect every step of the decision-making cycle before, during, and after. And when social and peer networks are factored in, the process becomes both expanded and approachable.

Information, research, and peer review still play a role, but the connected consumer follows a different path. In the realm of social consumerism, engagement has emerged as a critical role in persuasion and influence, having a one-to-one-to-many effect on decisions, outcomes, and experiences. It was through these studies many years ago, that I realized that the end of business as usual was closer than I imagined.

The patterns and engagement models I observed and participated in followed an elliptical path that spun inward toward resolution based on the state of the consumer decision and back outward through shared experiences. The state of the decision, however, was broadcast to friends and peers online and the resulting activity was open to observation and engagement.

In the June 2009 issue of *McKinsey Quarterly*, David Court, along with three co-authors, introduced a new model revealing how a new generation of consumers engages with brands. The report, titled "The Consumer Decision Journey," studied the purchase decisions of nearly 20,000 consumers across five industries—automobiles, skin care, insurance, consumer electronics, and mobile telecom.[12] The report uncovered a decision-making cycle not unlike the ellipse identified in my research.

In the funnel model, a consumer goes through a linear process of distilling many brands to fewer brands to a final choice that leads to the ultimate purchase. McKinsey's research, however, revealed a different path. The digital consumer as referred by McKinsey or, as I believe, the connected consumer, follows a decision journey that is more iterative than reductive and is segmented in four stages:

1. *Consider*—Options are much more refined and may expand or narrow based on input and active evaluation.

2. *Evaluate*—Consumers now actively evaluate options collaboratively by seeking input from peers as well as resellers, brands, and competitors. Remember, the connected consumer makes information come to them.

3. *Purchase/Buy*—The point of purchase is often held until the last minute and up until this point consumers are exposed to active evaluation. Thus, active engagement is critical through D2C interaction in *the last mile* of decision making.

4. *Experience*—The study found that 60 percent of skin care customers perform online research on the product *after* purchase. If they "like" it, they're actively referring the product to others online, setting in motion a powerful form of advocacy that taps into the worldwide reach of the network effect.

The funnel model doesn't vanish. (See Figure 14.4.) It is still how traditional consumers evaluate options toward making a purchase, which affects resulting loyalty. In the elliptical model, brand strength is tested much like in the funnel as connected customers carry with them only a handful of brands in the initial stage of consideration.

The research also surfaced a loyalty loop that shortcuts future decision cycles and leads to repurchase if the experience is enjoyable. This shortcut also applies to referrals, hence the importance for designing and delivering positive experiences at every step. It is these experiences that form a powerful advocacy program that extends well beyond the reach of any brand alone.

Revisiting the car example, we need not look any further than yours truly. Throwing myself into the role of a connected consumer, I

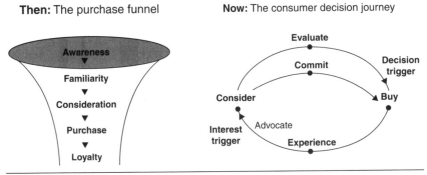

Figure 14.4   The Funnel Model

experimented with a public decision-making journey tapping the wisdom within my social graph. I wasn't 100 percent committed to making a new vehicle purchase, but I was curious to learn more about my options. I broadcasted that I was looking for a vehicle that was sporty, stylish, economical, and known for its stellar fuel economy. While I had a few options in mind, new considerations were presented. I think about McKinsey's research here as any business hoping to compete for the future will need to also take note. Connected consumers believe that information is inundating and product choices are overly abundant. Faced with too many choices and marketing messages flying at them, consumers will fall back on a limited set of brands that managed to cut through the dense forest of information. As McKinsey found, "Brand awareness matters: brands in the initial-consideration set can be up to three times more likely to be purchased eventually than brands that aren't in it."

When I invited feedback within my digital networks, peers, local dealerships, brands, and experts chimed in. My process of evaluation was largely focused on social feedback through Facebook and Twitter. My options were steered in a different direction as a result. As referred to in McKinsey's research, my choices expanded as trusted voices filtered in. Also, some of the original options disappeared in the following steps. This is an important point, as brands that pay attention to this very public decision-making cycle can literally interrupt the process by either engaging directly with the consumer or connecting with a trusted advisor.

McKinsey found that the number of brands added in later stages differs by industry. For those shopping for personal computers, consumers added an average of 1 brand to their initial-consideration set of 1.7. Those shopping for cars added 2.2 to their initial set of 3.8 (sounds like me). The opportunity here is that this change in behavior opens up new touchpoints for marketers to engage. And, as McKinsey notes, brands already under consideration can no longer take that status for granted. This is in large part due to the reality that brands were heavily dependent on pushing messages to the consumer when in fact, consumer outreach to brands is now much more important. This signifies a shift away from push marketing, creating a need for brands to invest in a pull approach that helps people through their decision journey.

McKinsey's research found that two-thirds of the active-evaluation phase was driven by online reviews, word-of-mouth recommendations, in-store interactions, and past experiences. Only a third of the touch points involve company-driven marketing.

Back to my experience. Now that I had a manufacturer and make narrowed down, I still needed to select a local dealership. Because of the trust for those who offered insight and direction, I opted to buy the vehicle from a dealership over two hours away from where I lived. Yes, there were closer locations, but all input and topline research pointed me in this direction. I contacted the person that I was referred to and the transaction was seamless. I didn't have to set foot in the dealership because all the paperwork was handled by email. The car was even delivered to me.

This is where the post-commerce experience begins. I would say that in this case, the purchase experience was exceptional. I've since referred this brand and dealership to my offline and online networks. I actively sought additional information online, specifically in online social groups, to proactively share my positive experience with the transaction as well as the splendid ownership experience that continues today.

Now, the post-purchase experience shapes the opinion for every subsequent decision, creating a never-ending consumer journey. This means that the brand's job is never done. Just because it earned the transaction, to earn the support of the customer requires ongoing engagement. For example, in the skin care industry, McKinsey found that more than 60 percent of consumers will go online *after* the purchase to conduct further research. This again opens up a new touchpoint that is nonexistent in the traditional funnel.

In the post-purchase stage, McKinsey discovered two types of post-purchase loyalists who may profess support or adoration, those who are active and those who are passive. To make a complex subject all the more complex, active loyalists will stick with the brand and persuade others to do so as well. Passive consumers will, despite their claims of allegiance, remain open for a potential switch down the line. Many factors play into these states, starting with the product experience. Naturally, it must deliver as promised and perhaps even more. As mentioned earlier, some consumers will also continue to research options even after they make the purchase. This is because of the onslaught of available options as well as the psychological notion to validate the purchase.

In the automotive insurance industry in particular, McKinsey's study surfaced a huge sixfold difference in the ratio of active to passive loyalists. To say there's room for interruption in the loyalty loop is an understatement.

There are a couple of important questions to ask at this moment:

1. Do you know what your customers value in their decision-making journey and are you marketing and engaging on the basis of their needs?

2. Are you giving consumers a reason to stay or unknowingly causing them to consider leaving?

■ THE DECISION-MAKING CIRCLE

From the digital consumer journey we get the decision-making circle, a continual approach to discovering information, acting upon it, and sharing the experiences that follow, both good and bad. To summarize my work along with McKinsey's research, I created a decision ellipse to visualize the steps a connected consumer may take, and also the new touchpoints that emerge as a result. (See Figure 14.5.)

The journey is divided by four important stages:

1. *Formulation:* The moment or instance that triggers interest and the steps a connected customer takes to boil down her initial options.

2. *Pre-Commerce:* Based on the initial consideration, the connected consumer conducts open research to validate her initial choices and surface new opportunities.

3. *Commerce:* When the decision is made, the consumer journey is only just beginning. Touchpoints unlock to shape and steer the ensuing customer experience.

4. *Post-Commerce:* Following the purchase, connected customers bond with the product, but to what extent defines their loyalty and advocacy.

The four stages are merely the acts in a grander production known as the business circle of life. In Act 1, the consumer is ready to begin the process of consideration based on a trigger, something that pushed an individual to take action—even if that action is merely consideration and nothing more. A trigger can be based on an event or simmering consideration that finally boils over. From there, the brands that they value and those that have caught their attention are brought along for the ride. Here, brand strength counts for everything. When a consumer enters this step, the first of many touchpoints emerges. Their interest can be interrupted by a brand that recognizes their needs and offers a solution. Brand strength is tested as those carried in may or may not make the next phase. New brands will indeed make the cut. This is why businesses' marketing, day in and day out, determines whether they are effective in earning a place of value heading into the consideration phase.

In Act 2, the connected customer makes the turn and as such, brand engagement, combined with peer interaction, weighs heavily into evaluation. Peer reviews, word of mouth, and also direct-to-consumer (D2C) interaction will help connected customers navigate their next steps.

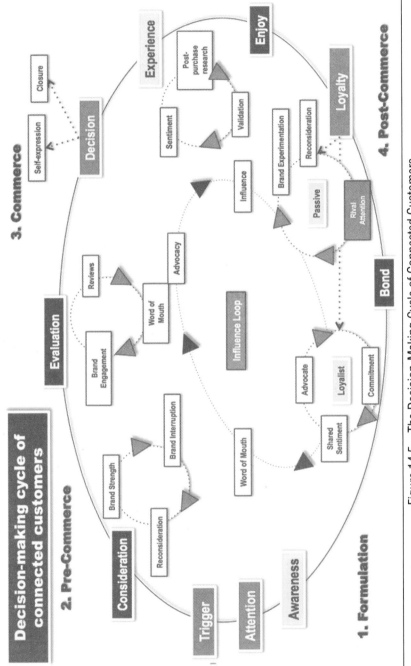

Figure 14.5 The Decision-Making Cycle of Connected Customers

On to Act 3, a consumer takes action. Once a decision has been finalized, it will be broadcast. Doing so is part closure and part self-expression. Consumers are excited and relieved that they made a decision. At the same time, a purchase says a lot about someone, and for those who share, it is a form of saying, "Hey, look at what I got. This is me!"

Not to be confused with a finale, Act 4 is nothing less than an encore. Following the commerce stage, customers now dive into the post-commerce product experience. As we see in McKinsey's study, consumers must validate their purchase. They will therefore begin to research the product again to learn more about the experiences of others, how they align with their experience, and in turn reassess their exposure to date. These acts motivate them to not only share their findings, but also influences where their loyalty will lie in the long term.

Again, another touchpoint emerges when the brand they're currently supporting, as well as those of competitors, can directly engage to shape the experience and ultimately set the stage for either advocacy (active loyalty) or brand hopping (passive loyalty). Allegiance is fickle, and in some ways, is open to either the brand that invests in a solid experience with or without follow-up, that is, design, documentation, functionality, performance, and so on, or the brand that spends the time to monitor and respond to those in need. In this case, Apple would be an example of the former and Dell the latter. The connected customer is otherwise open to rival attention, secondary peer input, or will explore alternatives based on personal experience.

For those customers who form a bond with the product, they will actively reinvest in the decision circle to help others in need. Doing so evokes a sense of catharsis, but equally gives back to the egosystem because others like them face similar crossroads. This creates an influence loop that serves as the axis for all future decision making. Shared experiences create a center of collective intelligence that influences customer decisions and shapes perceptions and future experiences.

It's important to note that connected customers, whether they're passive or active, will share their experiences within the decision circle. Brands must define the experience pre- and post-commerce to ensure that the extended network of your customers (the audience with an audience) feel vested and rewarded. This is the recipe for influence. It comes down to this: Making decisions is an emotional endeavor. While logic and information shape considerations, people naturally apply varying degrees of emotional filters to every situation. Therein lies the opportunity for engagement, personalization, and partnership. What we learn from this exploded view of decision making is that the brand promise, the product value proposition and differentiators, and the acts of empathy and guidance must be integrated into all that you do. From print to digital to signage to social and new media to your front line representatives, the story they tell must be aligned to make an emotional connection. As a very sage CMO once said, "Every touchpoint is a teaching point."

What McKinsey's research and my experience bring to light is that a connected consumer requires a different and dedicated approach to steer experiences and actions favorably. The funnels of old no longer apply directly to this savvy and networked consumer, and investing time, money, and resources in marketing to this rapidly emerging (and influential) segment is not only ineffective, it may represent a general lack of appreciation for the customer collective. The decision-making cycles are unique to traditional, online, and connected customers. The future of commerce is social. Experiences require design, deployment, and engagement. Without the architecture and implementation of intentional, empowering, and shareable experiences, brands will drift from a lucrative position of relevance to a decaying position of irrelevance in the decision-making cycle of connected customers—from the top of one's mind to out of sight and out of mind.

An interesting twist in this model is how peer-to-peer communication and a brand's direct-to-consumer (D2C) engagement affect the flow. Steps are sometimes eliminated, and in other cases, the process restarts.

The intelligence that a brand can extract from listening to the activity of the social customer is unprecedented. To learn from it and steer it in desirable directions requires nothing short of new methodologies and processes. Dedicated resources at every step are essential. The future of connected consumerism is tied to shared experiences. Through engagement, brands now have the ability to steer positive experiences before, during, and after the sale. Executed properly, the likelihood for loyalty and advocacy grows exponentially and scales one-to-one engagement. Through every touchpoint, brands must scale reach through an investment in goodwill and leadership.

Intelligence is just that, intelligence. Knowing the connected consumer and exposing their decision-making and experience-sharing behavior is instrumental in developing on-target engagement and marketing strategies, improving service, designing better products, activating effective loyalty programs, investing in goodwill, and steering influential advocacy initiatives. This is an uncharted, but bustling landscape in which the brand is measured in dynamic stages between relevance and irrelevance.

Centers of Attention

➤ Shared experiences and relationships are at the heart of on-line interaction between connected customers.

➤ At the center of shared experiences is emotion, which fuels greater levels of activity and interaction.

➤ Shared experiences are either negative or positive and you have a say in which way they gravitate: It's your choice.

➤ Experiences span across networks and influence the decisions of others in real time and over time.

➤ To the connected customer, a brand must come alive and speak at a personal level.

➤ Brand essence requires redesign to cast hooks to the heart and mind to earn transactions and engender positive experiences.

➤ Affinity, loyalty, and advocacy are byproducts of positive engagement and experiences.

➤ The decision-making cycle is evolving away from a linear process to an elliptical cycle that publicizes touchpoints for brand connection.

➤ Brands are either part of the conversation or they're not and as a result, they're either part of the decision-making cycle or they're absent from the heart, mind, and actions of the connected customer.

➤ Positive experiences take the shape of advocacy and help scale a brand's reach across the human network.

➤ The value of listening and the resulting intelligence that is discovered is priceless. Prioritize it within your organization.

Chapter 15

Aspiring to Reach beyond Conformity to Inspire Customers

Connected customers look beyond ordinary. They never settle for uninspired products and services. They don't have to. Their expectations for usefulness and value are unparalleled and undeniable. Yet, brands are still holding a singular view of the customer.

While they study the customer: who they are, what they want, and how and why they remain loyal, businesses still approach markets as if they are made up of one type of customer, creating one audience. Mass marketing tends to be driven by objectives and designed around demographic data and supported by paid and earned media to reach desirable consumers. CRM is designed to lure and cultivate high value customer relationships and boost customer lifetime value. A dizzying array of processes, programs, and methodologies are then inserted into the mix to attract new customers, boost sales, solve problems, activate and convert existing customers, and streamline processes.

Many enterprise businesses strive to streamline procedures to build companies that are well-oiled, operations-driven machines. These operationalized businesses rely on their operators to perform against the bottom line, maximizing efficiencies, increasing margins, and growing revenue as part of their monthly objectives. Connected customers prefer not to align with faceless, emotionless businesses.

It's easy for a brand to assume that customers are alike. After all, they share the same needs, wants, and desires. They face the same challenges and hurdles in life, personally and professionally. They each follow the same routine in making purchase decisions. Customers equally subscribe to the same sources for information and idly wait by their smartphones, tablets, laptops, and TVs awaiting the next set of instructions from brands that reveal their next move.

Does this sound like you?

Of course not.

Businesses tend to generalize their audiences through marketing and communication which minimizes the individual's role in the market. If there's anything we learned in the last few chapters, it's that the shift in power between connected customers and brands is real and of vital consequence to the reach and effect of any brand. Yet, still today, even in the face of customers who demand that information reach them on their terms, the individual is still underrecognized and underappreciated by businesses, governments, media, and others.

In the Disney/Pixar production *Wall-E*,[1] we're given a sensationalized glimpse of the customer's role in operationalized business. Aboard the great ship Axiom that carries among the last generation of Earth's denizens, passengers are overweight overconsumers, who now meander through life in a state of constant distraction. There's no longer a need to walk or drive, as they are confined to mechanical chairs that transport them wherever they need to or are told to go. Their capacity to make decisions is essentially stripped to simple responses. Children learn their ABCs and the basics of excess at the same time ("B is for buy a large lunch in a cup"). In one scene meant to convey mindless consumerism, a female voice over the mechanical society, "Try blue—it's the new red." With one fell swoop of an index finger, a button on every chair is depressed and wardrobes immediately change color in accordance with the prescribed trend.

Connected customers will have no part in this society and are already leading micro uprisings, uniting to deliver the macro significance of a full-scale consumer revolution.

Apple shattered our view of conformity a quarter-century ago when it introduced the Macintosh during the Super Bowl in 1984. In a landmark commercial directed by visionary Ridley Scott, consumers were not unlike the mindless consumers aboard the Axiom. A dark and dreary vision of the future showed a world in which consumers are minions, led in herd mentality by Big Brother. Individuality is extinct. Free thought is eclipsed by absolute rule. This is a world in which consumers do as they're told and move through life as a pawn in a game envisioned by a higher authority.

The drones march to the impassioned speech of their dictator:

Today we celebrate the first glorious anniversary of the Information Purification Directives. We have created for the first time in all history a garden of pure ideology, where each worker may bloom, secure from the pests of any contradictory true thoughts. Our Unification of Thoughts is more powerful a weapon than any

fleet or army on earth. We are one people, with one will, one re-
solve, one cause. Our enemies shall talk themselves to death and
we will bury them with their own confusion. We shall prevail!

The future of humanity and free thought emerges in the form
of an athletic and determined heroine who races ahead of the storm
troopers who must stop her from introducing change. With the mighty
throw of a sledgehammer, our champion sets in motion the immediate
demise of the bleak dystopian future.

The large screen in which Big Brother stares down upon the drones
explodes in brilliant light.

Boom.

The commercial aired on television only once[2] and its effects on
shattering the idea of conformity still resonate today. In a 2004 article
in *Macworld,* author Adelia Cellini interviewed TBWA/Chiat/Day's
Lee Clow for clarification on whether or not Big Brother was meant
to depict IBM at the time. According to Clow, it was something much
more significant, "Apple wanted the Mac to symbolize the idea of
empowerment, with the ad showcasing the Mac as a tool for combating
conformity and asserting originality."[3]

Connected customers are not cogs in the business machine, but
they play an instrumental role in the progress of progress, the adaptation of business, and as such, become part of a new era of customer-
centric business mechanics.

Even though the balance of power is shifting, any loss in ground
or influence on behalf of the other side has yet to be recognized or
acknowledged en masse. It's a dangerous position. Today's leaders will
learn that leadership is an earned position and it is those visionar-
ies who recognize opportunities and rally teams to seize them who
become the leaders of tomorrow.

■ MARKET FRAGMENTATION LEADS TO DIVERSIFICATION

It's quite simple, really . . .

1. Businesses exist because of customers.
2. Customers have specific needs and wants and look to businesses
   to fulfill them.
3. Those needs are either satisfied or they're not.
4. Products and services represent varying levels of value to customers in addressing those needs before, during, and after
   the sale.

5. The state of a business is the derivative of performance against item numbers 2, 3, and 4.

What *is* complicated, however, is the reality that connected customers are people, too, and they are not a passive bunch. To borrow from economic and marketing concepts, the growing activities led by connected customers within online communities materialize the important segmentation that exists within markets.

Whether it's moms, dads, enthusiasts, professionals, or other potential influencers, markets are composed of concentrated interests, and each require a focus based on those that demand attention. These nicheworks are identifiable and reachable by market intervention. In turn, these communities respond similarly to market stimulus. These distinct markets are made up of a variety of needs and exhibit forms of diverse behavior as a result. It starts with applications, extends to peer-to-peer interaction around solutions, relies upon the expert advice from authorities and influencers, and ends with individuals reinvesting their experiences into the process. It doesn't end. The paths between their activity and businesses and brands are not yet paved nor are they defined for that matter. Depending on the existing positioning and product differentiation programs designed to attract various segments, they will require modification to suit the unique and discriminating behavior of the connected customer.

A new infrastructure is necessary to address the new state of business, which includes not just customer segmentation, but also customer fragmentation. This fragmentation extends beyond identifying the needs of the distinct roles of today's customers within traditional, online, and connected segments and also the active layers of segments within segments. Identifying who they are, what they do, where they connect with one another and why, their needs are available to those who wish to learn how to pinpoint opportunities for relevance and engagement.

The first step on the road to relevance and, ultimately, customer-centricity is acceptance. You can't be customer-centric if you don't know who customers are and what it is they value.

Customer-centricity struggles to find a home within the operationalized business, losing favor instead to the business of business. But it is market and customer segmentation and identification that allow businesses to compete for the future by recognizing the needs and wants of customers to set the stage for meaningful engagement.

Segmentation begins with the division of traditional, online, and connected customers. But while we understand the nuances within each, uncovering the links that unite them is equally important. Everything begins, of course, with understanding the varying roles of the connected customer and within that series of studies, surfacing their needs, challenges, and opportunities so as to introduce and continually deliver value.

The networks of connected consumers reveal the multiple dimensions of each consumer's role in the marketplace in each medium in which brands are either absent or disillusioned in believing that they are already building engaged communities. How companies approach new media today and how they approach it tomorrow must be gradual and adaptive.

In early 2011, I worked with the team at Pivot Conference to capture a moment in time to show how engagement with connected customers was isolated to just one department, thus missing the greater opportunity for engagement.

As reported by participants in the Pivot study, social media programming and engagement emanated from the following departments in order of ranking:[4]

1. Marketing
2. Public Relations
3. Sales
4. Customer Service

As David Packard of Hewlett Packard once said, "Marketing is too important to leave to the marketing department."[5] The same could be said for sales and customer service. The functionality of each role is to attract and satisfy customers. But the greater purpose they serve and the potential of what's possible when they work together is practically heroic.

Brands are under pressure, whether realized or not. What we don't know right now within these new markets is both empowering and overwhelming. Regardless of context or sentiment, tapping into the undercurrent of activity can be nothing less than illuminating. But what's clear is that most are missing the overall dynamics of what is actually necessary to satisfy the needs of those who are defining markets, regardless of whether the brand itself is active in the network. And, by *defining markets*, I don't just mean the singular conversations that randomly populate online social networks. This is about the collective consciousness that unites us online and presents the foundation for conversations to gather momentum, touch people, and thus trigger effects. (See Figure 15.1.) At any moment, an individual

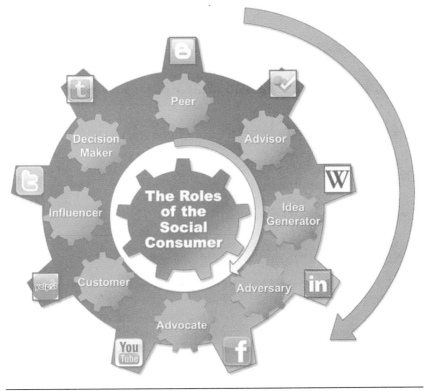

Figure 15.1   The Roles of the Social Consumer

possesses the capacity to show any number of faces toward a brand, including, but not limited to the role of:

➤ Peer
➤ Advisor
➤ Idea generator
➤ Adversary
➤ Advocate
➤ Customer
➤ Influencer
➤ Decision maker

The question is, in these or any network in which the roles of the social consumer are shaping experiences and guiding decisions, are you watching, engaging, and learning from every facet, or simply addressing one of the many opportunities that exist before you?

No one department owns new media or the overall relationship with the customer. Any person or department affected by outside activity in which public interaction affects decisions is obliged to plug in. That includes, at a minimum:

➤ Customer service
➤ Customer acquisition and retention
➤ Sales
➤ Product development/R&D
➤ Marketing
➤ Communications
➤ Intelligence and analysis

Still today, businesses tend to have a narrow view of the customer. But as we're learning, customer roles are expanding from prospect to advocate to adversary to influencer and everything in between.

Every organization will benefit from the acts of segmentation and differentiation as illustrated in Figure 15.2. Chances are this is already in play within the organization; the difference is that it is most likely not taking into account the varying roles of the connected customer

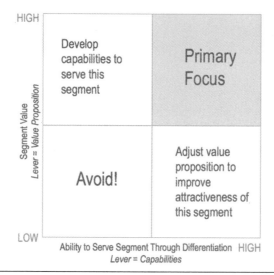

Figure 15.2   Target Segment Selection Matrix

nor is it profiting from the rich wells of insight that exist across the Social Web.

What are the levers to convey value and capabilities? Where should we focus and why? What elements are we missing to captivate the roles of the connected customer? What aspects of our value proposition could benefit from improvement or augmentation?

Revisiting a target segment selection matrix[6] helps us diversify our story and approach and identify areas for processes and workflow to help information move in and out efficiently and effectively while still hitting the internal touchpoints for organizational transformation, process innovation, and product innovation.

Customer-centricity is not about conversations on Twitter and Facebook or check-ins on Foursquare or videos on YouTube. These channels are the health monitors of our brand and business, and the readings tell us that we not only need to pay attention, we also need to improve the health of our reputation and relationships. This is an opportunity to build bridges to a new genre of customers and the people who influence their decisions. Our mission now is to pave those paths to our future relevance, perpetually.

We can blame the lack of current support on process, hierarchy, ignorance, old school thinking, lack of budget, and anything and everything standing in our way. Or, we can own the acts of socializing the company using relevance as a banner for customer centricity across the organization. Then grab a pair of self-sharpening industrial-grade scissors and run through the hallways of your organization to begin the long and arduous process of cutting red tape to free people to collaborate internally and externally. Or, to extend the example used earlier in this chapter, take hold of the sledgehammer and hurl it toward the screen that dictates corporate mediocrity and break free from this dystopian rule of operational commerce.

Someone has to do it.

Without you, even though we're operating with the best of intentions, we are still operating from silos. The customer, however, does not see silos; she sees the company as one. It's time for a holistic approach to create an adaptive business, a collaborative business, an aspirational business . . . a business of one.

■ BEHAVIORGRAPHICS

The connected customer lives and makes decisions through networks where they dwell, and not only are their needs divergent, the nature of their behavior and character are equally diversified. Much like the work that lies ahead in segmentation, customer psychology plays a critical role in ideation and engagement. It is quite literally a series of connected worlds in which we are at the center of our online experiences, a place where everything and everyone revolves around us.

Placing ourselves in the role of this emerging consumer for a moment, brands, businesses, and media aren't sure how to see or reach us directly yet. We're lured through creative attempts to follow them on Twitter or Google+ or to Like them on Facebook. But for the most part in new media, consumers are faceless consumers brought to life only through avatars, bios, and a history of our online activities and connections.

They are part of demographic studies, grouped by age, income, gender, education, and so on, or part of psychographic studies grouped by commonalities, shared interests and passions, and themes. We're often lumped together through keyword mentions or online influence scores. But the real question is, who are we in the egosystem, and what makes us connect, share, and live online? Finding these answers is revealing and, we hope, inspiring. Think of these as engagement levers based on the concentrated behavior that populates the fragmented market landscapes. (See Figure 15.3.)

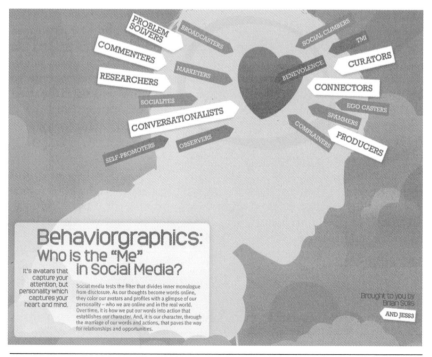

Figure 15.3   Behaviorgraphics

Do you know who your connected customers are and how they're interacting online? I worked with the team JESS3 to visualize the new consumer. The infographic introduced behaviorgraphics to help us see what drives him to engage online.

At the center of behaviorgraphics is the Benevolent—the unselfish and kindhearted behavior that engenders and promotes recognition and reciprocity, and in doing so, earns the goodwill of those around them. This is the hub of social networking with a purpose, mission, and a genuine intent to grow communities based on trust, vision, and collaboration.

Problem Solvers—One of the most common sources of conversations and updates in social media are questions . . . people seeking information in the hopes that commenters will respond with resolution or direction.

Commenters—Providing thoughts, opinions, observations, experiences, and sometimes, unfiltered reactions to the information shared online. They are less likely to produce original content, but are compelled to share their views.

Researchers—Peer-to-peer influence is prominent in social networks, and researchers rely on their social graphs for information and direction to make qualified decisions. They are also active in championing polls and surveys to truly learn about the thoughts and opinions of those connected to them.

Conversationalists—Conversationalists fuel threads within and across networks by participating in conversations through proactive updates and direct responses to other content.

Curators—Curators work diligently to find and share what captivates them as filtered by what they believe will interest their followers in their interest graphs.

Connectors—Individuals who take social networking literally. Connectors represent the most resilient and obliging roles in new media today, constantly investing in the quality and caliber of their networks and the nicheworks of those important to them.

Producers—Among the more elite group of online participants, their stature is earned by the amount of content they generate within multiple networks.

Broadcasters—Broadcasters are mostly one-way communicators who either intentionally or unintentionally push information to followers without injecting conversational aspects into the mix.

Marketers—Profiles dedicated to marketing ideas, products, or services and may or may not include content outside of their portfolio, unless the account is focused on funneling beneficial and value-added solutions to specific audiences, regardless of origin.

Entertainers—Entertainers feel responsible to satisfy and engage the social graph they weave. They use their channels to delight, occupy, or divert others, and they're often cherished by those who follow them.

Socialites—Individuals who have earned varying levels of *weblebrity,* these new Internet famous personae who earn recognition and attention in online networks, which increasingly spills over to real-world fame.

Self-promoters—Unlike broadcasters and marketers, self-promoters are unconcealed in their intentions through constant updating of activities, events, and accomplishments.

Egocasters—Egocasters contribute to the ego in the egosystem and represent the evolution of self-promoters. What they think and say is what they believe to be the reality for one and for all. They lose touch with perspective, as listening gives way to telling. . . .

Observers—Often referred to as inactives, lurkers, or simply consumers, observers represent the majority of the social web today, defined by those who read and also share information in the back channel, including email, and also in the real world.

Social Climbers—Social capital is not only something that is earned in social networking, it is something that is proactively pursued by those whose sole mission is to increase influence scores. These individuals intentionally climb ladders on the avatars, profiles, and social capital of others.

TMI—The things some share in social media continue to blur the line between what's relegated to inner monologue versus that for sharing with others in public. The state of sharing too much information is dictated by those on the receiving end of the update, not those who publish it.

Spammers—Those accounts and profiles that are created to push messages blindly. They're often tied to current events (using trending keywords or hashtags) or targeting influential voices to lure them into clicking through to their desired goal.

Leechers—Not included in the graph, but an important category to recognize, as leechers take the good work of others and channel it into their own accounts almost exclusively for the sake of promoting their own cause.

Complainers—When we love something, we tell a few people. When something bothers us, we tell everyone. Complainers are often sharing their discontent as a primary ingredient in their social stream. And, as customer service takes to the Social Web, these complainers are only encouraged to share their experiences to achieve satisfaction and earn recognition for their role as the new social customer.

Trolls—Certainly the bottom of the connected customer psychology chart, these individuals exist solely to suck the life out of engagement. These social vampires jump from thread to thread and profile to profile and community to community, feeding on the animation and productivity within each. While everyone is left void of intellectual or emotional resolve, trolls leave with a greater sense of self-worth. They are not worthy of engagement.

Understanding the role of individuals within the egosystem provides opportunities for engagement, empowerment, observation, or simply listening. If we align behavioral traits to the common culture of each network, we can reverse engineer positioning to personalize our value proposition for each of the distributed groups of connected customers important to our markets.

■ THE INTEREST GRAPH IS ALIVE: A STUDY OF STARBUCKS'S TOP FOLLOWERS

There's an expression that goes "By the time you hear the sirens, it's already too late." In an era of connected consumerism, it's quite the opposite. Your time to act is now.

The human network is maturing as are the people embracing its most engaging tools and networks. The maturation of relationships and how customers are expanding their horizons when it comes to connecting to one another is nothing short of remarkable. What started as the social graph, the network of people we knew and connected to in social networks, is now spawning new branches that resemble how we interact in real life.

This is the era of the interest graph—the expansion and contraction of social networks around common interests and events. Interest graphs represent a potential gold mine for brands seeking insight and inspiration to design more meaningful products and services as well as new marketing campaigns that better target potential stakeholders.

While many companies are learning to listen to the conversations related to their brands and competitors, many are simply documenting activity and mentions as a reporting function and in some cases, as part of conversational workflow. There's more to Twitter intelligence, however, than tracking conversations.

To identify the varying roles of the connected customer and complete the customer segmentation matrix, we must look beyond the social graph. While relationships count, surfacing interests, values, and the people who connect around them is our expressway to relevance.

To bring an example of an interest graph to life, I worked with the team at PeopleBrowsr and ReSearch.ly.[7] The goal was to show brands how to look beyond listening and monitoring to visualize demographics and psychographics, sentiment, bio data, profession, and the people connected through common bonds, not just keyword mentions or peer-driven networks.

The following example of audience profiling represents merely a sliver of intelligence available (Figure 15.4). But to demonstrate what's possible, we focused on @Starbucks because it is one of the most celebrated brands actively using Twitter today.

Figure 15.4   Bio Word Cloud—Top 100

We started by extracting 1 million follower profiles, sorted by follower count. The results were then further filtered to include only those who published a complete profile. ReSearch.ly provides the option to then organize the resulting information in any number of ways; in this case, we sorted the accounts by bio, location, and gender.

While we are what we say in our tweets, our bios also reveal a telling side of who we really are. In this study, we reviewed the complete bios of 50,000 of the top @Starbucks followers to learn a bit more about how they present their life story as well as their interests, opinions, and preferences.

We then created a word cloud to amplify the most common words used in each of the bios of these connected social consumers. Followers tended to use expressive words that suggest sentiment runs rich in the Starbucks interest graph. The top five words include:

1. Love
2. Life
3. Friends
4. Music
5. World

We also learned a bit more about Starbucks influencers by analyzing what interests them. Looking a bit deeper into the cloud, we can see that not only do emotions rise to the top, other revealing themes also surface:

➤ Family
➤ People
➤ Mom
➤ Wife
➤ Husband

This is just the beginning. The words associated with the brands demonstrate the emotional and personal connections Starbucks holds with these tastemakers. Campaigns can be a direct beneficiary of such data. As we submerge ourselves one level deeper into the study, we find that this information becomes paramount when we link it to individuals through demographics and psychographics. An important footnote is that the word *coffee* is among the least-used words in the bio, but used nonetheless.

We further reviewed each of the bios to find commonalities in how each person presents who they are in a few precious characters. (See Figure 15.5.)

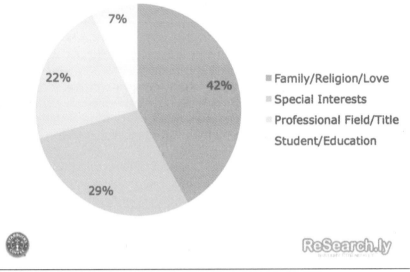

Figure 15.5   Bio Interest Breakdown—Top 100

Of those, we found that . . .

➤   Forty-two percent express strong ties to family, religion, and love.

➤   Twenty-nine percent boast special interests (which are further discernible).

➤   Twenty-two percent are professionals who state their current place of employment and position.

➤   Seven percent are students.

We can also extract the attributes of @Starbucks followers further to better symbolize their digital persona. Further review highlights that followers . . .

➤   Identify themselves as enthusiasts, geeks, addicts, junkies, creatives.

➤   Define the most popular areas of interest as music, food, coffee, and fashion.

➤   Potentially favor dogs to cats (2 to 1 as per their mentions).

➤   Work in either social media or marketing. (Note: If we were to change the scale of followers, we would open up the sample to a much broader set of professions.)

➤   Are still studying. Despite the low percentage, students still account for more than any single professional field.

Brands are more than aware that no single marketing strategy reaches and moves everyone in the same way. Beyond demographic marketing, brands must also focus on driving traffic regionally. Having access to location data isn't new, but using Twitter as a collective stream of intelligence to identify higher and underperforming locales and associative word clouds allow teams to surface the 3 Ws of real-time geo-loco marketing:

1. Where is negative and positive activity taking place?
2. Why is it leaning in that direction?
3. What can we do about it?

To give us an idea of where the top @Starbucks followers are tweeting, we zoomed in to their point of reference. We found that top users tend to tweet from . . .

➤ California
➤ New York
➤ Texas
➤ Florida
➤ Washington

Combining London and the United Kingdom, we find that the United Kingdom would actually join the ranks of the most-often-cited cities.

Grouping locations provides a holistic view for regional marketing metrics and areas in need of attention. (See Figure 15.6.)

The interest graph is defined by connections, but it is brought to life through self-expression. When we combine brand-centric relationships and conversations, the interest graph eventually evolves into what is essentially a brand graph. Within each brand-related graph is a group of highly connected individuals that serve as a company's network of influence. The ReSearch.ly team extracted 50,000 of the most recent tweets that included a mention of Starbucks. We then analyzed the connections between people and identified the top 100 individuals and the number of their followers who also mention Starbucks within the 50,000 mentions. We can then create a strategy to connect with Starbucks influencers as a representation of its brand graph and influential hubs. As we can see, the difference between monitoring and gathering intelligence allows Starbucks to now identify relevant networks and introduce personalized campaigns to further spur advocacy and loyalty.

Figure 15.6   Location Word Cloud—Top 100

We assembled a list of the top 100 most connected people within the group mentioning Starbucks and the number of their followers also discussing Starbucks are listed in Figure 15.7.

Accordingly, we visualized the interest graph as connections, showing how influencers are not only interconnected, but also capable of disseminating relevant information and influencing behavior to varying degrees beyond the traditional reach of Starbucks (Figure 15.8). Connected customers and their place within the social consumer hierarchy determine reach and, ultimately, outcomes. Everything begins, however, with recognizing who they are and what inspires them.

The era of analysis paralysis is officially over. We are now entering an era of Big Data. While the term *Big Data* might sound intimidating and even paralyzing, it is the shot of invigoration every business can benefit from in the new economy. But it does take work.

According to the "IBM Business Analytics and Optimization for the Intelligent Enterprise" study, one in three business leaders make decisions without the benefit of intelligence, and about half don't have access to the information they need to do their jobs successfully. The study also revealed that companies that excel at finance efficiency and employ mature business analytics and optimization can experience 20 times greater profit growth and 30 percent higher return on invested capital. Information to the rescue.[8]

Here are the top 100 most connected people within the group mentioning Starbucks and the number their followers also discussing Starbucks:

1. @Starbucks: 10196 followers
2. KChenoweth, 1976
3. chrisbrogan, 1896
4. MCHammer, 1486
5. El_Universal_Mx, 1144
6. adage, 1088
7. lizstrauss, 999
8. MandyJiroux, 892
9. MarketingProfs, 864
10. RayWJ, 774
11. barefoot_exec, 736
12. iTwitQuotes_, 725
13. DramaBeats, 722
14. MensHealthMag, 690
15. AdaDiskon, 657
16. StarbucksCard, 633
17. JasonFalls, 625
18. jacvanek, 607
19. mayhemstudios, 584
20. BuzzEdition, 579
21. refinery29, 549
22. Flipbooks, 534
23. orianthi, 524
24. SbuxIndonesia, 518
25. newmediajim, 506
26. LoriMoreno, 495
27. KellyOlexa, 472
28. pokwang27, 444
29. THR, 429
30. ChrisSpagnuolo, 426
31. ProfessionalOne, 419
32. BgirlShorty, 418
33. Starbucker, 408
34. mayaREguru, 405
35. aaronrgillespie, 385

36. CNNMoney, 384
37. coffeetweet, 383
38. BieberArmour, 376
39. robdelaney, 371
40. Uncharted_, 369
41. shannonleetweed, 367
42. sno_buny, 366
43. StarbucksJobs, 365
44. knealemann, 361
45. DealSeekingMom, 361
46. OfficialKat, 356
47. jonathanfields, 350
48. kyleplacy, 348
49. redeyechicago, 342
50. BlondeTXGoddess, 337
51. benpatrick90069, 332
52. melissaonline, 331
53. SbuxMel, 325
54. BreakingNewz, 325
55. sumaya, 324
56. iKissNTell, 312
57. andytelasai, 311
58. AaronStrout, 305
59. LisaJohnson, 301
60. glennhilton, 300
61. MomsofAmerica, 291
62. StarbucksKorea, 286
63. imalexevans, 285
64. PurseBlog, 278
65. smaxbrown, 276
66. heykim, 273
67. ElizandJames, 271
68. Quotalicious, 269
69. wespazforjb, 267
70. itsALDO, 267

71. OfficialFYRARE, 265
72. LaineyGossip, 264
73. InterviewAngel, 262
74. MomItForward, 257
75. wera_supernova, 254
76. CathyWebSavvyPR, 254
77. Bieberbucks, 254
78. jasonkintzler, 253
79. AlexBlom, 249
80. BethFrysztak, 248
81. daveweigel, 241
82. TimeOutMom, 240
83. nature_org, 232
84. MoneySavingMom, 232
85. KyNamDoan, 230
86. PhilipNowak, 226
87. organicguru, 224
88. StoryofMyLife, 224
89. scottparent, 222
90. fondalo, 222
91. paulwalker47, 219
92. djwaldow, 219
93. andipeters, 216
94. SocialGrow, 215
95. SAngelloLIVE, 215
96. LenKendall, 215
97. TheSavalots, 212
98. NickLongo, 212
99. kdpaine, 210
100. StephenHampton, 206

Powered by PeopleBrowsr

Figure 15.7   Interest Graph Report by Brian Solis and Research.ly

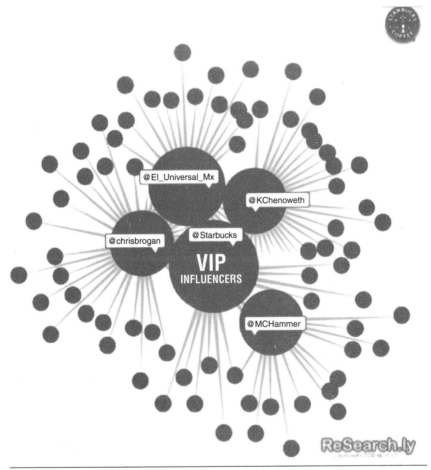

Figure 15.8   Starbucks Interest Graph

While many definitions abound, Big Data refers to the tools, processes, and procedures allowing an organization to create, manipulate, and manage very large data sets and storage facilities.[9] What we're talking about is taking the volumes of shared experiences, available data, and public information shared by desirable consumers to glean insights, interpret the trends, and identify the opportunities that contribute to innovation, productivity, and a new era of consumer relevance that directly translate to competitive advantages.

MGI and McKinsey's Business Technology Office published a report in May 2011, "Big Data: The Next Frontier for Innovation, Competition, and Productivity."[10] According to the report, the amount of published data "has been exploding and analyzing large data sets—so-called big data—will become a key basis of competition, underpinning new waves of productivity growth."

The report studied big data in five domains—health care in the United States, the public sector in Europe, retail in the United States, and manufacturing and personal location data globally. Following are seven key insights in the report:

1. Data is an important factor of production, alongside labor and capital.

2. There are five broad ways in which using big data can create value. First, big data can unlock significant value by making information transparent and usable at much higher frequency. Second, organizations can collect more accurate and detailed performance information to expose variability and boost performance. Leading companies are using data collection and analysis to conduct controlled experiments to make better management decisions. Other businesses use data for basic low-frequency forecasting to high-frequency nowcasting to adjust business levers just in time. Third, big data allows narrower segmentation of customer nicheworks and enable or deliver precisely tailored products or services. Fourth, sophisticated analytics can substantially improve decision making. Fifth, big data can be used to improve the development of the next generation of products and services.

3. The use of big data will become a key basis of competition and growth for individual firms. In most industries, established competitors and new entrants alike will leverage data-driven strategies to innovate, compete, and capture value from deep and up to real-time information.

4. The use of big data will underpin new waves of productivity growth and consumer surplus. For example, we estimate that a retailer using big data to the full has the potential to increase its operating margin by more than 60 percent. Big data offers considerable benefits to consumers as well as to companies and organizations. For instance, services enabled by personal location data can allow consumers to capture $600 billion in economic surplus.

5. While the use of big data will matter across sectors, some sectors are set for greater gains. We compared the historical productivity of sectors in the United States with the potential of these sectors to capture value from big data (using an index that combines several quantitative metrics), and found that the opportunities and challenges vary from sector to sector. The

computer and electronic products and information sectors, as well as finance and insurance, and government, are poised to gain substantially from the use of big data.

6. There will be a shortage of talent necessary for organizations to take advantage of big data.

7. Several issues will have to be addressed to capture the full potential of big data. Policies related to privacy, security, intellectual property, and even liability will need to be addressed in a big data world. Organizations need to not only put the right talent and technology in place, but also structure workflows and incentives to optimize the use of big data. Access to data is critical—companies will increasingly need to integrate information from multiple data sources, often from third parties, and the incentives have to be in place to enable this.

Social media, new and mobile media, the Internet of things, and data are gold mines of insight that give brands the potential to improve business efficiencies, innovation, relevance, and, more importantly, deliver improved customer experiences. What we're talking about here is the ability to personalize experiences that go beyond demographics and start to employ psychographics and behavior graphics—the ability to connect with groups of people by interest and how they interact based on what's important to them.

As this practice develops, brands can also gather the intelligence necessary, and widely available, to improve products, processes, and productivity. Doing so builds not only an adaptive business, but a sustainable business, while improving relationships to convert customers into stakeholders.

Centers of Attention

➤ There is no market for conformity today.

➤ Connected customers expect better products and services.

➤ Not listening or adapting is a risk you take at your own peril.

➤ The connected customer is not a cog in the operationalized business machine.

➤ Connected customers scream individuality to the point that entire market and customer segments rise, hoping for recognition and engagement.

➤ Businesses must build diversification into processes to appeal to the flavors of customers populating traditional, online, and social channels.

➤ The roles of the social consumer require different aspects of recognition and engagement and will eventually demand the complete *socialization* of your business.

➤ Human intelligence is available that gives you insight into your customers beyond demographics and hunches and it requires study in the last mile of engagement.

➤ Big Data is a big opportunity.

The Last Mile: The Future of Business Is Defined through Shared Experiences

Simple in nature, but complex in reality, the design of customer experiences is an important role in sharing. Meaningful design is created with intent, personalization, and useful incentives—all which form the essence of triggered sharing.

By visualizing the connected customers we want to reach, we gain a heightened level of understanding and awareness. The adaptive business approaches the market and market segments through the lens of connected customers to address their needs while acknowledging the various roles they play in the decision-making process. The adaptive business maintains dedicated two-way channels that connect outside activity internally to listen, learn, and adapt. The adaptive business earns relevance by then connecting with customers and those who influence them based on this intelligence directly through contact and indirectly through products, services, and processes. This is how a business becomes one with the customers defining new market opportunities.

The emergence of these new media touchpoints creates new opportunities for engagement. But engagement in the human network requires a new outlook, a new approach, and a new model for conveying empathy and leadership and creating *magical* and shareable experiences. We've come far enough in our journey to where the heart of what's next for business is implied implicitly: The business must emanate heart and soul for a brand to create a presence in the human network. And at the heart and soul of that business, a culture must take shape, for it is the culture that lures affinity. It is then the ensuing experiences that foster loyalty and allegiance.

In this chapter, we review the customer-centric approach of two celebrated brands that have captured the attention of connected customers and built thriving communities around them. For Apple and Virgin America, the common threads are an undeniable focus on the customer experience and the infrastructure to support it at every level.

■ THE APPLE OF MY EYE: DESIGNING MAGICAL (AND SHAREABLE) EXPERIENCES

Apple is a company that is unique unto itself. To say that its success is a formula would be a great injustice to the brilliance of the Apple brand. But you don't have to be Steve Jobs to recognize the importance of empowering customers through creative marketing, innovative product development, and the creation of what it calls magical experiences at almost every touchpoint.

When compared to the electronics industry at large, Apple has long been the underdog. But over the years, consumer electronics, gadgets, mobile phones, and computers migrated toward becoming commodities as margins eroded and features were mostly comparable. Even in the face of tablets, a brand new market opportunity, competitors took the same route as they do with every other form of digital device: focusing on creating products that are immediately commoditized rather than delivering unique, meaningful, and shareable experiences.

As competitors in each industry continued to leapfrog the status quo with every new product release and update, Apple instead focused on innovation and experiences, placing the special recipient of its work front and center, the alpha customer who doesn't follow drones to consumer conformity, but instead "thinks different." And thus, everything is designed around creative, enriching experiences that capture the heart, mind, and soul of its desired customers. Apple creates products that become an extension of our personas. Striving for average is a settlement that ultimately prohibits ingenuity. Think different. Think about the possibilities. Then, bring them to life.

For the purpose of this discussion, I will only highlight the aspects of what Apple does around its culture and the experiences it creates for its customers before, during, and after the sale. For the fourth straight year and probably a fifth as you're reading this, Apple topped *Fortune*'s Most Admired list.[1]

Starting with Apple.com, the company's website is consistently regarded as a beacon for design inspiration. It immerses the visitor in an architected experience: clean, elegant, stylish, and innovative. (See Figure 16.1.) It invites you to aspire to this digital

Figure 16.1   Elegance in Simplicity: The iPad 2 Page on Apple's Website

lifestyle. But it's also incredibly functional in its simplicity. Everything neatly arranged to tell a story, it's clear that Apple.com is created as the brand essence and voice of Apple. In brevity there's clarity, and such is true for Apple's narrative. The company's storytelling appeals to its customers and extends beyond the website to evoke a digital lifestyle. And that's the difference. Apple is selling innovation, yes, but one can argue that the brand is also selling a lifestyle. The products become extensions of an individual's personality and hence, we're now a global nation of earbudsmen.

Apple continues to connect with its customers by bringing the company's brand essence to life in the retail environment.

At the iPad 2 launch event in San Francisco in March 2011, Steve Jobs discussed the importance of the company's retail stores in the success of the iPad 2, "One of the things that enabled us to roll out this technology so fast was our Apple retail stores. They were built for moments like this. They were built to take new technology, to roll it out, and educate customers about it, and be there when they have questions and issues. And without these stores, I don't think we would have been as successful, either."[2]

Indeed. Walking into any Apple retail store is to technology enthusiasts what Disneyland is to children. The stores are as functional in design as they are refined. Need information? An Apple representative is within reach, but not hovering over your every step. Need to pay? An Apple representative will bring the cash register to you.

Have a problem? Make an appointment and an Apple Genius will spend one-on-one time with you to ensure that the customer product experience is exceptional. Brilliant!

The experience continues to unfold after the purchase. Every aspect—from the product packaging to the unpacking—is almost magical. Customers take pictures of every step of the boxbreak to savor the moment. The connected customer shares every moment of this purchase through pictures on Twitter or video on YouTube throughout the entire ownership lifetime. Again, brilliant!

Apple isn't selling products as much as they are experiences. This is an important distinction, as it seems they leave the features game to everyone else. In that light, let's return to the iPad 2 launch. From a feature perspective, the iPad 2 certainly eclipses its first-generation predecessor. But, rather than focus on these features throughout the launch event, Apple instead showcased how the original iPad "changed the world."

The iPad was portrayed as a magical device that helped people see and navigate their worlds their way. The first quarter of the event showcased magical moments in which people used the iPad in wonderful, personal ways.

Gazing into the stars.

DJing an event.

Reviewing patient records.

Sharing visual progress with patients.

Helping students learn.

Encouraging co-workers to collaborate more effectively.

Working with autistic children.

The audience was shown magical moment after magical moment of people whose lives were touched and changed because of the iPad.

To close the event, Steve Jobs set the stage for the adaptive business, for the business leader, and for you, "This is worth repeating. It's in Apple's DNA that technology is not enough. It's tech married with the liberal arts and the humanities. Nowhere is that more true than in the post-PC products. Our competitors are looking at this like it's the next PC market. That is not the right approach to this. These are post-PC devices that need to be easier to use than a PC, more intuitive."[3] (See Figure 16.2.)

What is your company doing to shape experiences and create shareable moments?

Figure 16.2   At the Intersection of Technology and Liberal Arts: Steve Jobs at the Launch of the iPad 2

■ THE LAWS OF ENGAGEMENT

With the ability to connect to the connected through myriad social touchpoints, businesses will lead transformation from within, from the top down, the bottom up, and inside out. Activating touchpoints requires engagement—the intersection at which customers and businesses encounter one another. At that moment, experiences unfold and impressions are shaped, only to be taken away as a memento of the interaction. That impression is yours to define, at every step, through every touchpoint, now and time again. The adaptive business reengineers or creates new customer-facing roles to manage these touchpoints and shape productive and memorable experiences. The idea of new engagement, however, is somewhat elusive in the province of connected customers. One of the challenges around the word *engagement* and helping businesses understand its promise is its definition.

Is engagement simply defined as a conversation, a comment, or @ reply?

Is it an email or phone call to offer resolution or direction to a customer in need?

Is engagement viewed as a conversion from a state of consideration to one of action?

Does engagement occur before, during, or after the sale?

Does it take a human touch or could that touch come alive in the form of content?

Is it a coupon or a trigger during the shopping experience?

Can the consumer walk away with a tangible or intangible form of recognized value?

Finally, is engagement an act of acknowledgment in ways to improve products and services?

The answer is yes. It's all of it. The resulting impressions that develop through each interaction are created with or without you when each touchpoint emerges. This is our opportunity.

In researching this chapter, I attempted to find a working definition of engagement. While there were many definitions of engagement, none really seemed to capture the crux of its significance nor represent its true potential in the last mile of the adaptive business. I therefore assembled the best pieces and principles to draft a definition of engagement for our purposes here.

Engagement starts with the recognition of existing and emerging touchpoints surfaced by traditional, online, and connected customers. It is defined by how a brand and customer connect and interact within their networks and channels of relevance. Engagement then creates an experience that is internalized, weighted, and in turn shared. It is measured by the takeaway value, sentiment, and resulting actions following the exchange. The combination of these elements reveals the potential for generating customer impressions and customer value.

Engagement unlocks touchpoints that inherently carry network effects and as such, presents brands with opportunities to shape and steer experiences to earn relevance and influence the decisions of connected customers. And through sustained engagement, businesses can increase sales, reduce churn, and most importantly, transform connected customers into connected advocates, united and motivated by exceptional brand engagement and product experiences.

The mission of an adaptive business in any engagement is to address the needs of the customer. But that's just the beginning. While customer needs tell us the what, we also need to explore the how and why. This is why social science becomes paramount to the adaptive business. New media landscapes and the communities in which connected customers dwell resemble real-world society in which behavior, culture, structure, and customs reveal the elements that facilitate connections in the last mile of business. Anthropology, sociology, and ethnography add a human layer to business intelligence that actually humanizes products, stories, services, and ultimately the processes that accelerate business relevance among the connected. By understanding their needs, behavior, desires, and culture, businesses can explore ways to activate the 4 A's of social consumerism. This is the switch that activates the human network to trigger the powerful social effect inherent among those who have audiences with audiences. The 4 A's transform customers into influencers and advocates. And it is through intelligent, genuine, and value-added engagement that brands can shape experiences, trigger action, create stakeholders, and inspire trust. (See Figure 16.3.)

1. Action
2. Advisory
3. Affinity
4. Advocacy

Touchpoints are present throughout the various stages of the decision-making process, and continue well after purchase. But connected customers pick their channels of relevance; they won't be pulled toward artificial touchpoints. The adaptive business will need to invest in these new channels to open opportunities for

Figure 16.3 The 4 A's of Social Consumerism

engagement. Doing so also serves as an investment in defining customer experiences and increasing customer lifetime value as well as sparking brand awareness and brand lift. The channel is ancillary to the relationship need, however, and all facets of engagement require a customer perspective to enliven the 4 A's.

■ LIKE A VIRGIN: TREATING CUSTOMERS LIKE THEY WERE TOUCHED FOR THE VERY FIRST TIME

Like Apple, Virgin America is a model citizen in the small but important world of businesses that design company products and services to steer customer experiences. Razorfish, one of the largest global interactive marketing and technology agencies, studied how Virgin America engages customers in a groundbreaking study, "Liminal: A Razorfish Analysis of Customer Engagement in Transition."[4] The report was designed to surface the answers for any brand seeking new customer insights.

The Razorfish Liminal report is revealing in so many ways. Most notably, it took a customer perspective in its approach to defining engagement. It also studied Virgin America's approach to engaging the connected customer and shared its findings.[5]

As Razorfish noted, Virgin America is a brand built around customer loyalty. In the report, Virgin America's vice president of marketing, Porter Gale, shared why: "We felt early on our customers were likely to use social channels, and the following we have gotten confirmed this. However, we realized we didn't know nearly as much as we wanted about what our customers wanted to get from us in these places. And, we didn't know what the value of our more social customers was. Especially when one takes into account the ever-expanding roster of channels, we needed to look beyond our customers' self-reported insights and beyond our customer base, to get a full picture of how we might better engage with our customers."

To find these answers, Razorfish and Loyalty Lab drew from a survey of 5,600 Virgin America customers. The team also sourced anonymous social data from 100,000 Internet users, existing information from Virgin America on its customers' engagement and lifetime value, self-reported attitudes and preferences, and independently tracked behavior.

In the Liminal report, Razorfish identified the six most important needs consumers possess when they reach out to a brand: feeling valued, trust, efficiency, consistency, relevance, and control, with the first three rating the highest in regard to importance. These elements of

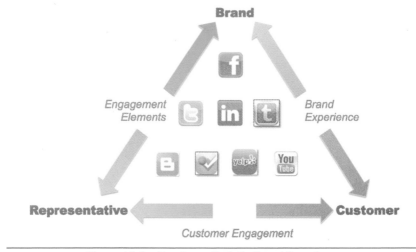

Figure 16.4   Creating a Holistic Brand Experience

engagement (or as Razorfish calls them, *engagement elements*) are the attributes of successful connections in the last mile. These elements require attention and design first and foremost to enrich customer interactions. Possessing these elements, and not merely having a presence, is paramount to steering meaningful customer engagement.

In my last book, *Engage!*, I introduced the importance of identifying consumers' needs within their channels of relevance before attempting engagement. But engagement is just the entry point. The entire experience that follows is as important as the engagement itself. (See Figure 16.4.)

The challenge to businesses, however, is that these engagement strategies require design if each of these encounters are to foster positive experiences. Without this, businesses are, in fact, diluting their brand, leaving customers feeling disconnected, unsatisfied, or confused. Everything begins with a shift in perspective from viewing stakeholders as a separate entity, "us versus them," to a singular view of "us," as this enlivens a new era of community-focused marketing and engagement.

Studying the needs of our customers and identifying the best ways to deliver through six elements of engagement will help businesses connect with connected customers.

Valued: In the Liminal report, consumers cited "feeling valued" as the most important element of brand engagement. Connected customers expect companies to go out of their way to support their needs and value their business. This is in direct contrast to how most businesses view customer engagement today. Businesses are designed to make the customer come to them and jump through hoops to get information, satisfaction, or resolution. For Virgin America, almost every step of the experience is designed around communicating customer value and appreciation. It starts with the flattering messages on its website and in all of its marketing materials. It continues when arriving at the ticket counter at the airport. You recognize immediately that there's something special here...the red carpet, slick music, stylish furniture, prevalent smiles, and the sincere desire to help. Customers know they're in for a treat. Once the customer boards the aircraft, the experience continues. Cabins are lit with a low-level of purple ambiance combined with fashionable beats. Passengers are then greeted by attendants who are as pleasant as they are stylish. Customers can't help but feel accepted.

Efficiency: Second, customers expect efficiency and quick, decisive actions in each engagement. If a company can demonstrate that it respects customers' time and energy by promptly addressing their needs, it will earn their appreciation and support. With Virgin America, efficiency is incorporated into multiple steps of the customer cycle. The website is designed to expedite the delivery of information and the process of purchasing tickets. Before leaving home, customers can check in online to upgrade, change seats, and print tickets. At the airport, customers are greeted by glossy white kiosks to make travel changes or print out boarding cards.

Trust: Customers need to feel that the companies that they do business with can be trusted. Trust is earned as a measure of a culmination of business actions and experiences. Credibility is at the heart of the matter and through honest, transparent, sincere, and authentic engagement, businesses earn a critical differentiator and value-add in the market, believability. Over time, I've come to trust Virgin America. Through every interaction, at every step, the company has communicated with me as defined in this paragraph. But more importantly, I feel appreciated in my experiences and also in my interactions with company representatives in my channels of relevance.

Consistency: As I trust Virgin America through the reinforcement of experiences and interactions, the fabric of my relationship with the company is woven in consistency. Communication, sales, service, policy, attitude, and representative behavior are all uniform across every Virgin America experience. I've yet to have such consistent service with any other airline, which is why I am loyal to Virgin America, as well as a vocal advocate.

Relevance: A mantra that you'll hear time and time again throughout my work is the importance of relevance in engagement with the empowered customer. Again, this customer is at the center of their own egosystem. The connected customer is immune to generic attempts at engagement. If the information is personalized or material to their world, they'll pay attention. If it's designed to make them feel valued with a click to action integrated into the engagement, they just might take action. Relevance is the net a brand casts to lure customers into its culture and its story. Then, and only then, can we hope for advocacy.

Control: This is my favorite subject when discussing new consumerism, and it is the very thing that executives fear losing should they attempt engagement with the connected customer. The reality is that control was never theirs to lose, as they held only the reins to the semblance of it. Engaging, however, allows businesses to become part of the process and thus, take some control in shaping and steering the experiences of their customers. Also, customers enjoy the empowerment of control within the dynamics of business and customer relationships. To them, it was the least important, but still important element that they shared in the Liminal study. In the egosystem, the connected customer is in control of the relationships that they weave and how and when information and people (and businesses) swim into their social streams. To this genre of discerning customers, control is a switch they turn on and off when they decide to initiate engagement or are open to contact. But control is also a way for a brand to empower customers to become advocates. By putting them at the center of the experience, customers feel appreciated and as such, are appreciative in return. For example, one of Virgin America's key value propositions is its in-flight entertainment network, Red. Red is one of the first truly on-demand systems deployed by any airline with which the customer can watch movies, videos, shows, talk to other passengers, play games, order food and drink, make playlists and listen to the music they want. Combine this with the in-flight Wi-Fi, and passengers feel compelled to tweet, update their Facebook status, and email friends to share the Virgin America experience.

The results of this research demonstrates a series of processes that every business will endure, studying the roles, needs, and connection points for connected customers. It only helps to get to know these customers, as doing so will inspire the shift from static business models to a more adaptive framework. The Liminal report introduces us to four customer engagement types. Let's get to know them a little better.

➤ Engagement Type 1: Socially Savvy

As Razorfish discovered, the value of the socially savvy is incredible. They are frequent flyers on Virgin America and thereby have high lifetime value (LTV). They are likely to be Elevate members (Virgin

America's loyalty program) and have the highest consumer influence score. They also use the Internet more than any other engagement type and rank second in mobile users. Introducing demographics into the mix, the group is well-educated and earns a high income. More importantly, however, they are incredibly influential in social networks. Engaging this socially savvy individual is key, as positive engagement and experiences are likely to trigger influential activity. As one customer shared in the interview process, "I look forward to a long flight."

> *Excerpt: The Socially Savvy need an optimized digital experience if Virgin America is to keep a long-term lock on them. As they demonstrate a strong propensity to influence, Virgin America will also need to tap into their social media behavior, by making it easy for them to share their experience with their extended network.*

> ➤ **Engagement Type 2: Traditionally Engaged**

Business is undergoing a metamorphosis driven by the state of an evolving customer landscape. With three customer segments, connected, online, and traditional, Razorfish distinguished the nuances between them, learning that (traditional) online customers required a different approach. They have high lifetime value and are therefore important when defining an engagement strategy, but they are not interested in social media and have a limited amount of time for engagement. "I only have so many hours in the day," quipped one customer during the survey.

This group, however, is loyal, representing the largest percentage of Elevate members. Interestingly, they use the most mobile apps and are also most likely to open emails from Virgin America.

> *Excerpt: The Traditionally Engaged may not be social, but they are certainly worth retaining. There are two ways to do this: by optimizing some older touchpoints, like email, and focusing more on mobile.*

> ➤ **Engagement Type 3: Up-and-Comers**

Representing a customer in transition between traditional, online, and connected, this group is inching closer to mobile and social media engagement. They're avid texters and are active online for recreation and networking. Of all the social networks, they are flocking to Facebook in droves. Their loyalty is Virgin America's for the taking, which was brought to light by one such customer, "I'm loyal if I have a good, personalized experience."

The onus is on the airline to deliver on the brand promise and bring to life meaningful and shareable experiences. No amount of engagement is going to engender loyalty without building a business around high-touch experiences.

> *Excerpt: While their income does not allow them to be frequent flyers on Virgin America, The Up-and-Comers can be very vocal about their experiences. This potential emerging customer has the ability to influence others in his or her network and should not be neglected. By ensuring positive experiences, future relationships with them will be secured.*

➤ **Engagement Type 4: Conventionalists**

In the exploration of the three types of customers during this market in transition, this group squarely hits the traditional customer or, as Razorfish categorizes them, conventionalists. They are not the most technical of the bunch and in the grand scheme of demographics, their education and income are among the lowest of the group. The more traditional customer desires personal interaction, but obviously not through social or mobile channels. For them, the phone or face to face is what it takes to satisfy their needs. By combining the factors discussed earlier, conventionalists are ranked with a lower lifetime value.

> *Excerpt: Since The Conventionalists are not technologically sophisticated, and desire a personal connection, Virgin America will have to focus on efficiency to drive the bottom line if it's to cater to this audience. The question becomes whether this investment will be worth it, as some of this Engagement Type will have the potential to get closer to center stage by becoming Traditional Engagers as their travel profile changes.*

■ **DISTRIBUTION OF ENGAGEMENT RESOURCES AND STRATEGIES**

Identifying the varying roles and engagement types of Virgin America's customers encourages personalized engagement strategies. It also reveals to what extent the company will need to focus resources to nurture relationships and improve customer lifetime value. Much like the Starbucks report shared earlier in the book, getting to know customers is the only way to deliver on the elements of engagement:

➤ Feeling valued
➤ Efficiency
➤ Trust
➤ Consistency
➤ Relevance
➤ Control

As such, research must fuel consumer-driven engagement through the collection of:

➤ Consumer data
➤ Social data
➤ Behavioral data

With the existence of multiple types of customers, it takes a personal touch to motivate each group uniquely. These groups connect through different channels across the board. Some expect engagement directly, while others don't want it at all. This is the new reality of business, and companies need to invest in data and intelligence to reveal the opportunities. As Razorfish explains, varying levels of focus, investment, and approach are required for Virgin America to meet the needs of their diverse customers, increase their value as customers, and tap into their influence and reach to grow the customer base. (See Figure 16.5.)

Socially Savvy: These are Virgin America's most valuable customers because they are both willing to buy and reach out to others. The engagement strategy will need to satisfy both needs. Channels that meet their engagement priorities—accompanied with ways to share that experience—will help their LTV [long-term value] and influence feed off one another. For this group, Virgin America could stress both email and major social platforms such as Facebook and Twitter; it can optimize email by making sure the content meets this group's needs, and also make that content easily shareable, therefore taking advantage of the The Socially Savvys' LTV and eLTV [electronic long-term value].

Traditionally Engaged: These customers, while not as high value as The Socially Savvy, deserve a more focused engagement strategy of their own—particularly because of their heavy mobile usage.

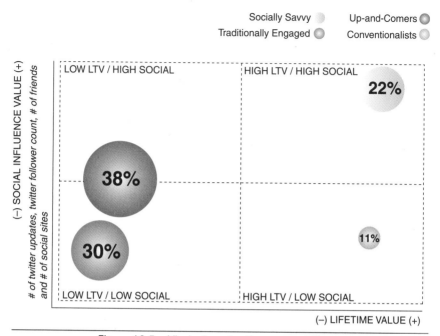

Figure 16.5   Virgin America Engagement Types

Since Virgin America isn't currently very active in the channel, it should consider building mobile touchpoints that fit the group's engagement priorities. Especially in mobile, airlines have a major opportunity to bring consumers utility; in Virgin America's case, this is a channel it can no longer overlook.

Up-and-Comers: The customers that are part of this Engagement Type are neither as social as The Socially Savvy nor as heavy on mobile use as The Traditionally Engaged, and their income doesn't allow them to travel as much as either of those two groups. However, what makes them stand out is their potential—they could be The Socially Savvy and Traditionally Engaged of the future. Because they are transitioning into heavier social and mobile use, some of the same touchpoint refinement that Virgin America could undertake for the preceding two groups might also work for them. Building out the current Virgin America Facebook page—which is primarily a fan site—would also be a smart move, given The Up-and-Comers' heavy presence on that social platform. And, Facebook would be a low-cost channel making it an easy place for Virgin America to experiment. One thing to remember about The Up-and-Comers: despite their relatively low value, they should be treated with special consideration because they have few experiences with the brand, and each experience will play a big part in their perception, positive or negative.

Conventionalists: This group presents a challenge, because of their low social influence and interest in personal interaction instead of more cost-effective digital platforms. While they may adapt to some of the newer touchpoints, the best fit for them might lie in the future, when technology is more able to emulate the personal touch they desire.

Engagement is key to creating meaningful and shareable experiences. But to stay relevant, businesses must continuously evaluate how every engagement point and strategy contributes to the top line and bottom line. In addition to engagement strategies, adaptive businesses must also examine the performance of the channels in play and those on the horizon.

■ A MARKET IN TRANSITION BEGETS A BUSINESS IN MOTION

The Razorfish Liminal report injects a dose of reality into today's business if they indeed desire to compete for tomorrow. We are not just competing for the moment; we are competing for the future through earned relevance. Markets are indeed in transition and therefore require a more agile business, a business that can learn, react, and adapt to the needs of distinct customer groups.

Knowing this, designing and delivering value is now your mission. But businesses also need to put their money where their engagement is by investing capital in the development of engagement protocol externally and internally. This and only this, allows business to effectively bridge the existing gaps to connect in the last mile. Meaningful engagement contributes to the long-term customer lifetime value. The net result is increased top-line sales and bottom-line results. It comes down to meeting needs, delivering value, and shaping experiences. If brand experiences serve as a form of self-expression, then let's give customers something to talk about.

Centers of Attention

➤ Businesses must design products and services that create meaningful and shareable experiences.

➤ The adaptive business will weave customers into its culture, development, process, and story.

➤ Customer-driven engagement is the key to relevance.

➤ To ensure that a customer will not only connect with a business, but do so over time, potentially in multiple channels, businesses must answer several questions before attempting to engage the connected customers.

➤ Where are customers connecting and sharing experiences?

➤ Understand that engagement strategies will differ based on the nature and culture of each channel and how customers are interacting with one another.

➤ Why are customers engaging or attempting to engage with businesses, especially your business?

➤ What touchpoints emerge and how are they prioritized?

➤ What do customers expect from engagement?

➤ How can the engagement experience improve now and over time?

➤ What investment is necessary to effectively engage?

➤ How will you measure customer satisfaction and also the all-important quandary of return on investment?

➤ Design effective engagement programs to spark the 4 A's of connected customers.

Chapter 17

The Culture Code: When Culture and Social Responsibility Become Market Differentiators

There's an old saying in business that seems to have found a new audience in today's networked economy: "People do business with people they like."

Customer-centricity, or getting closer to customers, is often the focus of many executive meetings I attend these days. The question always arises, "How can we use new media to get closer to customers?" The answer is, change. Any organization that focuses on operations, margins, and efficiencies over customer experiences will hasten the erosion of market relevance. It's difficult to see the customer or empathize with him if you're focused on a spreadsheet. It's impossible to change if you can't see what it is they value.

While we talk of humanizing our brand and our business or becoming a more consumer-facing brand, the reality is that we are merely at the beginning of an important shift in business philosophy. Customer-centricity begins with internal transformation and the willingness to adapt or create processes and programs that break down internal silos. It's not just about communicating with customers; it's about showing them that listening translates into action within the organization to create better products and services and also foster valuable brand experiences and ultimately relationships with customers. It's also about empowering employees to improve those experiences and relationships in the front line and to recognize and reward their ability to contribute to a new era of customer engagement and collaboration. They have to care, not just because they're human, but because it's part of the corporate culture . . . and a recognized contribution at that.

Innovation and collaboration is an outside-in and an inside-out process. It is living. The activity we tap into in networks inhabited

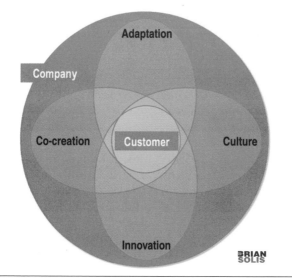

Figure 17.1   Customer-Centricity Starts with a Culture of Change

by connected customers forces a groundswell that inspires top-down transformation from the bottom-up.

Customer-centricity begins with creating a culture of change (see Figure 17.1). It starts with leadership and is brought to life through employees, their vigor, and the products and experiences they develop, support, and improve. A culture of change is built upon four pillars that are essential in building bridges to customers and promoting internal transformation:

1. Adaptation
2. Innovation
3. Co-creation
4. Culture

This is just the beginning of how we create a more customer-centric organization and how disruptive technology, new media, and consumer insights drive meaningful engagement and constant learning to foster change and earn relevance.

The roles of new consumerism demand that business units collaborate in a united effort around engagement and adaptation. As a result, the silos that dominate the infrastructure of businesses are not conducive to reaching the very customers who are forcing this market transition. Therefore, adaptive businesses, for the foreseeable future, must remain in motion.

It's up to you to change your business by investing in the relationships that yield insight and impact. It's also up to you to help your business earn affinity, loyalty, and advocacy through ongoing relevance. This all requires learning and adaptation. But most importantly, it takes a supporting culture to recognize the importance of the connected customer and a management infrastructure that supports the change necessary to adapt.

The days when great companies, products, and services organically connected with their markets are numbered. In this highly competitive attention economy, businesses must purposefully connect with connected customers and deliver exceptional experiences. It takes a leader and culture of engagement to navigate this market in transition.

An adaptive business, at a minimum, is a customer-centric organization that invests in a data and support structure that is plugged into traditional and emerging touchpoints. Also, the adaptive business invests in a fully engaged enterprise in which a philosophy of customer-centricity connects all departments. Doing so creates a collaborative infrastructure in which insights are shared and customer touchpoints are distributed, managed, engaged, and productive.

Culture may exist naturally, but not unlike the mission statement, the mission of the brand should be refreshed in light of the connected customer and customers overall. Culture and its perception in the market is a differentiator. As such, customer-centricity is now a competitive advantage. It requires definition, architecture, and a top-down infrastructure that supports adaptation and collaboration every step of the way.

■ THE ZAPPOS STORY: THE CUSTOMER SERVICE SHOE IS NOW ON THE OTHER FOOT

Delivering happiness and creating culture are large parts of Zappos's ingredients to success and customer adoration. Building a loyal following of emphatic customer loyalty and advocacy doesn't just happen, it comes as a result of design and delivery. Around the time that I interviewed Jack Dorsey for *Entrepreneur* magazine, I also spent some time with Zappos CEO Tony Hsieh to discuss the importance of change and culture and how revisiting it often can help lead the company in rewarding directions.[1]

To call Zappos an online shoe store takes away from the brilliance behind the 13-year-old e-commerce powerhouse. While its original premise was based on helping people find the shoes they want in one place, online, and discounted, the company certainly evolved into something nothing short of disruptive. As we hear so often with technology startups, Zappos was born in a college dorm room.

Already a success by any startup standards in just a few short years, Tony Hsieh looked at the $32 million his company generated in 2002 and challenged his team to do better.

Roughly four years into the game, Tony decided it was time to look beyond shoes and move his company toward a more significant mission. His epiphany was the result of learning through research that companies serving customers with a higher purpose outperformed those that focused on market leadership and profitability in the long run.

■ ZAPPOS: PUTTING THE CUSTOMER IN CUSTOMER SERVICE

In 2003, the Zappos brand evolved from an online shoe e-tailer toward a customer-centric organization powered by service. Everything started with looking at the pains customers were experiencing and the options they faced when making purchase decisions. One of the biggest sore spots for customers was something that was out of the company's realm of control, a significant number of customer complaints stemmed from issues with shipping. Zappos at the time relied on drop shipping, a means of selling products that the e-tailer doesn't actually stock. The manufacturer or a distributer fulfills the order directly. While drop shipping equaled 25 percent of the annual revenue at the time, it was also the very thing that prevented the company from keeping its promise of delivering exceptional customer service. If the company were to become truly customer-focused, it would need to take control of the entire experience, from beginning to end. As a result, Zappos did away with drop shipping and moved everything it stocked into its warehouse. After taking control of its inventory, Zappos's new customer service program resembled that of industry retail giant Nordstrom, for which the customer experience is paramount. Leaders for both companies will say that doing so directly correlates service to loyalty, repeat business, word of mouth, and increased revenues.

"If you're looking for a pair of shoes, and we're out of your size, we made it part of our policy to refer them to a competitor that had it in stock," said Tony.

Almost immediately, the team noticed a difference. Customers weren't the only people singing Zappos's praises. Employees were more engaged and passionate. The new focus gave them something they could stand behind. Customers could hear the passion of the person on the other end of the phone. They cared. And vendors noticed too. Suddenly their onsite visits increased in frequency and length to see what the new Zappos was all about.

Focusing on customer service caused a snowball effect that helped Zappos soar to new heights. At the end of 2003, Zappos nearly doubled its revenues to $70 million. In 2004, the company earned $184 million.

■ ZAPPOS: THE CULTURE OF CUSTOMER ADVOCACY

Business leaders, especially innovators, are continually looking at what's working, but more importantly, what's possible. By the close of 2004, the Zappos team believed that focusing on customers and their experiences had not only boosted revenues by 600 percent, it also created a global community of enthusiasts and advocates behind the Zappos brand. In 2005, the team was set for its biggest transformation yet.

Tony Hsieh says, "We never really paid much attention to what other companies were doing. We never knew that the decisions we made were in direct contrast to those of our competitors."

Tony believed that if making customers happy would help improve business, then focusing on company culture was a natural progression. Making company culture the number one priority resulted in the creation of a pipeline team, a group of trained professionals who host more than 40 classes to help improve morale and career development. Courses ranged from career and interdepartmental training to Zappos history, and personal development programs such as strength finders, the science of happiness, and optimism. In 2005, early Zappos investor and professional life coach Dr. Vic moved into the Zappos headquarters. He offered onsite coaching to employees looking for empowerment and direction and as a result, employees continued to evolve from a role driven by passion to one of company stakeholder. The evidence of success was in the sales. The year 2005 hit a new high with $370 million in sales and in 2006, they reached almost $600 million. With a customer- and employee-focused organization, the company managed to hit $1 billion in 2008.

■ ZAPPOS: DELIVERING HAPPINESS

In 2009, Zappos sought to reinvent Zappos once again, this time by focusing on employees, customers, and other companies through one powerful, yet uncommon business term ... happiness.

Tony Hsieh said then, "Customer service is about making customers happy, company culture is about making employees happy, so let's just simplify it and at the same time, amplify our vision for our customers, employees, vendors, and peers."

Following the success of investing in company culture and customer service, Tony was introduced to positive psychology. So the team took a step back and looked at the science of happiness to help them develop the company's next growth strategy, delivering happiness to the world.

It started within.

Zappos management introduced elements of progress into its career advancement program to help employees stay happy consistently. Rather than give big promotions every 18 months to deserving employees, management introduced incremental advancement every six months.

Zappos also formalized the definition of culture into 10 core values:

1. Deliver *wow* through service
2. Embrace and drive change
3. Create fun and a little weirdness
4. Be adventurous, creative, and open-minded
5. Pursue growth and learning
6. Build open and honest relationships with communication
7. Build a positive team and family spirit
8. Do more with less
9. Be passionate and determined
10. Be humble

Following in the footsteps of the Walt Disney Company, Zappos looked externally to find ways to share its experience with culture and service to help others reinvent their businesses. As a result, Zappos introduced its Insights program, a series of immersion workshops designed to bring other businesses into the world of Zappos.

Tony deeply believes openness and transparency are the pillars for a successful business and the corresponding culture they create. But he wasn't content with keeping these philosophies within the walls of Zappos. He created a university program for other businesses to learn the Zappos way. Zappos Insights (ZI) was then created to invite other businesses to a series of workshops that shared exactly how the

Zappos family does business. It provided attendees with the tools and methodologies needed to develop the culture they desired.

By exposing its company secrets around happiness, culture, and service, Zappos could teach other organizations how to improve relations with customers and employees.

To date, the Insights program has helped many businesses, many of which report that learning the Zappos Way helped increase sales and morale almost immediately. Zappos didn't do too bad, either. It closed 2009 with $1.2 billion in revenue and was acquired by Amazon for $928 million in November of that year.

The deal with Amazon proved gratifying. Over the years, Amazon attempted to eclipse Zappos with Endless.com, but Tony credits Zappos's success to its unique championing of employees, customers, and happiness. Under Amazon, Zappos now runs as an independent brand, a brand that only continues to excel under the banner of happiness.

When you create an empowered workforce that is not only happy, but evangelical, placing them in front of social networks such as Facebook and Twitter ensures that the company's mission, purpose, and culture scales as social media become pervasive as next generation platforms for sales, marketing, and service. At current count, 436 Zappos employees use Twitter, including CEO Tony Hsieh, who has more than 1.7 million followers.

As Tony says, "Your culture is your brand. Customer service shouldn't just be a department, it should be the entire company."

■ THE NEW CEO: CHIEF EXPERIENCE OFFICER

In his book, *Delivering Happiness,* Tony Hsieh explains how an emphasis on corporate culture can lead to unprecedented success.[2] Most notably, he shares how to apply the science of happiness as a framework to increase collaboration and employee commitment, which nets in increased profits through passion and purpose. While Tony describes himself as a "chief happiness officer" (CHO), in the real world, proposing a title or role of this nature to your organization might be met with opposition if not outright disbelief.

To compete for the attention, business, and loyalty of the connected customer, a new type of CEO is needed, however. If the future of business is connected through shared experiences, those experiences require design and direction. In many ways, the essence of Tony's CHO role is focused not only on delivering happiness, but also designed experiences. Tony's role is representative of a new class of CEO, in which the *E* represents *experience.* I would also say the same thing about Apple's Steve Jobs, Best Buy's Brian Dunn, Dell's Michael Dell, Starbucks's Howard Schultz, and Virgin's Richard Branson. These individuals belong to an elite club of executives who are designing businesses to create unique customer experiences. It is these experiences that unite connected customers and increase the market for earned relevance. Their vision looks beyond the operation of the business. They strive to bring to life the future they see. The difference is that they don't overlook streamlined operations, increased profitability, improved morale, and continued growth. Instead, those become the metrics of customer-centricity. The new CEO invests in the culture of the organization, benchmarking performance against the opportunity, not the competition. By default, competing for the future succeeds competition while also focusing on a higher mission and purpose.

The culture code equals the path toward relevance in the future of business and new consumerism. The importance of revisiting the culture of the organization, however, is as much about what the outside world sees as it is about what the inside projects. Again, to collaborate externally, we must first collaborate internally. Like the mission statement, businesses must revisit the culture of the organization to unite the workforce around a common mission and a significant purpose. Leaders who choose not to recognize this opportunity to compete for relevance force us to question their leadership. Leadership is earned and its performance in the near future will be based equally on profits and growth along with the health and prognosis of the company's internal and external stakeholders. Employees and customers are increasingly becoming connected and without paving a foundation for experiences, what are they to share?

Leaders, too, must relearn everything they thought they knew about customers. Traditional management infrastructures taught in the most prestigious schools of business have yet to fully understand the impact of connected consumerism on business models. The adaptive business pivots on agility and can only evolve and succeed if the management infrastructure is designed to foster change.

Zappos is not alone in its mission to help businesses create magical experiences or inspire businesses to reimagine their corporate culture and mission. Twenty years ago, Disney responded to an increasing demand for behind-the-scenes tours with the creation of the Disney Institute, an experiential educational program to teach leaders the "Business Behind the Magic." Going back to the opening of Disneyland, admiring executives and entrepreneurs sought to learn the secrets behind Disney's eye-catching best practices and pioneering procedures in people management, team building, customer service, leadership, and customer loyalty.

Since debuting in 1986, The Disney Institute has hosted more than one million individuals from every industry worldwide. Bruce Jones, the Institute's programming director, shared one of the Institute's special attractions in an article published in TrainingIndustry.com, "Attendees come from many countries and industries, from companies of all sizes and from all levels within organizations. They are seeking knowledge and skills about Disney's proven business practices. A special attraction is Disney's ability to achieve consistency across a broad base of employees in the areas of HR practices, management philosophies, leadership development, customer loyalty, creativity and innovation."[3]

In its book, *Be Our Guest: Perfecting the Art of Customer Service,* the Disney Institute shares this pearl of wisdom, "Anything that does not support and enhance the Quality Service experience will, by definition, detract from it."

■ IN GOOD COMPANY: PHILANTHROPIC CAPITALISM AND THE NEW ERA OF CORPORATE SOCIAL RESPONSIBILITY

Bill Gates and Warren Buffett, two of the world's richest billionaires, shared the stage at the New York Public Library with one mission, to urge the world's richest families to pledge at least half their fortunes to charity. By August 2010, the "Giving Pledge" movement was promised a collective sum of $125 billion to charitable causes.[4]

This act was regarded as the seminal movement for what we now recognize as philanthropic capitalism—the merger of philanthropy and capitalism. This historic event changed the world and set the stage for a new era of socially responsible business.

Matthew Bishop, co-author of *Philanthrocapitalism: How Giving Can Save the World*[5] and U.S. business editor and New York bureau chief of *The Economist,* marked the occasion as the beginning of a global phenomenon: "That struck me as a genuinely unique moment in history, and a moment which needed to be understood. It raised many, many questions about the responsibilities of wealth, the opportunities that wealth gave, and about the future and nature of capitalism."[6]

In addition to acts of philanthropic capitalism, the business world was introduced to new socially conscious frameworks that blend non-profit and for-profit sectors as operation models. This important shift required that investors accept a decrease in financial returns while increasing a positive impact in driving economic and social change. Thus, humanistic capitalism creates a market in which businesses and customers work together to make the world a better place through everyday commerce.

To demonstrate the evolution of this market in transition, Bishop cited the example of Goldman Sachs in an interview with INSEAD Knowledge, "[The company] had a deep culture in philanthropy, but [it] is now fighting for its life because the investment bank has failed to understand how the public is demanding higher standards from business. It faces the danger of becoming a much diminished firm through government action and through their own customers leaving them."

Perhaps better known as corporate social responsibility (CSR), businesses, to varying levels, have long embraced the responsibility for their impact on society and the environment. For many businesses, CSR serves as a guideline for operating as a good corporate citizen. Others embed the importance of helping society and the environment in their foundation and ethical mission. But leaders who possess the gift of awareness realized long ago that CSR presents unique emotional channels through which companies can differentiate their products and services and help create shared value (CSV) by working with customers and stakeholders to make a difference through profitability.

CSR isn't a business strategy, but is instead a mission and promise. This isn't about employing CSR as a "have to" to show customers that your business actually cares about the community or important causes. Nor is this about the tax write-off. Good business is now about aligning the values of the organization with the values of connected customers to seed deeper relationships. As Willis Harman said in his pioneering paper "Humanistic Capitalism: Another Alternative," published in 1974, "Good business policy must become one with good social policy."[7]

The adaptive business is not just socially responsible, it is culturally significant. Aligning connected customers and stakeholders to inspire something greater than business is soon to become business as usual. Those that embrace this philosophy sooner than later will find themselves in good company.

■ GIVING BACK IS THE NEW . . . RED

If giving back is the new black, to Starbucks, it's the new red.

Starbucks is no stranger to the CSR or the need to create shared value. The company's business model is designed to help reinvest in the communities where it does business as well as reaching the most remote parts of the world where its coffee is sourced.

One such program is the active investments the company makes in the livelihood of African citizens. Each time customers buy a Starbucks Red product or pay with their Red Card, Starbucks contributes to the Global Fund to help people living with HIV/AIDS in Africa.[8]

Starbucks's mission is to save lives, "We have deep relationships with many coffee growing communities of Africa. Their health and prosperity are important to us. Through our relationship with Product (RED), we have an opportunity to help them thrive. To use our size for good. And to bring our customers new ways to do good every day."

To spread the word, Starbucks actively creates in-store and online experiences that evoke customer contribution through purchases and advocacy. Customers become benefactors in the greater mission of saving lives, but also serve as recruiters by inviting people to join them in the cause for change by sharing these experiences. Starbucks developed a compelling video titled simply, "40 cents can save a life." It featured international celebrities, including Penelope Cruz, Bono, Hugh Jackman, and Julianne Moore, among a cast of A-listers who shared anecdotes of what 40 cents could buy. The point was to introduce everyday people to the power that they held in helping save lives simply by purchasing a cup of coffee. The morale of the story is that 40 cents pays for the daily dose of pills that can keep someone infected with HIV alive.

Starbucks, as well as the other brands supporting Red such as Belvedere Vodka, Bugaboo, Apple, American Express, and Hallmark, unite people around the effort through events and marketing in the real world as well as activating the connected customer to fuel philanthropic capitalism through social activism. Facebook, YouTube, Twitter, and various blogs compel social customers with moving information packaged in shareable social packages to contribute to an AIDS-free generation by 2015.

Indeed, participating companies profit through this activity, but it is done so to support an honorable cause. As a result, human beings profit as well.

◼ ONE DAY WITHOUT SHOES: A MARCH TOWARD PROSPERITY AND SOCIAL RESPONSIBILITY

In 2006, Blake Mycoskie, an American traveler, visited Argentina. He was struck by the number of Argentinian children he met without shoes to protect their feet, and thus a new business was born. TOMS Shoes started with a simple but powerful mission. Flying under the banner One for One, the company would match every pair of shoes purchased with a pair of new shoes given to a child in need. Blake returned to Argentina later that year with 10,000 pairs of shoes—all made possible by TOMS customers.

According to company reports, as of September 2010, TOMS had given more than 1 million pairs of new shoes to children through Giving Partners around the world.

TOMS realized that by using the purchasing power of individuals, the company could benefit the greater good. Forthrightly, the company states its mission is to transform, "our customers into benefactors, which allows us to grow a truly sustainable business rather than depending on fundraising for support."[9]

How the company grew from an idea to a movement is equally compelling. The company wisely pursued the connected customer from the onset. Realizing that marketing and advertising is not an inexpensive endeavor, nor is return on investment guaranteed, TOMS sought out to inspire those who cultivated social nicheworks around related interests, passions, and missions. Through an artful, dedicated, and sincere series of engagements, TOMS used storytelling to evoke empathy to trigger word of mouth. This word of mouth would, as TOMS intended, drive commerce and turn customers into benefactors. More importantly, benefactors would ultimately be transformed into advocates, extending TOMS's mission through the audiences of audiences within the human network to increase sales, grow donations, and help children around the world. TOMS and its customers united to make an impact and the shoes became a badge of honor, a form of self-expression that screams, *"I'm making a difference!* What are you doing?"* Social networks also became the platforms for self-expression and equally served as the corporate hub for social propaganda.

The company focused its marketing and sales investments on Facebook, YouTube, Twitter, and its blogs to recruit customers and affiliates, all bound by a high purpose of profit and charity. At the time this chapter was written, TOMS had built a community of almost one million benefactors each on Facebook and Twitter. The company's channel on YouTube has amassed over 2 million views. The company's blog became a global epicenter for change, celebrating the stories of the people who have been touched by the company's benefactors as well as how customers could or were already contributing to the movement on their own.

Each year, TOMS organizes "One Day Without Shoes" when, according to the company's people, "We take off our shoes to raise awareness of the impact a pair of shoes can have on a child's life." In 2010, more than 1,600 events were held around the world and more than 250,000 people went without shoes.

The connected customer connected the world to an important cause, and TOMS, stakeholders, and children in developing nations benefited equally.

In the words of TOMS, "This is not a trend, this is a movement. And you keep it in motion."

■ EMPATHY LOVES COMPANY

Michael Porter and Mark R. Kramer shared their vision of next-generation business in a stirring essay published in the *Harvard Business Review*, "The Big Idea: Creating Shared Value."[10]

These leading business scholars believe businesses can achieve success through CSR, social progress, and relevance, "The solution lies in the principle of shared value, which involves creating economic value in a way that *also* creates value for society by addressing its needs and challenges. Businesses must reconnect company success with social progress. Shared value is not social responsibility, philanthropy, or even sustainability, but a new way to achieve economic success. It is not on the margin of what companies do but at the center. We believe that it can give rise to the next major transformation of business thinking."

Everything comes down to empathy and empathy is something that companies can't invent; it must be felt. It is also something that businesses can plug into by tapping the wisdom of the crowds. Like the Razorfish Liminal report that said businesses can learn about engagement by asking their customers what's important to them, businesses can crowdsource customer communities for opinions and ideas on how to tackle certain issues. Doing so transforms customers into stakeholders in change and impact.

The combination of connectedness, empathy, and philanthropy creates a powerful elixir that when ingested, transforms the culture of any business into a stronger, more adaptive, and benevolent organization.

PR agency Weber Shandwick and KRC Research interviewed 200 corporate executives who have oversight for corporate philanthropy, social responsibility, and community relations within their organizations.[11] The resulting study demonstrated the benefits of tapping the wisdom of the crowds for CSR programs. If we apply the results to the examples of TOMS and Starbucks, imagine the possibilities when CSR becomes part of value proposition and customers become catalysts for change through commerce.

The most valuable aspect of crowdsourcing for CSR was the ability to surface new perspectives and diverse opinions, according to

36 percent of the executives surveyed. Twenty-five percent felt that crowdsourcing created a way for businesses to build engagement and relationships with key audiences. Another 16 percent believed that the process of inviting customer participation introduced new energy into the process of generating ideas.

It's all of these and more.

Your takeaway is to draft a new social contract between your business and your customers to co-create a business model that profits through positive impact and builds relationships through purpose and partnerships for good.

The contract should clearly communicate:

➤ Intention

➤ Mission

➤ Promise

➤ Ethics

➤ Consumer Expectations

➤ Societal and Environmental Impact

➤ Consumer and Benefactor Rewards

➤ Outcomes

Simon Mainwaring introduced a template for a new social contract between businesses and consumers through his work at We First[12] and his book by the same name:

➤ We believe companies have a right to innovation, entrepreneurship, and profit making while consumers have a right to a healthy society and planet to live on.

➤ We recognize an interdependent, global community requires an expanded definition of self-interest that acknowledges the needs of all inhabitants of the planet.

➤ We define success through prosperity that means the well-being of many, not the wealth of a few.

➤ We believe that future of profit is purpose.

➤ We believe that the interests of companies and consumers are best served through a sustainable practice of capitalism—economically, morally, ethically, environmentally, and socially.

➤ We believe that corporations and consumers owe each other an equal duty to operate with transparency, authenticity, and accountability.

➤ We believe that social technology, business, and shopping have the potential to change our world through new modes of engagement, collaboration, and contribution.

➤ We believe the values that inform our daily practice of capitalism include: sustainability, fairness of rewards, fiscal responsibility, accountability, purposefulness, engagement, and global citizenship.

➤ We believe that corporations and consumers are duty-bound to serve as custodians of global well-being for this and future generations.

➤ We believe that the private sector must cooperate, collaborate, and coordinate with governments and NGOs to create a unified force for social good.

Introducing purpose into the business model and operating under a veil of transparency, customers and businesses collaborate in something bigger than they are.

Revisiting the words of Tony Hsieh once again, those businesses that focus on a higher purpose outperform those that focus on operations.

Centers of Attention

➤ Organizations must define meaningful experiences.

➤ Experiences are shared and they unite those who feel connected to the emotions they evoke.

➤ Company culture is embodied through stakeholders and their actions. What does your company culture project?

➤ Culture must support change to create an adaptive business.

➤ Transparency is a genuine value proposition.

➤ Philanthropic capitalism nurtures empathy into a competitive advantage.

➤ Giving back is the new black.

➤ Develop a new social contract.

Chapter 18

Adaptive Business Models: Uniting Customers and Employees to Build the Business of Tomorrow, Today

If you are currently working within the confinements of a large or matrix organization, you'll find this chapter of great significance. Even if you're not a leader today, operating as a change agent will make you a leader tomorrow. The infrastructure of customer relationships within business today is usually managed by a combination of methodologies, operations, and technology known as CRM, or customer relationship management. Connected customers, however, are inherently elusive and designing an adaptive infrastructure around engagement requires a new and dynamic approach. These incredibly influential consumers don't simply wish to connect with brands in new interactive landscapes, they expect more. As such, the mission of adaptive business is to design experiences that deliver tangible value in return for the attention, endorsement, and resulting activity data of the connected customer.

In the rise of social media, the need for CRM to socialize became paramount. However, social CRM (or sCRM), like its predecessor, was governed by processes and technologies designed to sell or *manage* customer relationships and introduce value throughout the relationship. As good friend and author of *CRM at the Speed of Light*, Paul Greenberg, shared in his blog post, "Social CRM—Getting Down to Reality":

Social CRM is the company's programmatic response to the customer's control of the conversation.[1]

We're learning that the connected customer is in control of their experiences and thus also in control of the relationships they maintain with whatever brands they support. As a result, the role of sCRM is to support the creation and sustainability of collaborative experiences and engagement that deliver and nurture value.

■ THE ADAPTIVE BUSINESS LEARNS THROUGH REFLECTION AND LEADS THROUGH PROJECTION

If a brand is defined in social networks through the culmination of shared experiences, it is now the responsibility of the brand to lead experiences toward customer satisfaction, loyalty, and, of course, profitability.

Now, businesses must start to construct a unified experience that addresses the needs of all consumers, online and offline. This isn't an overnight transformation, nor is it an overnight fix. Businesses will have to redesign and socialize CRM to facilitate collaboration and co-creation to effectively manage and lead customer relationships at every touchpoint.

Remember, the customer sees the various departments within an organization as one. Using the airline example earlier in the book, this experience starts with the research into a particular trip, the purchase of the tickets, the arrival at the ticket counter and the path through the gate, the flight itself, baggage handling, and everything in between.

Connected consumers might expect human inputs during trip research, check-in, and during the flight. Should something go wrong or simply not live up to expectations in any phase of this experience, the human network can activate touchpoints that require response, learning, and potentially, adaptation. In the fight for greater relevance, new adaptive frameworks are necessary for enlivening sCRM, expanding its capacity beyond operations and technology to now add a human touch.

In its study "From Social Media to Social CRM—What Customers Want," IBM studied just that, what customers expect from brands in the egosystem.[2] IBM surveyed more than 1,000 consumers worldwide and 250 executives to uncover disconnects and opportunities for connection in the emerging era of connected consumerism.

Similar to the Razorfish report, IBM learned that customers seek to obtain tangible value as the top reason they seek out businesses through social sites. In a true example of perception versus reality, the IBM report identified the separation between business as usual and the adaptive business. Sixty-five percent of businesses view social media as a new source for revenue but not as channels for offering discounts, coupons, or social commerce. Ironically, consumers claimed otherwise. In fact, receiving discounts or coupons, offering the ability to purchase products or services, and the ability to read the experiences of others were reported as the top reasons they would interact with businesses through new media.

Also, IBM's report revealed another key perception gap. Businesses are three times more likely to think consumers are interested in interacting with them to feel like part of a branded community. Equally, businesses overestimated consumers' desire to engage to feel connected to the brand. As before, these activities are among the least interesting from the consumer's perspective. (See Figure 18.1.)

Not surprisingly, *connected* consumers are open to interaction if they trust the company and believe there's something in it for them. While intimacy is not a driver, meaningful engagement that delivers tangible value may result in a feeling of connectedness.

The net result? The adaptive business will think more like a customer, considering their needs and their needs within each new channel rather than telling them what they think they want to hear. If you are unsure, ask.

As IBM noted, "A successful Social CRM strategy facilitates collaborative experiences and dialogue that customers value."

■ THE DILEMMA'S INNOVATOR

If necessity is the mother of invention, relevance is the mother of innovation.

Just as the role of the CEO is now responsible for leading a business toward a new generation of relevant and shareable experiences, businesses can benefit from the revitalization of the role chief information officers (CIOs) will play in transformation. Whereas the *I* in CIO represented "information technology," it now must also symbolize "innovation." Implementing technology across the organization today is sluggish, and by default, prevents an organization from fostering agility. The role as it's designed today is intended to operationalize departments and increase efficiencies through technology. The role of innovation in the new CIO department must now track technology and trends in addition to its focus on technology support and deployment across the organization. Innovation can live elsewhere within the business construct, but the point is that it does need to live. It needs an operator or owner to ensure that businesses compete for relevance and not mediocrity.

If we revisit the companies where experience is already part of the new CEO role (such as Starbucks, Apple, Dell, Zappos, Best Buy,

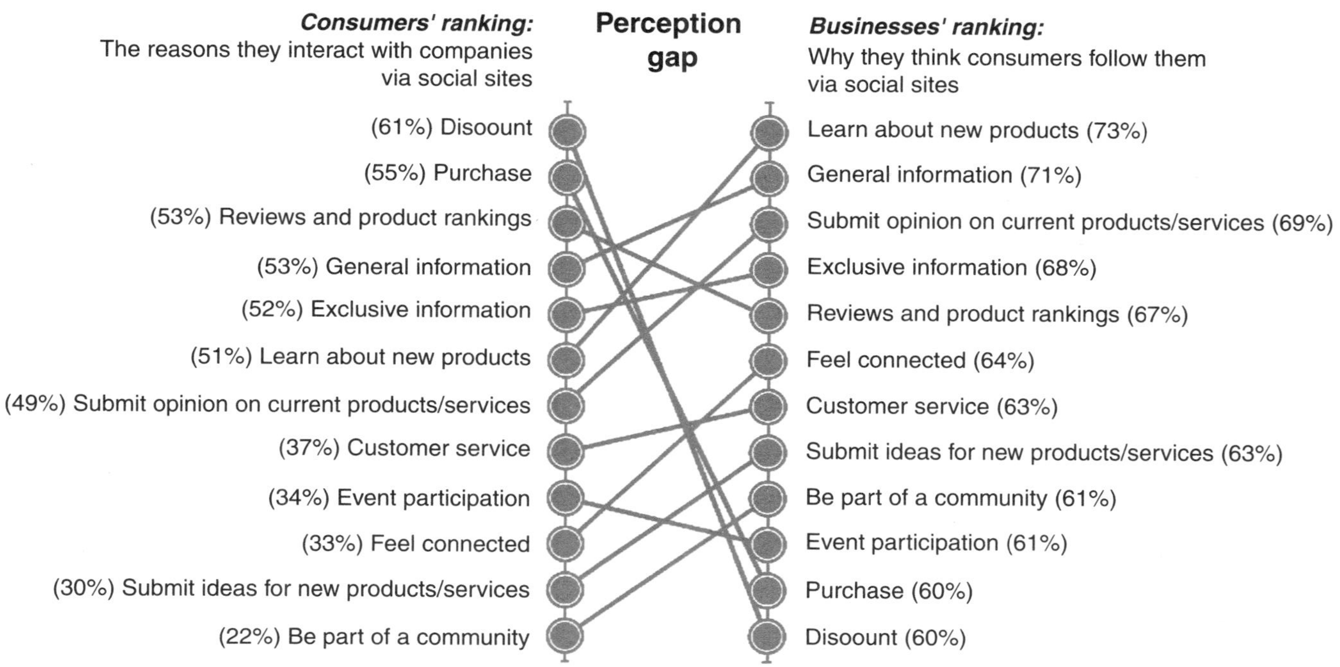

Consumers' ranking:
The reasons they interact with companies via social sites

(61%) Discoount
(55%) Purchase
(53%) Reviews and product rankings
(53%) General information
(52%) Exclusive information
(51%) Learn about new products
(49%) Submit opinion on current products/services
(37%) Customer service
(34%) Event participation
(33%) Feel connected
(30%) Submit ideas for new products/services
(22%) Be part of a community

Perception gap

Businesses' ranking:
Why they think consumers follow them via social sites

Learn about new products (73%)
General information (71%)
Submit opinion on current products/services (69%)
Exclusive information (68%)
Reviews and product rankings (67%)
Feel connected (64%)
Customer service (63%)
Submit ideas for new products/services (63%)
Be part of a community (61%)
Event participation (61%)
Purchase (60%)
Discoount (60%)

Figure 18.1   IBM sCRM Report: Perception Gap

Source: IBM Institute for Business Values, February 2011.

Figure 18.2   Mediocrity Sucks by Hugh MacLeod

Virgin, and Disney), the common trait they share is a significant investment in the role innovation plays in the greater scheme of business mechanics. Technology is used to connect with customers, earn their loyalty, and increase the business opportunity. Like culture, innovation becomes a business differentiator.

Why?

Innovation is instrumental to the transformation of business from a static state to one far more dynamic. (See Figure 18.2.) Changing the technology infrastructure, like its culture, is problematic, but not impossible. The challenge is that innovation happens with or without you. Every day it seems, new technology is introduced. In many cases, connected customers spur adoption, and just as you possess a strong grasp of the current trends, a new shift emerges that's worthy of your attention and analysis.

To be clear, I'm not insinuating that businesses need to react to every new shiny object with an engagement strategy, but rather every business have a system in place that examines how existing customers and prospects are adopting disruptive technology and in turn how it changes their behavior and to what extent. Those emerging trends that appear to gain traction are theoretically recognized and understood by the new CIO or innovation team and thus, ideas for engagement programs are already conceived or set for deployment.

Starting with a small task force of change agents to pursue the connected customer allows a business to experiment, learn, and adapt. As a result, best practices are documented and thus spread across the organization to standardize new processes and metrics.

The adaptive business is keenly aware of the top-line trends already in play. For the most part, the longer-term technology that's driving connected consumerism is a combination of the Four Screens and the Golden Triangle. Before we go any further, allow me to explain.

The Four Screens represent the devices that people use to consume or share information or both. They include:

1. PCs
2. TVs
3. Smartphones
4. Tablets

The Golden Triangle then extends the Four Screens into day-to-day applications that divide into three concentrated trends:

1. Social
2. Real time
3. Gaming

Without getting too abstract, the Four Screens bring the Golden Triangle to life and connect connected customers through the cloud. (See Figure 18.3.) No matter how many new products, services, and devices emerge over the next few years, they will represent one or multiple facets of this model. However, innovation always has a way

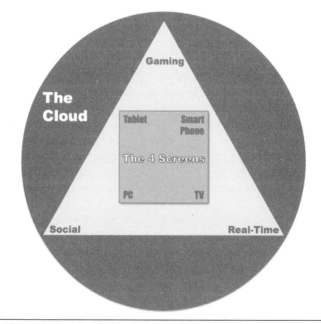

Figure 18.3   The Golden Triangle Extends to the Four Screens

of surprising even the most astute technologists and futurists. Hence, the need for the CIO.

The importance of innovation doesn't just lie in the development of brilliant ideas, deployment of new technology, or the creation of new processes or systems, innovation is now also necessary in the development and execution of these ideas and how corresponding infrastructures erect and evolve to support and scale with them. The modern schools of business management suddenly appear old school in the face of human networks. And with the rise of the connected customer, tomorrow's business leaders are now forced to rewrite the books that help grow companies and markets today.

Innovation is an essential ingredient for not only the survival of emerging companies, but for business in general. We are forced to compete for the future, right here, right now.

■ RETHINKING THE FUTURE OF BUSINESS: BUILDING THE FRAMEWORK

In 2010, my colleague at Altimeter Group, Jeremiah Owyang, reviewed the frameworks of enterprise businesses recognized for their prowess in new media. In his report, we were presented with a view of organizations in transition and the genesis of next-generation models as they were unfolding. Studying this data allows us to visualize new possibilities to design organizations that are more customer aware, socially responsible, and adaptable.

How a business embraces social media and ultimately how it organizes resources around engagement, learning, and leading is directly tied to the internal influence of change agents and their ability to shape an interactive culture within the business. I'm talking about you. This is a critical discussion that will help businesses excel today and over time. This is also an inflection point for you and your career. Your success is tied to the success of the change you bring about.

Owyang shared five ways companies currently organize for social media in his Altimeter report, "The Two Career Paths of the Corporate Social Strategist."[3]

Of the 150 businesses Altimeter studied, 41 percent employed a hub-and-spoke model to support social media (Figure 18.4).

This framework represents a centralized resource for guidelines, governance, best practices, and policies that support cross-functional teams and business units. Many times, a specialized unit represents the hub, usually a social media task force or board of advisors made up of internal and external stakeholders. This team usually reports directly to the chief marketing officer (CMO) or chief executive

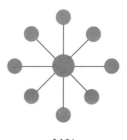

41%

Hub and Spoke
A cross-functional team
sits in a centralized position
and helps various nodes
such as business units.

Figure 18.4   The Hub-and-Spoke Model

officer (CEO), or in some cases, an executive vice president. Its members consist of human resources, legal, information technology, marketing, sales, heads of business, customer service, and so on. However, these organizations are rather far along in the new media adoption cycle. And, it should be said, that this is only one stage in the maturation of an adaptive business.

For the more evolved and experienced organizations, the hub-and-spoke model scales to what Altimeter refers to as the dandelion, or the multiple hub-and-spoke model (Figure 18.5). While only 18 percent of businesses are currently structured to support new media and the connected customer in this fashion, we start to see the fluidity of such a schematic. A centralized system allows for effective top-down leadership as well as amplifies the need for harmony and direction. (See Figure 18.6.) When we combine the two hub-and-spoke models, 60 percent of participating organizations represent the foundation for a majority of emerging adaptive businesses.

Centralization is a key theme for businesses in transition—28.8 percent of companies manage new media in one department, similar to that of corporate communications. In my work, you'll see a fusion of the multiple hub-and-spoke archetype combined with this centralized approach. This means the adaptive business requires cross-functional support and distributed responsibility to address the unique needs of connected customers in the capacity they expect engagement.

Altimeter also found that almost 11 percent of organizations are not yet structured around new media or the connected customer. The

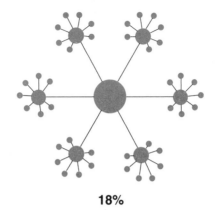

18%

**Multiple
Hub and Spoke**
Similar to Hub and Spoke
but applicable to large
multinational companies
where "companies within
companies" act nearly
autonomously from each other
under a common brand.

Figure 18.5   The Multiple Hub-and-Spoke Model

act of exploring new media is instead decentralized, setting the stage
for potential chaos and brand dilution. (See Figure 18.7.)

Of all of the companies interviewed by Altimeter, only 1.4 percent
of businesses employ a holistic methodology in their migration to
adaptation and relevance.

In principle, the holistic model is representative of a business in
transition that empowers employees to become part of the business
at large in all that they do. (See Figure 18.8.) Chris Heuer, a leading

28.8%

Centralized
One department
(like Corp Communications)
manages all social activities.

Figure 18.6   The Centralized Model

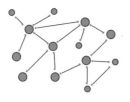

10.8%

Decentralized
No one department
manages or coordinates;
efforts bubble up from
the edges of the company.

Figure 18.7   The Decentralized Model

thinker in new media and business consultant at Deloitte, shared his views on this subject in a rousing article, "The Time Has Come for Holistic Business Strategy."

> ... [I]t is time ... for organizations large and small to adopt a holistic business strategy that empowers more employees to think about the whole of the business; to more fully understand the ins and outs of the product/service offering; and ultimately focus on serving their markets instead of serving the stock market.[4]

Considering the level of sophistication combined with varying roles of the connected customer, perhaps the framework for the future of business combines the mission of a holistic approach with the distributed model of multiple hub-and-spoke formations.

1.4%

Holistic
Everyone in the company
uses social media safely
and consistently across
all organizations.

Figure 18.8   The Holistic Model

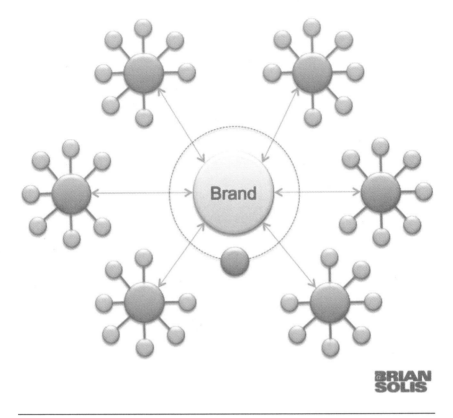

Figure 18.9   The Framework for the Social Business

(See Figure 18.9.) This enables an adaptive business to listen, learn, engage, and adapt through a virtuous cycle that fosters market relevance.

The executive management team responsible for the direction of the brand is, of course, at the center. This is where leadership, culture, and a holistic view of empowerment take shape. Orbiting the hub is a center of excellence (COE) designed to lead transformation from the top down, helping business units learn and collaborate with one another. This COE is also responsible for ensuring the creation of new business processes within the organization to ensure the self-sufficiency of each line of business. The role of the COE also improves the processes necessary and introduces new structures to activate the emerging touchpoints and opportunities rife in new media. It functions as an internal consultancy to lead transformation from within and thus has a sense of autonomy within the organization. As it most likely includes stakeholders from critical business units on its advisory board, the COE's mission is to improve business processes and internal methodologies and align business priorities with opportunities. This creates an optimized flow for guidance, intelligence, leadership, and employee empowerment and recognition throughout the organization—up, down, inside, and out.

Management combined with new roles within each division will introduce adaptive elements to each division relying on the COE to provide the insight and support necessary to lead internal and external stakeholders.

Eventually, each business unit is empowered to engage through new channels operating under a renewed vision and mission. This hub projects and protects the company's brand promise, mission, and purpose to ensure brand integrity in each engagement. This new resource center maintains best practices, sets policy and governance, introduces new methodologies and guidance, and also provides the training and technology necessary to achieve desirable outcomes.

■ FROM BOTTOM UP TO TOP DOWN AND OUTSIDE IN TO INSIDE OUT

Over the years, it seems that the world of business and media placed process roadblocks, technology, and automated intermediaries between the brand and the people who define success. Innovation by default was inhibited.

Businesses are approaching new media differently and no one formula prevails. But it's less about what *is* and more about what needs to be. New media and the resulting behavior of connected customers introduce new or long forgotten elements that serve as the foundation for relationships and affinity. Culture and leadership are at the root of adoption and, ultimately, how the organization embraces change. It's not easy. The truth is that the bigger an organization is, the greater the challenges and politics to introduce the change necessary for ongoing relevance. But that doesn't mean that we should cower in complacency.

Our opportunity is to introduce collaboration internally before we can do so externally. It's the difference between remodeling and rebuilding.

The adaptive business opens up doorways between silos to foster collaboration within (Figure 18.10). The framework for sCRM and engagement introduces a human touch into the process, in which

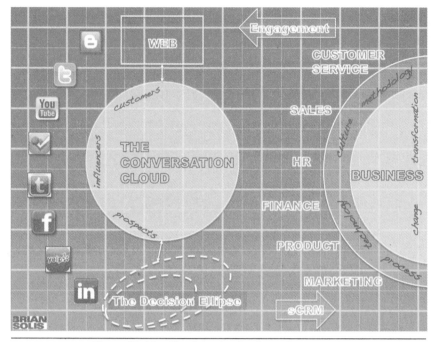

Figure 18.10   The Adaptive Business Framework

operations, technology, and people align around new touchpoints and the unique needs of customers in emerging channels to engage and nurture noteworthy experiences.

It begins with listening and monitoring not only conversations, but also tracking recognized touchpoints within each channel of relevance. When engagement is necessary, it is then managed through the affected person or department with a sole intention of introducing value. Significant experiences are routed through the organization to provide insight to improve products and processes, deliver greater value, and introduce extraordinary experiences.

Businesses must look within so as to more clearly see what's required. What we'll learn is that the business of tomorrow takes a human touch, and new media provides stepping-stones, leading us to a new era of relevance. Businesses will have no choice but to lead and respond as the rise of the connected upsets the balance of power between brand and customer. It's up to you to ensure that the organization adapts accordingly. Your experience and vision are instrumental in designing an organizational chart and workflow that integrate the roles of listening, engagement, learning, and adaptation departmentally and across the company.

■ DELL'S BELLS

Dell is among the most-often-cited examples when it comes to new media and business, and for good reason. While many articles and news stories studies focus on the use of new media tools such as Twitter, Facebook, and wikis, the real story for you is how a business pivots its culture. Michael Dell, with the help of some amazing people along the way, designed a new infrastructure from scratch and erected an adaptive business from within.

But Dell didn't learn or change overnight. In fact, the company's path to relevance began through what seemed at first to be a march toward irrelevance. The company's previous direction was diverted through brute force and is an example to all businesses that dismiss the overall influence of connected customers. The saga, now recorded in history books as "Dell Hell," was not the result of one experience, but the culmination of years of customer dissatisfaction. A perfect storm brewed, and through a relentless series of shared negative experiences, Dell's transformation played out on the stage of new consumerism. Dell was forced to listen, learn, and adapt.

In July 2005, noted media thought leader Jeff Jarvis published a blog post that chronicled his contempt for a brand that he felt failed him. His post was aptly titled "Dell hell: Seller beware."[5] While Jarvis concentrated his energy on Dell, it wasn't just about one company. It was about the need for businesses to care about the customer again, if not by choice, then by force. It served as a shot across the bow of every business. Businesses were now introduced to the reality that loomed ahead. Customers could now share their experiences to trigger a backlash that could tip traditional media but more importantly, give rise to a consumer revolution that will forever change the face of business. That post and several that followed sparked years of conversation in new and traditional media.

The age of caveat emptor is over.

Now the time has come when it's the seller who must beware. Caveat venditor.

A company can no longer get away with consistently offering shoddy products or service or ignoring customers' concerns and needs.

For now the customers can talk back where they can be heard. Those customers can gang up and share what they know and give their complaints volume. Of course, they can use their reviews and complaints to have a big impact on a company's reputation and business.

Jarvis's words ring truer today and every day, and while these were dark days for Dell, it presented consumers everywhere with hope for a brighter future. It gave connected customers hope that their voice would one day be heard, that their experiences matter, and that their patronage equates to appreciation and value. While Dell embraced the opportunity, others still turn away. This is the fate that awaits all businesses that ignore the importance of this new class of customer. For connected customers do not wish to have their needs and desires placated through new media channels. They, we, demand that businesses cater to our needs on demand. The egosystem reigns supreme. Divided we stand, united they fall. . . .

Jarvis concluded his epic post with words that echo as businesses still question the importance of the connected customer. . . .

> *You know what: If Dell were really smart, they'd hire me (yes, me) to come to them and teach them about blogs, about how their customers now have a voice; about how their customers are a community—a community often in revolt; about how they could find out what their customers really think; about how they could fix their customers' problems before they become revolts; about how they could become a better company with the help of their customers.*
>
> *If they'd only listen.*

Dell listened. But it did more than that; it adapted. In doing so, Dell paved the way for other businesses to follow, learn, and adapt. Dell's new adaptive business plan wasn't simply about social media; it was about improving customer experiences through better products and service.

■ THE DELLWETHER OF CUSTOMER SENTIMENT

Among the many changes Dell immediately implemented, Michael Dell sought to make a sincere and powerful statement to customers. He invited his trusted advisors over to his house one weekend to brainstorm new ideas. As then vice president of communities and conversations, Bob Pearson, explained in a conversation we had years ago, Dell sought to introduce feedback loops in new channels to build an interactive organization that not only listened, but also acted on customer insight. This is when IdeaStorm was conceived. Bob discussed the possibility of building a channel through which customers could share ideas and challenges and interact with the ideas of others to vote up or down the ideas that were most relevant to them. Michael loved the idea and asked how long it would take to introduce. Bob replied with a realistic time frame of several weeks to which Michael replied, "Can we get it done by next week?" That was 2007.

Pearson was interviewed by *Ad Age* shortly after IdeaStorm hit the Web and was met with industrywide praise, "You can't do digital media from one group with one point of view on the world. It just doesn't work. In fact, that's too marketing-oriented. There's a big difference between pushing your story out versus becoming relevant in customers' conversations."[6] Pearson continued by focusing on the importance of the new customer landscape, "With the average focus group, you go in for an hour or two, give them some sandwiches and leave. We may be listening to conversation going on over two months. It's a totally different game." IdeaStorm is part of an effort "to make sure the customer is walking the hallways at Dell."

IdeaStorm continues today and as noted in an update released by the company in 2011, idea submissions have been on an upward trend.[7] By far, the most active idea category has been mobile devices, which is not surprising when one looks at the technology landscape and where the market is going.

The point of sharing a story that's years old is that change is only possible when the executive team feels that change is necessary. It's your job to show why they need to care. Since Dell Hell, the company has continued to push the boundaries of what's possible. Now Dell is finding comfort living outside of its comfort zones of the past. It's blazing the trail for other would-be adaptive businesses by building new frameworks that overturn classical business models to better compete for relevance among a new genre of customers that make businesses compete for their business, not the other way around.

Welcoming customers into the fold through empowering feedback loops placed Dell on the path to relevance. But it is this very philosophy that other businesses question for fear of losing control of the customer relationship. Control was never there, however. At best, businesses possessed the semblance of control. In a connected global society, customers are in control of the brand experience and it didn't take new media to bestow this power on them. That's the gift of free thought. Opinions are universal, and now the ability to share them with the masses and affect the impressions and decisions of others is equally democratic.

To that end, control is now something that is within the grasp of any business. Conversations and the resulting impressions will take place with or without you. Taking control is now simply a matter of improving those conversations through productive and shareable experiences.

As Pearson noted, "This isn't just crowdsourcing. This is crowd-managing. Companies still fear this. But, hell, if even Dell can lean back and let its customers begin to take charge, anyone can."

Here we are, years later, and Dell is constructing the model for the adaptive business of the future. Innovation is at the center of improving business, product relevance, and customer relationships through improved experiences across the board. Following IdeaStorm, Dell continued to introduce products and services built on customer insights. And, along the way, it identified new touchpoints and introduced effective feedback loops that solidified earning and imparting relevance as standard business protocol. To that end, Pearson later told *Brand Digital* in a piece that analyzed Dell's incredible transformation, "Michael Dell is the biggest proponent of making sure the company avails itself of any digital tools and behaviors that make listening to consumers easier and more productive."[8]

Dell transformed every division of the organization that was affected by stakeholder activity. Among the earliest divisions that gained immediate traction and support was Dell's customer service team led by Richard Binhammer (RichardatDell). Richard and his team showed the world what's possible when you bring help directly to customers in their communities. Most notably, the team operationalized the service infrastructure to facilitate proactive engagement in addition to traditional inbound support.

In July 2010, Dell's chief blogger, Lionel Menchaca, offered a glimpse at the evolving framework to support connected customers. In his words . . .

> People who have been following Dell's progression in social media know that we are in the midst of transitioning from a centralized team that carried out all social media efforts to a more decentralized hub and spoke model. It's really about scaling social media. For us to scale our efforts, we need to make social media a core part of Dell's business functions. In Dell's case, it's clear that providing support for our customers in the digital realm is one of the most vital aspects of our overall social media strategy.[9]

Highlighted in the center of Menchaca's graphic is customer service. (See Figure 18.11.) The company invested significantly in the creation of new feedback loops to ensure that customers could reach representatives within their channels of choice, when needed. Dell realized that to meet the needs of the connected customer, scale and efficiency would inevitably come into play.

In addition to the company's support forum, Support.Dell.Com, Dell developed a Facebook presence specifically for customer service.

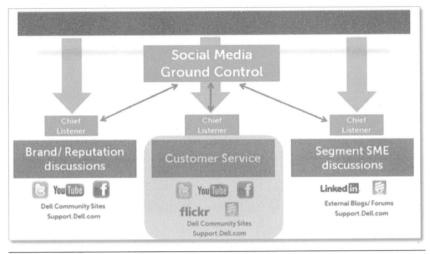

Figure 18.11   Listening Process

Through a custom widget, customers could receive live support without leaving Facebook. (See Figure 18.12.)

Also, Dell's dedicated Customer Facebook tab provides a variety of insights and solutions, again, without the customer having to leave their channel of relevance.

On Twitter, through the @DellCares account, Dell provides 24/7 global support in English and the team was expanding into other languages as well. (See Figure 18.13.)

Menchaca shared that the company is dedicated to improving the customer experience, catering to the behavior of each of the customer segments (traditional, online, and connected), "We are measuring

Figure 18.12   Dell Support on Facebook

Figure 18.13   Dell Support on Facebook

many aspects of this outreach in Twitter and Facebook. The initial results are promising: roughly 2/3 of the Dell customers we've helped claim a positive customer experience with Dell after our support interaction, and feedback from other customers has been very positive. Still, our goal here is not to replace traditional support methods. Instead, our goal is to be there for customers who wish to get support from us through social media."

In late 2010, Dell continued to innovate in its quest to adapt to the new world of connected consumerism when it introduced its social media listening command center. Like IdeaStorm and its other groundbreaking developments in Facebook, Twitter, blogs, and forums, Dell's command center introduced a new workflow for tracking customer insights and managing engagement across the organization. What the world was really witnessing, however, was the call center of the future, plugging in the adaptive business and all of its corresponding departments to new touchpoints and feedback loops. This, Dell realized, was the key to relevance.

In December 2010, CEO Michael Dell and CMO Karen Quintos officially launched the company's command center as the operational hub for listening and engagement across all social media, globally. As a result, Dell is embedding social media across the fabric of the company, connecting with customers to listen, engage, and act on every facet of business. The Web is now a point of convergence to build stronger customer connections and improve products, service, and business overall.

Michael Dell introduced the command center in a video that was shared on Dell's YouTube channel, "One of the founding principles of Dell is really about listening and learning from our customers, to take that feedback and improve."

Marcel LeBrun, CEO of Radian6, one of the technologies used to power the command center, highlighted the cultural impact of the announcement, "It's not just a superficial show that social media is cool and that we're listening, but it really is a reflection of this deeper cultural investment in listening."

As the video pans out, we see three important words that adorn the walls of Dell, "Listen. Engage. Act."

The social media listening command center tracks on average more than 22,000 daily topic posts related to Dell, as well as the mentions of Dell on Twitter that have a reach greater than the circulation of the top 12 daily newspapers in the United States.

Dell's command center tracks in real time:

➤ Topics and subjects of conversations
➤ Sentiment
➤ Share of voice
➤ Geography
➤ Trending across topics, sentiment, geographies
➤ Heat maps of problems or areas where support is needed

The reality is that conversations on the Social Web touch every aspect of Dell's business. As a result, Dell's efforts in social media and community are focused on hearing everything to ensure that the relevant people in Dell's businesses receive feedback and connect with customers directly. (See Figure 18.14.) More importantly, it's about learning and changing based on repeat feedback. With more than 5,000 Dell employees now trained in social media, many are actively listening across the Web as part of their jobs.

Manish Mehta, former vice president for social media and communities at Dell, expressed the company's commitment and vision for listening, learning, and engagement, "The goal is to enable every employee inside the company where they can listen to conversations. The command center will do it at the companywide level across 11 languages and across every country around the globe. We then give those tools down to every employee. Every function you can imagine inside the company is going to use social media and community tools and today is the day we emancipate those tools into the company."

To succeed, Dell empowers employees to act as intrapreneurs, individuals who behave like an entrepreneur, except within a larger organization. They work independently within the company to introduce innovation and revitalize and diversify business. Who are your intrapreneurs?

Comparing the infrastructure of Dell in 2011 to Dell just one year earlier, adaptation is instrumental to scale and business growth. The company is empowering every aspect of the organization to listen, engage, and act.

Dell is simultaneously building interactive channels that provide each division with a dedicated residence and voice to supply stakeholders with consistent and relevant information. (See Figure 18.15.) This includes customer service, legal, human resources, education, investors, enterprise customers, small business customers, communications and marketing, everyday customers, sales, research and development, and the overall corporate brand.

It is this customer-centricity and those words *listen, engage,* and *act* that has affected the entire organization. Dell connects with connected customers, prospects, and influencers uniquely through each of the following divisions (Figure 18.16):

➤ Product
➤ Marketing
➤ Services and Solutions
➤ Online
➤ Sales

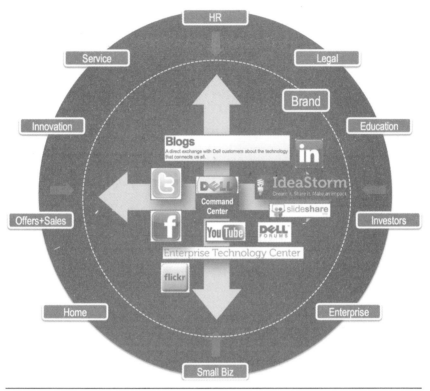

Figure 18.14 Dell Touchpoints and Feedback Loops

➤ Customer Services
➤ Communications
➤ Human Resources

This cultural renaissance has opened the doors between departments for collaboration internally and externally. In many ways, Dell is years into designing both a social and adaptive business. With the launch of its social media listening command center, customers officially become part of Dell's value proposition.

■ THE FUTURE OF BUSINESS IS UP TO YOU

As we're learning, many businesses may be blind to or blinded by the emergence of influential human networks and thus, we may

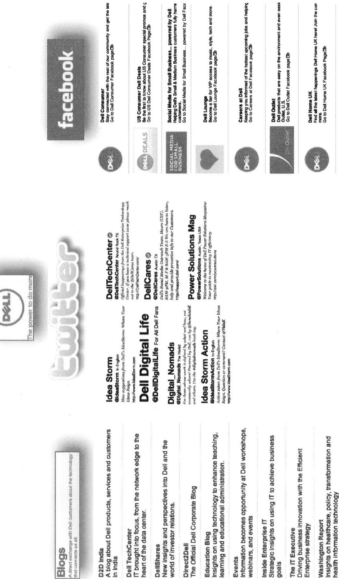

Figure 18.15   Dell Social Channels

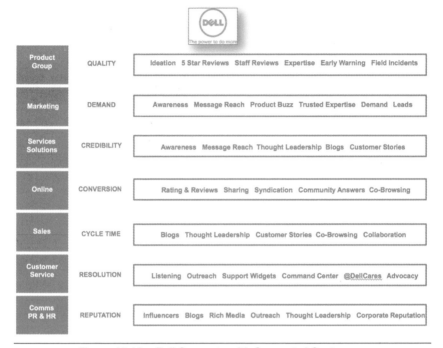

Product Group	QUALITY	Ideation 5 Star Reviews Staff Reviews Expertise Early Warning Field Incidents
Marketing	DEMAND	Awareness Message Reach Product Buzz Trusted Expertise Demand Leads
Services Solutions	CREDIBILITY	Awareness Message Reach Thought Leadership Blogs Customer Stories
Online	CONVERSION	Rating & Reviews Sharing Syndication Community Answers Co-Browsing
Sales	CYCLE TIME	Blogs Thought Leadership Customer Stories Co-Browsing Collaboration
Customer Service	RESOLUTION	Listening Outreach Support Widgets Command Center @DellCares Advocacy
Comms PR & HR	REPUTATION	Influencers Blogs Rich Media Outreach Thought Leadership Corporate Reputation

Figure 18.16   Dell Connects with Connected Customers

miss the intimacy, intelligence, and urgency necessary to learn, adapt, and succeed.

In a world full of demanding customers who use multiple channels to engage with one another, businesses have no choice but to change. They must adapt to continually add value to the customer experience and foster relationships rooted in collaboration. If businesses hope to use these channels to influence other potential customers, it's clearly time to build new, cross-departmental engagement strategies that can be introduced through multiple touchpoints. At the same time, these touchpoints must activate internal paths for modification and personalization.

Not every company is led by an open leader such as those executives who are profiled in this book. Yet, to change, businesses ultimately require support from the top. This is where you come in. You know better than most that businesses should not require a baptism by fire to force the proverbial business hand to shake that of the connected customer. Unfortunately, that is how many will learn. But, under your leadership and championship, you will align with the most influential partners within your organization to devise an evil plan that leads your company to relevance now and over time. Muhahaha!

Indeed, the challenge we face is great, but without your work, without your dedication, and without your inspiration, change is impossible. With your leadership, change *is* inevitable. Take this book and the many lessons and insights to devise your evil plan. Your job is to stay inspired and inspiring!

As a wise CEO of a leading global brand once told me, "If you come to me with a request for budget and resources for mobile and social media, to make it a priority for our business, you will lose every time. If you tie it to our business priorities and objectives and demonstrate how engagement will enable progress and improve customer relationships, you will win every time. New media must be an enabler to our business; just show me how."

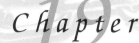

Chapter

Change Is in the Air: The Inevitable March toward Change Management

You're approaching the final pages of this book, but not the final steps in your journey. Take the time to chart your course, as we're at the beginning of a transformation that will unfold over the years ahead. To keep you and those around you motivated, build in milestones to chart progress and appreciate your progress and accomplishments.

Changes call for new direction.

Change is an opportunity that needs new leadership.

Seek not inspiration in the words of others when change is on the horizon, for it is your words that will inspire others to change.

If you've ever watched the hit show *Undercover Boss* on CBS, you've most likely watched the transformation of an executive officer or operator into a human being. The show is quite magical in that it asks leaders of some of the most recognized and renowned brands to leave their senior executive post for a week to experience their business from the perspective of everyday employees—all while doing so undercover. Employees don't realize who this new recruit really is and as such, these executives are treated as a peer, not as "the boss."

The real magic of the show occurs when the audience (us) witness the moments when executives gain a new sense of appreciation and humility while working alongside their employees. Like this book, these executives learn through immersion. They see the effects that their decisions have on others. They get a first-hand view of where the problems lie within their organizations, the challenges employees face, and they learn the importance of people over numbers and processes. When we talk about the humanization of business, nothing is more powerful than getting to know the real people behind the scenes, the unsung heroes who make every company excel. These stakeholders offer insights that rarely get a stage for an executive audience. This show demonstrates the effects of leadership looking within to grow.

Through this incredible and emotional journey, executives walk away with a deep sense of empathy and inspiration. At the end of each show, as they reveal who they really are to each employee, tears and laughter ensues. And, usually, the employees are rewarded for the insights and experiences they shared along the way. The company, too, is rewarded, benefiting from stakeholder perspectives to inspire change, inside and out.

■ THE FUTURE OF BUSINESS STARTS WITH CHANGE AND ENDS WITH CHANGE MANAGEMENT

The journey we each take as leaders of change within our business or organization is similar to the steps of those executives in *Undercover Boss*. Representing leading businesses, including Frontier Airlines, DirecTV, MGM Grand, Subway, NASCAR, and 7/11, we are presented with business models not unlike our own. And, regardless of shape, the only thing that separates you from the insights they experienced is the perspective of your employees, peers, and your connected customers. It comes down to openness and the capacity to let their experiences and stories touch you. . . . It comes down to empathy.

It starts within. . . .

It starts with getting back to basics.

At the center of an adaptive business is a culture that supports change. Change is something that requires design, support, and execution. And everything begins with understanding the gaps between business and its connected, traditional, and online customers. Also, businesses must measure the gaps between this new direction and the current state of employee perception, happiness, and needs. Attempting to build an adaptive business without a comprehensive study to surface these insights is akin to building a business on a house of cards. It will fail eventually and waste everyone's time, money, and resources in the process. More importantly, we will have spent hopes and trust in the pursuit of a fast track when, in fact, change requires management, systems, and tools. Answers serve as the conduits for strategy and planning and it is this and only this that reveals the scope of change management, the process, and the desirable outcomes.

Many businesses today are attempting to lead change, drafting the popularity of new media channels and networks. While the intent of getting closer to customers is genuine and a top priority for CEOs, it is how businesses are designed to support that effort now and in the long term that defines success or failure. Revisiting the IBM 2010 CEO study, we see that today's businesses are "fervently building social media programs to do just this."[1] But as IBM notes, customers are not enthusiastic and most do not engage with companies through new media channels just to "feel connected." If the adaptive business wishes to connect, it must appreciate that connected customers are far more pragmatic. Companies must strive to a higher purpose to design shareable experiences that deliver tangible value in return for customers' "time, attention, endorsement and data."

Customers represent only one side of the equation, however, and for the adaptive business, engaged and empowered employees represent the balance. To bring about change, change agents cannot focus on technology or the emergence of new media channels, but instead develop a banner of aspiration, "We're all in this together and together we will achieve great things!" Remember, this is about embracing and projecting a new mission of customer dedication, a promise of new leadership and collaboration, and the pursuit of a higher purpose that rallies both customers and employees alike.

The methodologies, systems, and associated rewards for all participants are what require definition and construction to successfully pursue and engage the connected customer. The adaptive business as a result must be built in real time.

Change begins with change management.

■ THE MARCH TOWARD CHANGE LEADS TO RELEVANCE: A BLUEPRINT FOR CHANGE

While change is never easy, its outcomes remind us of its importance. Here, relevance is monetizable. To manage change, however, takes an entire organization. And while there are many schools of thought on change management and organizational transformation, we will focus on the basics to serve as a checklist for preparing for, unfolding, and reinforcing change. Ultimately, your mission, the culture of the organization, and the state of your connected customer define how change management plays out.

Defining what change management is and isn't, is a strong place to begin. Many change agents are not necessarily new to innovation, but may be new to the process of change management. Its name seems ominous and arduous. But understanding what it is will help us in our quest toward relevance. Change management is the processes, tools, and techniques for managing the people side of change.[2] The process is designed to reduce friction and resistance and promote opportunity.

Change takes time, and throughout this process everything is exposed to transformation from business processes to product development and quality management to organizational development and continuous process improvement. It's all about managing change to realize business goals and results. Dividing change into stages allows for all those affected to chart progress, feel a sense of advancement, and allow for everyone to support the new direction without upsetting the balance.

■ PHASE 1: SETTING THE STAGE

Here we prepare for change by documenting the need for it. The first step is formally interviewing key stakeholders, including connected customers and employees. This allows us to size the scope of change, how people are affected, and the nuances that will define success or represent significant hurdles. Also, analyzing the market and internal stakeholder research surfaces needs and opportunities. Benchmarking competition and industry best practices also contribute to the definition of our goals. Working backwards, we prepare for change by . . .

➤ *Readiness:* Conduct a readiness study based on objectives.

➤ *Audit:* Perform an audit of external activity and internal employee sentiment and engagement.

➤ *Needs:* Identify the needs of customers and front-line employees and the capacity to execute now and over time.

➤ *Understand:* Change triggers a deeply psychological reaction, and understanding how people go through changes will help in planning, communication, and motivation.

➤ *Strategy:* Define your change management strategy.

➤ *Vision:* Develop the mission and purpose of the need for change.

➤ *Change Team:* Identify and prepare your change management team.

➤ *Sponsors:* Secure executive sponsors and stakeholders to help champion the transformation at the top and introduce visible opportunities to demonstrate support.

➤ *Progress:* Document goals and milestones.

➤ *Communication:* Define messages and the communication plan.

   ➤ Shape the messages for each stakeholder group.

   ➤ Build awareness and validate the process.

➤ Avoid loss of key employees.

➤ Set expectations.

➤ Reduce fears.

➤ Promote progress.

■ PHASE 2: MANAGING CHANGE

In the second phase, we document everything into a detailed plan that is then circulated among the change management team to secure buy-in. The aim of this step is to shift from planning to implementation and to ensure the buy-in of the organization at large. More importantly, we must secure the acceptance of the market.

Eleven steps include:

1. *Planning:* Finalization of change management plans and measurement models.

2. *Buy-in:* Circulation among stakeholders to ensure credence and support.

3. *Metrics:* Definition of outcomes that communicate success.

4. *Best practices:* Development of best practices to visualize the effort and the benefits of change.

5. *Playbook:* Documentation of guidelines and guardrails to help people follow the right steps to personal success and achievement.

6. *Training:* Creation of training and education regiment to scale the transformation across the organization and ensure everyone can perform as expected.

7. *Communications:* Implementation of a communications strategy that paves the way for change and internal support.

8. *Workflow:* Introduction of new processes for collaboration and decision trees.

9. *Recognition and rewards:* Creation of reward system for internal stakeholders to ease the burden of change and acknowledge achievement in a new paradigm.

10. *Implementation:* Roll out change management program through an inspiring event supported by the internal champions who inspire at every level.

11. *Help:* Proactively help employees transition through the change process to prevent a reaction akin to organ rejection.

■ PHASE 3: REINFORCING CHANGE

The mission of change is only as strong as its perseverance and its ability to inspire the team as well as the market. The implementation of change will be met with varying levels of support and opposition, and the management side of change management allows for alignment. The goals of the change management team are to...

➤ *Assess:* Collect and analyze reactions, extent, and feedback.

➤ *Measure:* Document progress and communicate to stakeholders.

➤ *Engage:* Continue support and contend with opposition to eliminate threats or potential revolutions.

➤ *Plan:* Identify gaps and define, introduce, and communicate corrective actions.

➤ *Celebrate:* Continually recognize achievements of the organization and individuals.

■ CONNECTING VALUE PROPOSITIONS TO PERSONAL VALUES

The greatest assets of the adaptive business are its customers and its employees. It comes down to people regardless of the medium they use to connect, discover, and share. To succeed, employees must stay motivated and aligned with the new or renewed vision and mission. With the introduction of a new culture, there are two sides of the equation necessary to drive enthusiasm and convert employees into stakeholders, the mind side and the heart side. Businesses must activate levers on each side to activate emotional and intellectual advocacy. This is a lesson I've learned time and time again.

During the writing of this book, I had the opportunity to work with Frank Mendicino, Danna Vetter, and Kerri Drozd and a dedicated executive team at ARAMARK on an important change management initiative driven by the desire to engage the growing market of connected consumers. This new initiative was rolled out to more than 230,000 employees over the course of one year. Recognizing the importance of employees, ARAMARK set out to learn more about their needs, concerns, and aspirations. While the details are confidential, the team of change agents prioritized internal engagement strategies that concentrated on the hearts and minds of employees. Reaching the "mind side" and "heart side" of employees would be instrumental in guiding adoption of a renewed culture and redefined ARAMARK brand to lead the company toward a new chapter of

Figure 19.1   Four Levers of Cultural Adoption

business and stakeholder relevance. The following lessons were inspired by ARAMARK's change initiative to help your business create and introduce a renewed promise and supporting culture by connecting the hearts and minds of employees and ultimately connected customers.

The mind side of the equation requires four key levels to attain intellectual engagement necessary to assure cultural engagement and adoption (Figure 19.1):

1. Accountability
2. Resources
3. Reward
4. Authority

The heart side of the equation helps change agents connect with personal values to champion cultural change. Triggering emotional advocacy requires beginning with an understanding of how people's experiences at your business connect with their personal values. Integrating the following catalog of experience types into change and defining how they connect with personal values promotes success (Figure 19.2):

➤ *Achievement:* The ability to accomplish great things.
➤ *Belonging:* Working in the trenches together, having someone to count on and vice versa.

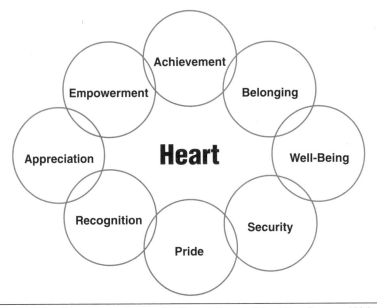

Figure 19.2   Culture and Change by Connecting and Enabling Personal Values

➤ *Well-being:* The small things, not money, such as a personal letter, congratulations on a life or work event, knowing my place of employment is where I can share my life.

➤ *Security:* Keeping promises and consistent information (career path and support).

➤ *Pride:* Being part of something bigger than yourself and knowing you make a difference.

➤ *Recognition:* The appreciation of your contribution among peers and management without your need to promote your good work.

➤ *Appreciation:* Recognizing good intentions and the role you play in day-to-day outcomes.

➤ *Empowerment:* Given the capacity to execute or offer resolution.

In the final stages of cultural adoption, businesses will need to pull the unique cultural levers within the organization to align strategic recommendations with the stakeholder needs and the everyday reality in which they operate. Introducing a filter model to the heart and mind equation drives cultural adoption to introduce change while minimizing friction. (See Figure 19.3)

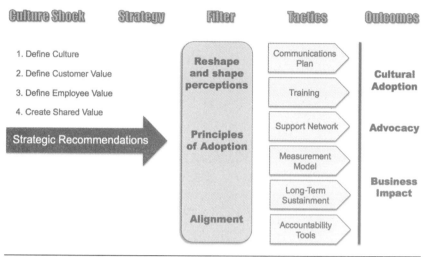

Figure 19.3   Driving Cultural Adoption

With every culture change comes culture shock. It's inevitable. Planning and managing change through value and a strategy that communicates empowerment and benefits shifts the vibration of shock into reverberation for adoption, advocacy, and impact. Everything must pass through the filter, however, to that change, and communication is vetted for optimized engagement. When strategic recommendations and rollout pass through the filter, change . . .

➤ Shapes and reshapes perceptions
➤ Introduces the tenets and principles of adoption
➤ Aligns with personal values

Once through the filter, relevant messaging and the connection to personal values are enlivened for effective engagement to front-line employees through . . .

➤ A communications plan
➤ Training
➤ Employee rewards and incentives
➤ Support network
➤ Measurement model
➤ Long-term sustainment
➤ Human resource and accountability tools

Finally, these tactics are measured in their efficiency and efficacy in the current state and ongoing evolution of

➤ Cultural adoption
➤ Advocacy
➤ Business impact

Change is overwhelming. Therefore, to engage with the front line as a new fabric of culture is rolled out, we must make it personal. We must transfer ownership. And, we must enlist advocacy. Perhaps most important, we must keep our promises and continue to inspire our employees to, in turn, inspire our customers.

■ THIS IS YOUR TIME

This is your time to lead, not follow.

This is your time to make a difference.

This is your time to bring about the change in your business that you expect as not just a connected customer, but a valued customer.

The very essence of the adaptive organization is change, and it is continuous. This is not about change for the sake of change; it is not about change for the sake of survival. This is about leadership. Embracing this reality allows us to compete for the moment, for the future, and ultimately, for relevance. You are not in this alone, however. The emergence of the connected customer will force every business to undergo deep cycles of reflection and transformation. The good news is that we are all in this together. The challenges you face are in fact your own, however, and looking to other businesses for guidance is not where to begin this journey. Benchmark not just against the competition, but against the opportunity, as it is unique to you and your business. Your connected customers will dictate the nature of the adaptation required to earn and impart relevance.

➤ Benchmark against ourselves
➤ Benchmark against competitors
➤ Benchmark against customer needs
➤ Benchmark against opportunities

What we know is what we know. It is pursuing what we don't know, however, that opens the gates to transformation.

And here you are, ready to transform your business into an adaptive business ready to engage and inspire connected customers through meaningful and shareable experiences. In the end, we'll learn that the rise of a new class of customers only makes our organization stronger, significant, and sincere, which amounts to an organization rich with relevance and value.

In the immortal words of Walt Disney, "You build the best product you can. You give people effective training to support the delivery of exceptional service. You learn from your experiences. And you celebrate success. You never stop growing. You never stop believing."

Chapter 20

What's Next? The Evolution of Business from Adaptive to Predictive

Customer-centricity begins with intention and it is brought to life through vision, execution, and adaptation. How a company evolves and adapts to this growing need for customer-centricity is based on a variety of factors. The prevailing corporate culture, the processes and systems in place, and of course employees' alignment toward a greater mission and purpose are integral in this evolution. The state of the customer is reflected through various stages as a company focuses on customer experiences.

Good friend and Executive Vice President of Global Innovation and Integration at Edelman Digital, David Armano, and I set out to document those stages to help inspire progress. Over the years David Armano and I have talked at great lengths about how changes in society, technology, and business would eventually affect organizations and, as a result, create new business models. As companies aspire to get closer to customers, our work together focused on documenting the transformation stages businesses undergo in the process. David and I would joke about what company is going to look at these models and say, "Aha, yes, that's the problem! We're a rigid business." Yes, we recognize that this is not how it works. While it's difficult to see their own reflection in the great mirror of reality, it's critical for any leader to recognize the attributes of each business and identify with the characteristics that ignite ambition. Specifically for this book, David and I worked together to visualize the development stages an organization may inevitably go through to achieve customer-centricity.

The stages are seen in Figure 20.1.

Rigid: An organization or business focused on traditional operations and one-way communication. Its ability to evolve is tied to rigidness of its own infrastructure and silos. As changes in the

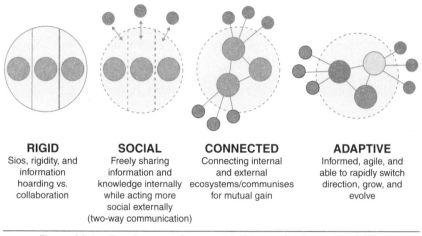

RIGID	SOCIAL	CONNECTED	ADAPTIVE
Sios, rigidity, and information hoarding vs. collaboration	Freely sharing information and knowledge internally while acting more social externally (two-way communication)	Connecting internal and external ecosystems/communises for mutual gain	Informed, agile, and able to rapidly switch direction, grow, and evolve

Figure 20.1   Development Stages of Achieving Customer-Centricity

environment occur, it is difficult to detect new opportunities and act upon or make the substantial changes needed to move in the right direction in a timely manner. The risk is losing ground to competitors and overall relevance to connected customers.

Social: A social business or enterprise has built a monitoring infrastructure to track conversations, activity, and sentiment. As it grows, a social enterprise then shifts to listening and engagement with customers, becoming increasingly social as time passes and conversations increase. These social dynamics begin to influence the fabric of the organization itself, making hard silos more "permeable." As "social expands from department to department, the organization becomes more social on the outside and inside and as a result begins to work more collaboratively and communicates interactively. A social business assumes a hub-and-spoke formation, where the hub becomes the resource for helping individuals and factions, and executives realize the benefits of engagement.

Connected: A connected business, brand, or organization not only acts social but also introduces layers and connective tissue that connect key stakeholders, people, processes, and groups (such as business units), functions, and external operations (such as the supply chain and distribution). Listening evolves into learning, where legacy systems are evolved to tap into social data both externally and within the organization. Social gives way to a multiple hub-and-spoke formation, where the responsibility of internal and external engagement is distributed across the enterprise. Employees are directly connected not only to other employees, but directly to customers as well. Social becomes additive to how each individual, group, or process touches customers and employees.

Adaptive: An adaptive business becomes smarter and faster, able to evolve with conditions so effectively that it ultimately becomes predictive or able to see opportunities or threats before they present themselves. A connected company integrates customer experiences and feedback loops into the organization to demonstrate opportunities for improvement, new products, and service programs. Listening and learning are expanded to analyze data and extract insights for short-term and long-term innovation and transformation. Both social and connected, an adaptive business makes sense of data—transforms it into intelligence it can act upon and evolves its people, process, and technology to be able to respond in real time. The goal starts with aspirations of new relevance and eventually develops into market and thought leadership.

As we learned in this book, becoming an adaptive business is key to establishing relevance and, ultimately, preference in a market that is very much in transition. At the core of adaptation is the ability to recognize needs or opportunities for improving customer experiences or driving business transformation. This requires learning systems and processes that enable the translation of data into actionable insights and, in turn, response and progression. This is where businesses must strive to be; but what is beyond that?

Although you have reached the end of this book, becoming an adaptive business is not the final stage of evolution. It is how information is studied and behaviors put into practice that set the stage for the next model of business, one rooted in adaptation but inspired by prophecy. To be successful in this endeavor, one's aspirations cannot rest with simply reacting to or creating remarkable customer experiences; you must also predict them. Thus, the next level for companies is to become a predictive business. By gazing into the crystal ball and interpreting behavior, sentiment, and experiences businesses can anticipate customer experiences and increase opportunities and likelihood for relevance, preference, and desired experiences.

Predictive: Only the most connected, agile, and progressive organizations will realize the potential in shifting from a reactive customer-centric approach to that of proactive, and ultimately predictive. The predictive business is social, connected, and adaptive. Data not only feeds intelligence for improvement and innovation, but can also predict customer needs, experiences, and

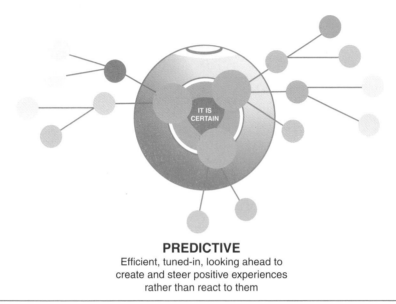

PREDICTIVE
Efficient, tuned-in, looking ahead to
create and steer positive experiences
rather than react to them

Figure 20.2 The Predictive Business

new opportunities. In order for this to occur, the organization as a whole becomes so proficient at making meaning of the intelligence it analyzes and acting upon it, both locally and globally, that it can predict scenarios before they occur, thereby maximizing opportunity and limiting risk. See Figure 20.2.

The capacity to transcend the various models of business is not necessarily an end game. The essence of evolution and the ability to outpace digital Darwinism lie in the ability to embrace change and illustrate the attributes of those models that improve opportunities for relevance and leadership. The recipe is dictated by customers and their experiences and measured by the caliber of relationships and the outcomes they yield.

Your next step begins with an understanding of where you are today and a vision of where you need to be tomorrow and over the course of the next 3, 5, and 10 years. This must also align with your vision for defining and shaping customer experiences along the way. Through clarity and the ability to articulate this vision, and being both inspirational and focused, you must convince stakeholders of the need for and value in change. You are the catalyst for change, transformation, and the architect of relevance.

Notes

■ CHAPTER 1 A QUIET RIOT: THE INFORMATION DIVIDE AND THE CULTURAL REVOLUTION

1. Emily Post, *Table Manners for Kids* (New York: HarperCollins, 2009).
2. Bruce Feiler, "Should You Google at Dinner?" *New York Times,* December 10, 2010.
3. AVG Technologies press release, "Digital Birth: Welcome to the Online World," October 6, 2010.
4. Laura Zimmer-Tamakoshi and Brian Cross, www.theanthropologist inthefield.com/ (1996).

■ CHAPTER 2 YOUTHQUAKE: MILLENNIALS SHAKE UP THE DIGITAL LIFESTYLE

1. Melissa S. Bristow, "Make Way for Generation Y," *Kiplinger,* December 28, 2010.
2. Edelman Digital, "Why Millennials Matter to Every Brand," www.edelman digital.com/2011/02/14/why-millennials-matter-to-every-brand/ (February 14, 2011).
3. CIA World Factbook, https://www.cia.gov/library/publications/the-world -factbook/fields/2177.html (accessed January 20, 2011).
4. Alex Abraham, "Why Millennials Matter to Every Brand," *Consumer Action- ism*, Edelman Consumer Marketing Intelligence, February 1, 2011.
5. Joshua Norman, "Boomers Joining Social Media at Record Rate," *CBS News,* November 16, 2010.
6. Brian Solis Blog, "The Social Media Manifesto," www.briansolis.com/ 2007/06/ (June 11, 2007).

■ CHAPTER 3 THE MEDIUM IS NO LONGER THE MESSAGE

1. Nielsen Wire Blog, "What Americans Do Online: Social Media and Games Dominate Activity," http://blog.nielsen.com/nielsenwire/online_mobile/

what-americans-do-online-social-media-and-games-dominate-activity/
(August 2, 2010).

2. Experian Hitwise press release, "Facebook Was the Top Search Term in 2010 for Second Straight Year," December 29, 2010.

3. Facebook Press Room (accessed January 30, 2011).

4. Jeffrey Van Camp, "Facebook's U.S. Traffic Has Grown 55 Percent since 2009," *Digital Trends,* November 19, 2010.

5. The Facebook Blog, "Democracy in the UK: Results of the Social Media Election," www.facebook.com/blog.php?post=387348402130 (May 5, 2010).

6. Democracy of UK on Facebook, "A Snapshot of Facebook in 2010," December 31, 2010.

■ CHAPTER 4 THE ATTENTION DEFICIT CRISES AND INFORMATION SCARCITY

1. "Mom's on Facebook," *Saturday Night Live* (s. 36; ep. 3), www.hulu.com/watch/184577/saturday-night-live-moms-on-facebook.

2. Paige Chapman, "Social Networking Can Bring Students Stress as Well as Connection, Survey Finds," *The Chronicle of Higher Education,* October 7, 2010.

3. AP-mtvU, Technology and Mental Health poll, October 2010.

4. Alan Fram and Trevor Tompson. "AP-mtvU Poll: High Tech Tools Connect College Students but Also Bring Stress, Vulnerability," *Chicago Tribune,* October 7, 2010.

5. Jon Hurdle, "Social Media Can Rule Your Life, College Finds," *Reuters Life!* September 21, 2010.

6. Retrevo Blog, "Preserve Your Facebook Privacy, Post Cautiously," www.retrevo.com/content/node/1371 (May 13, 2010).

7. Matt Richtel, "Growing Up Digital, Wired for Distraction," *New York Times,* November 21, 2010.

8. Caroline McCarthy, "Survey: Over Half of U.S. Workplaces Block Social Networks," *CNET.com,* October 6, 2009.

9. Nucleus Research, "Facebook: Measuring the Cost to Business of Social Notworking," July 2009.

10. Brendan I. Koerner, "How Twitter and Facebook Make Us More Productive," *Wired,* February 22, 2010.

11. Thomas B. Ward, Ronald A. Finke, and Steven M. Smith, *Creativity and the Mind: Discovering the Genius Within* (New York: Basic Books, 2002).

12. "Facebook, Twitter Doesn't Kill Productivity," *The Times of India,* October 25, 2010.

13. Marshall Kirkpatrick, "Shocking News: Scientists Say Workplace Social Networking Increases Productivity!" *ReadWriteWeb,* April 2, 2009.

14. Stephen Cauchi, "Surfing the Net Good for Workers and for Business," *The Age.com.au,* October 24, 2010.

15. danah boyd, "Risk Reduction Strategies on Facebook," *danah boyd/apophenia,* November 8, 2010.

■ CHAPTER 5   THE EVOLUTION OF THE NETWORK ECONOMY AND THE HUMAN NETWORK

1. Joan O'C. Hamilton, "Separation Anxiety," *Stanford* magazine, January/February 2011.
2. Paul Adams, "The Real Life Social Network," Presentation at Voices that Matter Web Design Conference, San Francisco, June 28–29, 2010.

■ CHAPTER 6   THE NEXTWORK: DEFINING TOMORROW'S INFORMATION NETWORK

1. Kim Linton, "Top U.S. Newspapers Show Huge Circulation Losses," *Yahoo! Contributor Network*, April 27, 2010.
2. Frazier Moore, "CBS Wins Weekly Ratings, NBC Scores with Football," *Associated Press*, January 11, 2011.
3. Matt Rosenberg, "Current World Population," http://geography.about.com/od/obtainpopulationdata/a/worldpopulation.htm (accessed February 1, 2011).
4. Frigyes Karinthy, "Chains," in *Everything Is Different* (Budapest: Athaneum Press, 1929).
5. "Everything Is Different," Art and Popular Culture, www.artandpopularculture.com/Everything_is_Different (accessed February 6, 2011).
6. Michael Gurevich, *The Social Structure of Acquaintanceship Networks* (Cambridge, MA: MIT Press, 1961).
7. Ithiel de Sola Pool and Manfred Kochen, "Contacts and Influence," *Social Networks* 1, no. 1 (1978–1979): 42.
8. Stanley Milgram, "The Small World Problem," *Psychology Today* 2 (1967): 60–67.
9. Stowe Boyd, "Everything Is Different," Stowe Boyd, www.stoweboyd.com/post/934522936/everything-is-different (accessed May 14, 2008).
10. Duncan J. Watts, Peter Sheridan Dodds, and M. E. J. Newman, "Identity and Search in Social Networks," *Science* 296, no. 5571 (2002): 1302–1305.
11. Harris Interactive Newsroom, "Thanks to Social Networks, Americans Feel More Connected to People," October 21, 2010.
12. Christopher Mims, "Why Twitter Is the Future of News," *MIT Technology Review*, April 30, 2010.
13. Twitter Blog, "Celebrating a New Year with a New Tweet Record," http://blog.twitter.com/2011/01/celebrating-new-year-with-new-tweet.html (January 6, 2011).

■ CHAPTER 7   YOUR AUDIENCE IS NOW AN AUDIENCE OF AUDIENCES WITH AUDIENCES

1. Brian Solis Blog, "Discovering and Listening to Conversations in Twitter," www.briansolis.com/2008/03/discovering-and-listening-to/ (March 21, 2008).

2. Lee Odden, "Web 2.0 Expo—Microblogging and Micromedia," *TopRank Online Marketing Blog* (n.d.).
3. Digital Inspiration Blog, "Students Only Use Macbooks in This Classroom," www.labnol.org/software/university-students-use-apple-macbook-only/4947/ (October 14, 2008).
4. Joey DeVilla, "How Do You Like Them Apples?" *Global Nerdy Blog*, www.globalnerdy.com/2007/10/02/how-do-you-like-them-apples/ (October 2, 2007).
5. Jay Rosen, "The People Formerly Known as the Audience," *PressThink.org*, June 27, 2006.
6. Saul Hansell, "Zuckerberg's Law of Information Sharing," *New York Times Bits*, November 6, 2008.
7. Nielsen Wire Blog, "What Americans Do Online: Social Media And Games Dominate Activity," http://blog.nielsen.com/nielsenwire/online_mobile/what-americans-do-online-social-media-and-games-dominate-activity/ (August 2, 2010).
8. Facebook Press Room (accessed February 6, 2011).
9. Claire Cann Miller, "Start-Up Plans a More Personal Social Network," *New York Times*, November 15, 2010.

■ CHAPTER 8 CONVERGENCE: THE INTERSECTION OF MEDIA AND THE HUMAN NETWORK

1. Mathew Ingram, "Twitter Plus TV Creates 'Social Viewing,'" GigaOM, November 10, 2010.
2. Sarah Devlin, "The Real Mark Zuckerberg Confronts a 'Surprised' Jesse Eisenberg on SNL," *Mediaite*, January 29, 2011.
3. Peter Kafka, "NBC Sent Out Embeddable Clips..." Twitter, 7:23 A.M., by TweetDeck, January 30, 2011.
4. Jackie Rousseau-Anderson, "US Consumers Now Report Spending Equal Time with TV and the Internet," *Forrester Blogs*, December 13, 2010.
5. Dan Sewell, "Soaps' Sponsor Goes Digital," *Boston Globe*, December 10, 2010.
6. "Pauli Exclusion Principle," HyperPhysics, http://hyperphysics.phy-astr.gsu.edu/hphys.html.
7. Linda Stone, "Conscious Computing," *Linda Stone Blog*, June 27, 2010.
8. Jacqueline Anderson, "Understanding the Changing Needs of the U.S. Online Consumer, 2010," *Forrester Research*, December 13, 2010.

■ CHAPTER 9 MEASURES OF DIGITAL INFLUENCE AND SOCIAL CAPITAL: FROM NOBODY TO SOMEBODY

1. South Park Studios, "You Have Zero Friends," www.southparkstudios.com/full-episodes/s14e04-you-have-0-friends.
2. Brian Solis Blog, "The Value of Online Conversations," www.briansolis.com/2008/01/value-of-online-conversations/ (January 17, 2008).

3. Brian Solis Blog, "The Human Algorithm: How Google Ranks Tweets in Real-Time Search," www.briansolis.com/2010/02/the-human-algorithm-how-google-ranks-tweets-in-real-time-search/ (February 1, 2010).
4. Robert Putnam, *Bowling Alone: The Collapse and Revival of American Community* (New York: Simon & Schuster, 2000).
5. "Klout and Starbucks Team Up on Influential Twitterer Marketing," http://aerocles.wordpress.com/2010/03/25/klout-starbucks-team-up-on-influential-twitterer-marketing/ (March 25, 2010).
6. "Spotlight on Klout Perks: Virgin America Campaign," http://corp.klout.com/blog/2010/10/spotlight-on-klout-perks-virgin-america-campaign/ (October 12, 2010).
7. "Klout Clubs and Social Rewards: Coming to a Hotel Near You?" http://socialhospitality.com/2011/01/palms-vegas-using-klout-and-social-rewards/ (January 6, 2011).
8. "Klout Comes to Facebook Fan Pages," http://corp.klout.com/blog/2011/06/klout-comes-to-facebook-fan-pages/ (June 22, 2011).
9. Jessica E. Vascellaro, "Wannabe Cool Kids Aim to Game the Web's New Social Scorekeepers," *Wall Street Journal,* http://online.wsj.com/article/SB10001424052748704637704576082383466417382.html?mod=wsj_share_twitter (February 8, 2011).

■ CHAPTER 10   THE DAWN OF CONNECTED CONSUMERISM

1. The Phrase Finder, "Fifteen minutes of fame," www.phrases.org.uk/meanings/fifteen-minutes-of-fame.html (accessed February 2011).
2. "Social, SEO, & the Open Graph: What to Do Now," White paper, http://info.gigya.com/rs/gigya/images/OpenGraphToday.pdf.
3. Marshall Kirkpatrick, "Why We Check In: The Reasons People Use Location-Based Social Networks," *ReadWriteWeb,* June 28, 2010.
4. Brian Solis, "Change: Lessons on What's Next," *Entrepreneur,* December 31, 2010.
5. Giselle Tsirulnik, "Retailers Can Drum Up Awareness via Mobile Location-Based Services: Study," *Mobile Commerce Daily,* October 22, 2010.
6. "Why Location Is About More than the Check-In," *eMarketer,* January 11, 2011.
7. "Foursquare for Business," http://foursquare.com/businesses/ (accessed February 2011).
8. Ji Kyung Park and Deborah Roedder John, "Got to Get You Into My Life: Do Brand Personalities Rub Off on Consumers?" *Journal of Consumer Research* 37, no. 4 (2010): 655–669.

■ CHAPTER 11   THE RISE OF COLLECTIVE COMMERCE

1. Jane McGonigal, "Why 'I Love Bees': A Case Study in Collective Intelligence Gaming," February 2007.

2. Pierre Levy, *Collective Intelligence: Mankind's Emerging World in Cyberspace*, trans. Robert Bononno (Cambridge, MA: Perseus Books, 1997), 24.

3. Ibid., xi.

4. Olga Generozova. The diagram is based on the types and examples of collective intelligence discussed in the books *The Wisdom of Crowds* and *Smart Mobs*, http://en.wikipedia.org/wiki/File:CI_types1s.jpg.

5. David Armano, "The 4 C's of Community," *Logic + Emotion*, November 30, 2008.

6. Joseph Tartakoff, "Amazon Invests $175 Million in LivingSocial," *paidContent.org*, December 2, 2010.

7. Oliver Chiang, "Facebook to Launch Social Group-Buying Feature," *Forbes Blog*, January 25, 2011.

8. "Empedocles," *Encyclopedia of Human Thermodynamics*.

9. Hugh MacLeod, *Evil Plans: Having Fun on the Road to World Domination* (New York: Portfolio Hardcover, 2011).

10. Karen Karbo, "Friendship: The Laws of Attraction," *Psychology Today*, November 1, 2006.

11. Arie De Geus, *The Living Company* (Boston: Harvard Business Press, 2002).

12. Arie De Geus, *The Living Company*, Prologue as seen on Bloomberg Businessweek, www.businessweek.com/chapter/degeus.htm (n.d.).

■ CHAPTER 12 CREATING MAGICAL EXPERIENCES

1. "Confusion about ROI, Disagreement about Performance Indicators," *eMarketer*, September 24, 2010.

2. Matt Anderson, Nick Buckner, and Stefan Eikelmann, "As Smartphones Change Shopping, Retailers Face a Stark Choice," *Remodista.com*, November 29, 2010.

3. Chris Cameron, "Ben & Jerry's: How a Big Brand Explores Augmented Reality," *ReadWriteWeb*, July 12, 2010.

4. Rimma Kats, "Macy's Bolsters Designer Sales via In-Store Mobile Integration," *Mobile Marketer*, February 25, 2011.

5. Rheana Murray, "Target Implements QR Codes in Print Ads to Engage Readers," *Mobile Marketer*, February 25, 2011.

6. Miguel Bustillo and Ann Zimmerman, "Phone-Wielding Shoppers Strike Fear Into Retailers," *Wall Street Journal*, December 15, 2010.

7. "Announcing Google Shopper for iPhone," *Google Mobile Blog*, http://googlemobile.blogspot.com/2011/02/announcing-google-shopper-for-iphone.html (February 1, 2011).

8. Jason Ankeny, "The Rebirth of Retail," *Entrepreneur*, March 2011.

9. Ibid.

10. "SNAP Launches Social Media–Based Loyalty Program," *QSRWeb.com*, February 10, 2011.

11. Stephanie Kwak, "Seventeen.com and J.C. Penney's Augmented Reality Dressing Room," *fashionablymarketing.me*, August 18, 2010.

12. "More Proof that Near Field Communication (NFC) Is Headed to Future iPhones?" *iPhone Download Blog,* January 28, 2011.
13. Brian Solis, "Change: Lessons on What's Next," *Entrepreneur,* December 31, 2010.
14. Clint Boulton, "Starbucks Enables Mobile Payments via iPhone, Blackberry," *eWeek.com,* January 19, 2011.
15. Kyle Studstill, "Social Interactions Powered by In-Shoe RFID," *PSFK.com,* January 26, 2011.

■ CHAPTER 13 BRANDS ARE NO LONGER CREATED, THEY'RE CO-CREATED

1. Groubal, "About Us," www.groubalcsi.com/about/(accessed March 3, 2011).
2. Burson-Marsteller press release, "Large Global Corporations Now More Likely to Directly Engage Users on Social Media, Study Finds," February 15, 2011.
3. Fortune 500 Mission Statements, www.missionstatements.com/fortune_500_mission_statements.html (accessed March 3, 2011).
4. "Branding Glossary," Lippincott, www.lippincott.com.
5. Eric Hellweg, "The Eight-Word Mission Statement," *Harvard Business Review Blog,* October 22, 2010.

■ CHAPTER 14 REINVENTING THE BRAND AND SALES CYCLE FOR A NEW GENRE OF CONNECTED COMMERCE

1. Nate Riggs, "This Is Your Brain on Direct Marketing at Akron University," Nate Riggs Social Business Strategies, http://nateriggs.com/2011/01/28/this-is-your-brain-on-direct-marketing-at-akron-university/content-marketing-consulting (January 28, 2011).
2. Adam L. Penenberg, "Social Networking Affects Brains Like Falling in Love," *Fast Company,* July 1, 2010.
3. Kirk Phillips, Presentation on "The 9 Criteria for Brand Essence," Conrad Phillips Vutech, www.slideshare.net/kirkphillips/the-9-crit (April 2010).
4. Advanced Marketing Institute, "Emotional Marketing Value Headline Analyzer," www.aminstitute.com/headline/index.htm.
5. "What Is Experiential Marketing?" *Advent,* http://adventresults.com/2007/10/31/001-what-is-experiential-marketing/ (October 31, 2007).
6. Drypen, "Hierarchy-of-Effects Model," http://drypen.in/advertising/hierarchy-of-effects-model.html (accessed March 2011).
7. Proven Models, "AIDA Sales Funnel," www.provenmodels.com/547 (accessed March 2011).
8. Arthur Frederick Sheldon, *The Art of Selling: For Business Colleges, High Schools of Commerce, Y.M.C.A. Classes, and Private Students (1911)* (Whitefish, MT: Kessinger Publishing, 2009).
9. Solomon Dutka, *DAGMAR: Defining Advertising Goals for Measured Advertising* (Lincolnwood, IL: NTC Business Books, 1995).

10. Drypen, "DAGMAR—Defining Advertising Goals for Measured Advertising Results," http://drypen.in/advertising/dagmar-defining-advertising-goals-for-measured-advertising-results.html (accessed March 2011).
11. Robert Lavidge and Gary Steiner, "A Model for Predictive Measurements of Advertising Effectiveness," *Journal of Marketing* 25, no. 6 (1961): 59–62.
12. David C. Edelman, "Branding in the Digital Age: You're Spending Your Money in All the Wrong Places," *Harvard Business Review,* December 2010.

■ CHAPTER 15 ASPIRING TO REACH BEYOND CONFORMITY TO INSPIRE CUSTOMERS

1. Chris Wisniewski, "Lonely Planet: Pixar's *Wall-E*," *Stop Smiling*, June 27, 2008.
2. The ad technically aired twice. In December 1983, the ad ran on KMVT-TV in Twin Falls, Idaho, before the 1 A.M. sign-off. This was done to qualify the ad for the various advertising awards events the following year, giving Chiat/Day the ability to nominate the spot.
3. Christoph Dernbach, "1984—The famous Super Bowl Spot," *Mac History,* July 12, 2008.
4. Pivot Conference press release, "Study Shows Brands Ready to Make the Pivot to Pursue the Social Consumer," February 28, 2011.
5. "Marketing Is Too Important to Be Left to the Marketing Department," *ska: unmasked interrupts,* http://blog.pixelboxx.com/ska/stories/35/ (March 17, 2008).
6. Grace Kim, Presentation on Customer Segmentation, www.slideshare.net/gracekim1986/customer-segmentation (March 2009).
7. Brian Solis, "The Interest Graph on Twitter Is Alive: Studying Starbucks Top Followers," www.scribd.com/doc/48360698.
8. Cliff Saran, "What Is Big Data and How Can It Be Used to Gain Competitive Advantage?" www.computerweekly.com/Articles/2011/08/01/247472/What-is-big-data-and-how-can-it-be-used-to-gain-competitive.htm (August 1, 2011).
9. Dan Kusnetzky, "What Is 'Big Data?'" www.zdnet.com/blog/virtualization/what-is-big-data/1708 (February 16, 2010).
10. "Big Data: The Next Frontier for Innovation, Competition, and Productivity," www.mckinsey.com/mgi/publications/big_data/index.asp (May 2011).

■ CHAPTER 16 THE LAST MILE: THE FUTURE OF BUSINESS IS DEFINED THROUGH SHARED EXPERIENCES

1. "World's Most Admired Companies," *Fortune, CNNMoney.com,* http://money.cnn.com/magazines/fortune/mostadmired/2011/snapshots/670.html (2011).

2. "Steve Jobs: Retail Stores Helped iPad's Success," www.ifoapplestore.com/db/2011/03/02/steve-jobs-retail-stores-helped-ipads-success/ (March 2, 2011).
3. Joshua Topolsky, "Live from Apple's iPad 2 event," *Engadget,* March 2, 2011.
4. "A Razorfish Analysis of Customer Engagement in Transition," http://liminal.razorfish.com/ (January 13, 2011).
5. "Virgin America: Creating an Itinerary That Identifies and Leverages Customer Influence," http://liminal.razorfish.com?page_id=19.

■ CHAPTER 17   THE CULTURE CODE: WHEN CULTURE AND SOCIAL RESPONSIBILITY BECOME MARKET DIFFERENTIATORS

1. Brian Solis, "Change: Lessons on What's Next," *Entrepreneur,* December 31, 2010.
2. Tony Hsieh, *Delivering Happiness: A Path to Profits, Passion, and Purpose* (New York: Business Plus, 2010).
3. "Disney Institute Teaches the 'Business Behind the Magic,'" www .trainingindustry.com/training-outsourcing/supplier-spotlights/disney-institute-teaches-the-'business-behind-the-magic'.aspx (accessed March 2011).
4. Bradley Blackburn, "The Giving Pledge: Billionaires Promise to Donate at Least Half Their Fortunes to Charity," *ABCNews.com,* August 4, 2010.
5. Matthew Bishop and Michael Green, *Philanthrocapitalism: How Giving Can Save the World* (New York: Bloomsbury Press, 2009).
6. Karen Cho, "Philanthrocapitalism: Dawn of a New Era?" *INSEAD Knowledge,* August 12, 2010.
7. Willis Harman, "Humanistic Capitalism: Another Alternative," *Journal of Humanistic Psychology* 14, no. 1 (Winter 1974).
8. Starbucks Red, www.starbucks.com/responsibility/community/starbucks -red (accessed March 2011).
9. TOMS: Our Movement, www.toms.com/our-movement/movement-one-for-one (accessed March 2011).
10. Michael E. Porter and Mark R. Kramer, "The Big Idea: Creating Shared Value," *Harvard Business Review,* January/February 2011.
11. "Crowdsourcing Adds Value to Corporate Responsibility Efforts," *eMarketer,* February 23, 2011.
12. Simon Mainwaring, "A New Social Contract between Brands and Consumers," *The We First Blog,* http://simonmainwaring.com/future/a-new-social-contract-between-brands-and-consumers/ (March 6, 2011).

■ CHAPTER 18   ADAPTIVE BUSINESS MODELS: UNITING CUSTOMERS AND EMPLOYEES TO BUILD THE BUSINESS OF TOMORROW, TODAY

1. Paul Greenberg, "Social CRM—Getting Down to Reality," www.briansolis .com/2011/03/social-crm---getting-down-to-reality/ (March 23, 2011).

2. IBM Institute for Business Value, *From Social Media to Social CRM: What Customers Want* (Somers, NY: IBM Global Services, February 2011).
3. Jeremiah Owyang, "Altimeter Report: The Two Career Paths of the Corporate Social Strategist. Be Proactive or Become 'Social Media Help Desk,'" *Web Strategy*, www.web-strategist.com/blog/2010/11/10/report-the-two-career-paths-of-the-corporate-social-strategist-be-proactive-or-become-social-media-help-desk/ (November 10, 2010).
4. Chris Heuer, "The Time Has Come for Holistic Business Strategy," www.briansolis.com/2011/01/the-time-has-come-for-holistic-business-strategy/ (January 21, 2011).
5. Jeff Jarvis, "Dell Hell: Seller Beware," www.buzzmachine.com/2005/07/01/dell-hell-seller-beware/ (July 1, 2005).
6. Matthew Creamer, "Dell Quells Critics with Web 2.0 Tack," *Advertising Age*, June 11, 2007.
7. Bill Johnston, "IdeaStorm Update: 2/17/2011," *Direct2Dell Blog*, February 17, 2011.
8. Allen P. Adamson, "Q&A with Bob Pearson, Dell's Vice President of Communities and Conversations," *Brand Digital: Conversations*, November 18, 2008.
9. Lionel Menchaca, "Supporting Customers in Facebook and via @DellCares in Twitter," *Direct2Dell Blog*, July 23, 2010.

■ CHAPTER 19   CHANGE IS IN THE AIR: THE INEVITABLE MARCH TOWARD CHANGE MANAGEMENT

1. IBM Institute for Business Value, *From Social Media to Social CRM: What Customers Want* (Somers, NY: IBM Global Services, February 2011).
2. Change Management Tutorial Series, "Change Management—the Systems and Tools for Managing Change," www.change-management.com/tutorial-change-process-detailed.htm (accessed March 2011).

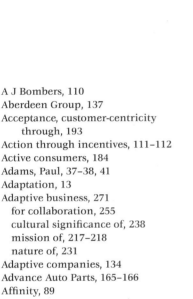

Index